THE FIRST PART

OF

HENRY THE FOURTH

EDITED BY

FREDERIC W. MOORMAN, B.A., Ph.D.

PROFESSOR OF ENGLISH LANGUAGE IN THE UNIVERSITY OF LEEDS

BLACKIE & SON LIMITED
LONDON AND GLASGOW

BLACKIE & SON LIMITED
16/18 William IV Street,
Charing Cross, London, W.C.2
17 Stanhope Street. Glasgow

BLACKIE & SON (INDIA) LIMITED
103/5 Fort Street, Bombay

BLACKIE & SON (CANADA) LIMITED
Toronto

Printed in Great Britain by Blackie & Son, Ltd., Glasgow

PREFACE

In sending forth this edition I should like to acknowledge my indebtedness to former editors and commentators.

In preparing the Notes, I have received considerable help from Mr. K. Deighton's edition of the *First Part of Henry IV*, and from Messrs. Halliwell and Wright's revised edition of Nares' *Glossary*.

In my treatment of Shakespeare's verse (see Appendix) I have closely followed the plan of Professor Herford's "Outline of Shakespeare's Prosody", appended to his edition of *Richard II* in the Warwick Shakespeare, and have also made use of Professor Schipper's *Englische Metrik* and Dr. Abbott's *Shakespearian Grammar*.

Among works consulted in the preparation of the Introduction, Kreyssig's *Vorlesungen über Shakespeare* and Brandes' *William Shakespeare* call for special notice. I also owe suggestions to an article by Professor A. C. Bradley, entitled "The Rejection of Falstaff", which appeared in the *Fortnightly Review* for May, 1902, and to which my attention was drawn by Mr. E. de Sélincourt of University College, Oxford.

Lastly, I should like to acknowledge my great indebtedness to my esteemed friend and former teacher, Professor C. H. Herford, for valuable suggestions in all stages of the work.

F. W. M

CONTENTS

ADDENDUM: SHAKESPEARE'S STAGE IN ITS BEARING UPON HIS DRAMA, by Prof. C. H. HERFORD, Litt.D.

THE WARWICK SHAKESPEARE. General editor, Professor C. H. HERFORD, Litt.D., F.B.A.

Play	Edited by
ANTONY AND CLEOPATRA.	A. E. Morgan, M.A., and W. Sherard Vines, M.A.
AS YOU LIKE IT.	J. C. Smith, M.A., B.A.
CORIOLANUS.	Sir Edmund K. Chambers, K.B.E., C.B., M.A., D.Litt·
CYMBELINE.	A. J. Wyatt, M.A.
HAMLET.	Sir Edmund K. Chambers.
HENRY THE FOURTH—Part I.	F. W. Moorman, B.A., Ph.D
HENRY THE FOURTH—Part II.	C.H.Herford, Litt. D., F.B.A.
HENRY THE FIFTH.	G. C. Moore Smith, D.Litt., Ph.D., LL.D.
JULIUS CÆSAR.	Arthur D. Innes, M.A.
KING JOHN.	G. C. Moore Smith.
KING LEAR.	D. Nichol Smith.
LOVE'S LABOUR'S LOST.	A. E. Morgan, M.A., and W. Sherard Vines, M.A.
MACBETH.	Sir Edmund K. Chambers.
THE MERCHANT OF VENICE.	H. L. Withers.
A MIDSUMMER-NIGHT'S DREAM.	Sir Edmund K. Chambers.
MUCH ADO ABOUT NOTHING.	J. C. Smith, M.A., B.A.
OTHELLO.	C.H.Herford, Litt. D.,F.B.A.
RICHARD THE SECOND.	C. H. Herford.
RICHARD THE THIRD.	Sir George Macdonald, K.C.B., D.Litt., LL.D.
ROMEO AND JULIET.	J. E. Crofts, B.Litt.
THE TEMPEST.	F. S. Boas, M.A., LL.D.
TROILUS AND CRESSIDA.	Bonamy Dobrée, O.B.E., M.A.
TWELFTH NIGHT.	Arthur D. Innes, M.A.
THE WINTER'S TALE.	C. H. Herford.

INTRODUCTION

1. LITERARY HISTORY OF THE PLAY AND DATE OF COMPOSITION

The literary history of the *First Part of Henry IV* is a history of success. The first (Quarto) edition of the play appeared in 1598, with the following title:—The | History of | Henry the Fourth; | with the battell at Shrewsburie, | *betweene the King and Lord* | Henry Percy, surnamed | Henrie Hotspur of | the North. | *With the humorous conceits of Sir* | John Falstalffe. | At London. | Printed by P. S. for Andrew Wise. . . . 1598. As the title indicates, this was only the First Part of the play; the Second Part issued from the house of the same publisher two years later. In the year 1599, a second edition of the *First Part of Henry IV* appeared, which, according to the title-page, had been "newly corrected by William Shakespeare". Three more quarto editions were produced before the author's death (dated 1604, 1608, 1613)—a sufficient indication of the popularity of the play with the reading public of Shakespeare's time. Of his other plays only *Richard III* reached a fifth edition by 1616.

The success of the play, which was largely due to the Falstaff scenes, is revealed in other ways. If tradition tell true, *The Merry Wives of Windsor* owes its creation to Queen Elizabeth's delight in Falstaff, and to her desire to see him in love. There is, further, a reference to Falstaff in the speech of Macilente which brings to a conclusion Ben Jonson's *Every Man out of his Humour*, 1599:

"Marry, I will not . . . beg a plaudite for God's sake; but

if you, out of the bounty of your good-liking will bestow it, why, you may in time make lean Macilente as fat as Sir John Falstaff."

But the most striking illustration of the popularity of the famous knight is that furnished by the frontispiece to Kirkman's *The Wits, or Sport upon Sport*, a collection of farces and drolls, published in 1673. The engraving represents the stage of the Red Bull Playhouse, on which appear such conventionally comic characters as the Simpleton, the Changeling, and the French Dancing-master; amongst these is seen Sir John Falstaff accepting a cup of sack from the hands of Dame Quickly. But this popularity was not won without the intrusion of a note of dissent. In the original version of the play, as delivered by the author to the actors, Falstaff bore the name of Sir John Oldcastle, the famous Lollard who suffered martyrdom under Henry V. The character of Oldcastle had after his death been travestied by the orthodox party in the church until, in spite of subsequent Protestant opposition, he assumed the form of a roysterer and profligate, the corrupter of Henry V during his youth. He appears in this light in the old play, *The Famous Victories of Henry V*, whence Shakespeare drew several hints for his own work, amongst others the name and a faint outline of the character of the Lollard knight. The fact that the Elizabethan public readily identified Shakespeare's knight with the Lollard martyr aroused the resentment of Henry Brooke, Lord Cobham, who claimed descent from Oldcastle. By making his grievances known at court, he forced Shakespeare to substitute the name of Falstaff for that of Oldcastle in the first quarto editions of both parts. To destroy effectually the idea that Falstaff was to be identified with the Lollard knight, Shakespeare makes a very definite statement in the Epilogue to *2 Henry IV*:

"If you be not too much cloyed with fat meat, our humble author will continue the story, with Sir John in it . . . where for anything I know Falstaff shall die of a sweat, unless already a' be killed with your hard opinions; for Oldcastle died a martyr, and this is not the man".

Yet even this did not satisfy the party which had taken offence at the name of Oldcastle. Attention was drawn to the real character of Sir John Oldcastle, and two plays, entitled respectively *The First Part of the Life and Death of Sir John Oldcastle*, and *The Second Part of Sir John Oldcastle with his Martyrdom*, were published in 1600. According to Henslowe, both plays were the joint work of Munday, Wilson, Drayton, and Hathaway. How far these plays were intended to be an antidote to Shakespeare's *Henry IV* may be judged from the following verses of the Prologue:—

> " It is no pampered glutton we present,
>   Nor aged counsellor to youthful sin,
>   But one whose virtue shone above the rest".

Traces of the earlier name of Falstaff are to be found in both parts of *Henry IV*, over and above the definite statement (already quoted) from the Epilogue. Thus in *1 Henry IV*, i. 2, the Prince addresses Falstaff as "my old lad of the castle", while in *2 Henry IV*, i. 2. 137, *Old* is by an oversight prefixed to Falstaff's speech in the first Quarto edition. Twenty years after the appearance of the first Quarto of *Henry IV*, we find that the name Oldcastle still clung to the person of Shakespeare's knight. In Nathaniel Field's *Amend for Ladies* (1618) the author asks:

> " Did you never see
> The Play where the fat knight, *hight Oldcastle*,
> Did tell you truly what this honour was?"

In substituting the name Falstaff for that of Oldcastle, Shakespeare probably had in mind the historic Sir John Fastolfe, a gentleman of Norfolk, a distinguished soldier in the French wars of Henry V, and at one time owner of the Boar's Head Tavern, Eastcheap. He is an actual character in *1 Henry VI*, and is banished by the king on the charge of Talbot, for cowardly flight at the battle of

Patay. As a matter of fact Fastolfe was no more a coward than Oldcastle was a profligate, and Holinshed himself makes it clear that the charge of cowardice was subsequently withdrawn, and Fastolfe restored to his former place of honour. Accordingly Shakespeare's use of the name Falstaff met with censure just as that of Oldcastle had done, and as late as 1662, Fuller in his *Worthies* calls attention to the injustice done by the dramatist to the memory of a valiant man:

"The stage hath been overbold with a great warrior's memory, making him a thrasonical puff, and emblem of mock-valour. . . Now as I am glad that Sir John Oldcastle is put out, so I am sorry that Sir John Fastolfe is put in, to relieve his memory in this base service, to be the anvil for every dull wit to strike upon. Nor is our comedian excusable, by some alteration of his name writing him Sir John Falstafe; . . . few do heed the inconsiderable difference of spelling of their name."

It need scarcely be added that in the creation of the character of Falstaff, Shakespeare had no satiric purpose in view, and that in calling him first Oldcastle, and then Falstaff, he had no wish to heap derision upon the historic bearers of those names. He took the first name, as we have seen, from *The Famous Victories*, and when objections were raised to it, recalled that of Sir John Fastolfe and the ignominious position in which that knight appeared in *1 Henry VI*. It may seem strange that Shakespeare did not choose a purely fictitious name for his knight when he found that objections were raised to the name of Oldcastle. The reason for his unwillingness to do this may perhaps be found in the fact that, as he was writing an historical play, he wished all the characters that were to take part in the serious plot—and Falstaff, it must be remembered, is one of these—to have something of an historic standing.

There is not much to say with regard to the relation of the various Quarto editions of the play to one another, and of their relation to the Folio editions of 1623 and 1632. The second, third, fourth, and fifth editions all profess on their title-pages to be "newly corrected by William Shakespeare", but are, on the whole, inferior to Q 1. The Cambridge editors state that the first Folio "seems to have been printed from a partially corrected copy of the fifth Quarto", and add that "in many places the readings coincide with those of the earlier Quartos, which were probably consulted by the corrector". The present edition follows in the main the text of the Cambridge editors: on the very few occasions on which another reading has been taken, an indication to that effect is given in the Notes.

It is generally agreed that the composition of *1 Henry IV* falls within the years 1596–1597. It must have been finished by February, 1598, for on the 25th of that month it was entered on the Stationers' Register under the title of "The Historye of Henry the iiiith", Date of Composition. while the fact that Oldcastle was the name originally borne by Falstaff in the Second Part as well as in the First Part, indicates that this Second Part must have been written before the appearance of the first Quarto edition of the First Part (1598), in which the knight appears under the name of Falstaff. The close connection between the two Parts suggests that they were written in direct succession, while slight allusions in *1 Henry IV* to events which happened in the year 1596 give us a time-limitation in the other direction. The evidence furnished by metrical tests also points to the years 1596–97 as the date of composition.

Popular tradition, which declares that Shakespeare wrote his *Merry Wives of Windsor* at the request of Queen Elizabeth, who, being delighted with the Falstaff of *Henry IV*, desired to see the knight in love, is our chief basis for assuming that the play was Stage History. well received on the Elizabethan stage. Apparently it was also popular with Elizabeth's successor; it was acted before James in 1613 under the title of "Hotspur".[1] Its popularity was maintained after the Restoration. Pepys saw it acted in London no less than five

1 Fleay: *Chronicle of the English Drama.*

times between 1660 and 1668. We read in his *Diary*, under entry of December 31, 1660: "At the office all the morning, and after that home, and not staying to dine, I went out, and in Paul's Churchyard I bought the play of Henry the Fourth, and so went to the new theatre and saw it acted; but my expectation being too great, it did not please me, as otherwise I believe it would; and my having a book I believe did spoil it a little". At a later representation he speaks of it as "a good play". The famous Restoration actor Betterton reckoned *1 Henry IV* as one of his greatest successes: up to the year 1700 he played the part of Hotspur, and then, growing old, fell back upon that of Falstaff. Genest, in his *Account of the English Stage*, mentions twenty-one performances of the play at London theatres between 1700 and 1826. Booth, Mills, and Quin all played the part of Falstaff with distinction. In 1803 the play was revised by Kemble, and performed by his company at the Covent Garden Theatre.

2. THE SOURCES OF THE INCIDENTS

The sources of *1 Henry IV*, as far as we are able to determine them, are: (1) Holinshed's *Chronicles of England, Scotland, and Ireland*, published first of all in 1577, and in a second and enlarged edition in 1587: it was this second edition which Shakespeare used; (2) a play by an unknown hand entitled *The Famous Victories of Henry V*, first published in 1598, but acted at least ten years before. The former work supplied Shakespeare with most of his historic material: his exact debt to the *Famous Victories* was slight, and is to be detected, as far at least as *1 Henry IV* is concerned, chiefly in the comic scenes.

Shakespeare's allegiance to Holinshed was of a different character from that which bound him to Plutarch. Whereas in his borrowings from the Greek historian his plan was to keep as closely to his authority as the conditions of a drama would allow, in the case of Holin-

shed he usually allowed himself much greater freedom.
Passages may be found in such a play as *Julius Cæsar*
which read like poetical paraphrases of North's noble
prose; but only very rarely is there such a correspondence
between the English historical plays and the pages of
Holinshed. Sometimes, indeed, Shakespeare finds a pic-
turesque phrase or word in Holinshed, and embodies it
in his plays; less frequently he gives a free rendering of
some of Holinshed's more eloquent passages. Thus we
read in Holinshed: "Thus were father and son reconciled,
betwixt whom the said *pick-thanks* had sown division";
and in *1 Henry IV* (iii. 2) the Prince, charged by his father
with disgraceful conduct, refutes the

> " many tales devised,
> Which oft the ear of greatness needs must hear,
> By smiling *pick-thanks* and base newsmongers".

In his rendering of Hotspur's speech to his men before
the battle of Shrewsbury, Holinshed rises to noble though
irregular eloquence: "Foorthwith the lord Persie (as a
capteine of high courage) began to exhort the capteines
and souldiers to prepare themselves to battell, sith the
matter was growen to that point, that by no meanes it
could be avoided, so that (said he) this daie shall either
bring us all to advancement and honor, or else it shall
chance us to be overcome, shall deliver us from the kings
spitefull malice and disdaine: for plaieng the men (as we
ought to doo) better it is to die in battell for the common-
wealths cause, than through cowardlike feare to prolong
life, which after shall be taken from us, by sentence of the
enimie".

An echo of these thoughts is distinctly heard in the
words which Shakespeare places on the lips of his Hotspur on the same occasion:

> " O gentlemen, the time of life is short!
> To spend that shortness basely were too long,
> If life did ride upon a dial's point,
> Still ending at the arrival of an hour.

An if we live, we live to tread on kings;
If die, brave death, when princes die with us!"
—v. 2. 82–87.

In adapting Holinshed's story to the requirements of a drama, Shakespeare made alterations, omissions, and additions, yet did not depart very widely from the main drift of the narrative. Most of these changes will be easily noticed when the quotations from Holinshed, found in the Notes, are read; but it may prove serviceable to summarize them a little at this point. Putting aside the comic scenes and the character of Falstaff, of which there is no suggestion in Holinshed, we may notice the following points of difference :—

(i) Shakespeare has introduced the following characters, of whom there is no mention in Holinshed's account of the first part of the Percy rebellion : Prince John of Lancaster, Lady Percy, and Lady Mortimer. Prince John is introduced probably in order to serve as a foil to the Prince of Wales; we hear his voice only when he is in his brother's company. Lady Percy and Lady Mortimer, on the other hand, are evidently introduced with the purpose of diversifying the characterization by the inclusion of women characters.

(ii) Shakespeare's Henry IV is less valiant, and his Prince of Wales more valiant, than Holinshed's on the occasion of the battle of Shrewsbury. Shakespeare departs from Holinshed in representing the Prince as the rescuer of his father and the victor over Hotspur. (See quotation from Holinshed prefixed to v. 3.)

(iii) Shakespeare has changed considerably the ages of King Henry and Hotspur. He represents the King as an old man (see v. i. 13, "To crush our old limbs in ungentle steel"), whereas he was only thirty-six at the time of the battle of Shrewsbury. Hotspur, who was in reality slightly older than the King, is made of exactly the same age as Prince Henry. The reason for these changes is to be sought for in Shakespeare's determination to represent Hotspur and the Prince as rivals at every point, and contending with one another in the first flush of manhood.

The above points indicate changes in respect of characterization; the following bear mainly upon plot-structure.

(iv) Shakespeare makes no use of Holinshed's statement that the Percies, when raising the revolt, circulated the report that Richard II was still alive.

(v) There is no suggestion in Holinshed of the contents of Act ii. scene 3, while in the case of other scenes, Shakespeare has introduced many new circumstances (compare iii. 1 with the quotation from Holinshed prefixed to the notes to that scene).

(vi) Shakespeare has removed the reconciliation scene between the King and Prince Henry (iii. 2) from its true position in Holinshed, and has introduced it at a much earlier period.

(vii) Shakespeare represents Glendower and his Welsh irregulars as being absent from the battle of Shrewsbury; Holinshed, though he does not mention Glendower as a sharer in the fight, says: "The Welshmen also which before had laine lurking in the woods, mounteines, and marishes, hearing of this battell toward, came to the aid of the Persies, and refreshed the wearied people with new succours".

Before considering Shakespeare's second source—*The Famous Victories of Henry V*—the reader's attention is drawn to the fourth book of Daniel's *History of the Civil Wars* as a possible supplementary source to Holinshed for the historic scenes of Shakespeare's play. Daniel published the first four books of his historical poem in 1595, and it is difficult to believe that Shakespeare was unacquainted with so important a work: whether he derived any ideas from it remains to be seen. In the fourth book of his *History of the Civil Wars* Daniel covers practically the same ground as Shakespeare in his two parts of *Henry IV*. His authority is apparently Holinshed, but he differs from him in several particulars, and these points of difference lie very close to those in which Shakespeare is at

variance with the chronicler. In the first place, he represents Hotspur as a young man, and as engaging in combat with the Prince of Wales in the battle of Shrewsbury:

> " There shall *young* Hotspur, with a fury led,
>   Meete with thy forward son, as fierce as he:
>   There warlike Worster, long experienced
>   In forraine arms, shall come t' incounter thee.
>   There Dowglas, to thy Stafford, shall make head;
>   There Vernon, for thy valiant Blunt, shall be.
>   There shalt thou find a doubtfull bloody day,
>   Though sickenesse keep Northumberland away."
>   (Daniel's *Civil Wars*, ed. Grosart, iv. 34.)

In the actual account of the battle Daniel tells of the
bravery of the Prince, but does not say that Hotspur fell
by his hand.

Secondly, Daniel departs from Holinshed, but is at one
with Shakespeare, in making the Prince rescue his father
from death at the hands of Douglas:

> " Hadst thou not there lent present speedy ayd
>   To thy indangered father, nerely tyrde,
>   Whom fierce incountring Dowglas overlaid
>   That day had there his troublous life expirde ".
>   (*Ibid.* iv. 49.)

(Holinshed's account of the battle will be found in the
quotation prefixed to Act v. sc. 3.)

Thirdly, whereas Holinshed represents the Percies as
receiving assistance from the Welsh in the battle of
Shrewsbury, Daniel agrees with Shakespeare—and with
historic truth—in declaring that they were not present on
that occasion:

> " The joining with the Welsh (they had decreed)
>   Stopt hereby part; which made their cause the worse ".
>   (*Ibid.* iv. 36.)

Lastly, it may be pointed out that Daniel represents the
troubles that encompassed Henry IV throughout his reign
as a righteous Nemesis falling upon him, because of the

"indirect crook'd ways" by which he procured the crown. Referring to Northumberland's absence from the battle of Shrewsbury, he says:

> "Who yet reserv'd (though, after, quit for this)
> Another tempest on thy head to rayse;
> *As if, still, wrong-revenging Nemesis*
> *Did meane t' afflict all thy continuall days*".
>
> (*Ibid.* iv. 35.)

Every reader of the two parts of *Henry IV* will be aware that this is precisely the view taken by Shakespeare (see *1 Henry IV*, iii. 2. 4–7, and *2 Henry IV*, iv. 5. 178–200).

It is of course possible—but in the present editor's opinion unlikely—that these points of agreement between Shakespeare and Daniel as against Holinshed are purely accidental, and that the two poets, in shaping an historical poem and an historical play respectively, made these changes independently, and with the same purposes in view. But inasmuch as it is unlikely that Shakespeare was unacquainted with Daniel's poem, it is reasonable to suppose that he had that poem in mind when he departed from Holinshed in his account of the battle of Shrewsbury.

The Famous Victories of Henry V is a short play, chiefly in prose, to which Shakespeare owed certain incidents of *1 Henry IV*, *2 Henry IV*, and *Henry V*. We have evidence of the popularity of this play in Elizabethan times, yet its intrinsic worth is very slight. It has a certain rollicking movement which no doubt appealed to the Elizabethan play-goer, but of true wit or humour there is scarcely anything. Yet, inasmuch as it was from this play that Shakespeare drew his idea of Prince Henry's comradeship with Falstaff and his satellites, it claims some notice here. Amongst the characters of the play are Sir John Oldcastle, Ned,[1] Tom, and Gadshill, while the incidents include the robbery by the prince and his confederates of the king's "receivers", and their retirement after the robbery to a tavern in Eastcheap, where their riotous mirth leads to a

---

[1] It should be borne in mind that Poins' name is Edward.

quarrel and the interposition of the sheriff and mayor of London, who afterwards make complaint to the king. Later in the play there is a scene of reconciliation between the prince and his father, which faintly suggests the circumstances of Act iii. scene 2 of *1 Henry IV*. Finally, the idea of the mock representation on the part of Falstaff and Prince Hal of an interview between the prince and his father (ii. 4) may have been suggested by the rehearsing on the part of Derick and John Cobler in *The Famous Victories* of the scene between the Prince of Wales and the Lord Chief Justice. (See quotation from *The Famous Victories* given in the Notes to ii. 4.)

But when the most is made of these points of resemblance, we cannot fail to recognize the illimitable gulf which separates the two plays. The comic scenes of the earlier work are mere horse-play, the wit consists in the bandying about of such oaths as "sowndes" and "Gogs wounds"; while in order to realize to the full the transcendent greatness of Shakespeare's characterization, we have only to compare Shakespeare's Falstaff with the Sir John Oldcastle (familiarly known as 'Jockey') of *The Famous Victories*.

3. PLOT AND GENERAL CHARACTERISTICS

An interval of three or four years—1593 to 1596-97—probably separates the *First Part of Henry IV* from its nearest predecessor in the field of the history-play—*Richard II*. During those four years Shakespeare's dramatic powers had developed rapidly, he had freed himself from his dependence on Marlowe, and had established his position as an independent playwright. Comedy in its various forms had been his chief concern since he brought his first series of historical plays to an end with *Richard III* and *Richard II*, and to these years belong such comedies as *The Merchant of Venice*, *A Midsummer Night's Dream*, and *The Taming of the Shrew*. Returning to the history-play in 1596-97, he produced in rapid succession *1 Henry IV*, *2 Henry IV*, and *Henry V*; and then, except for his share in *Henry VIII* at the end of his dramatic career, relinquished this form of drama entirely.

The two plays of *Henry IV*, together with *Henry V*, form a trilogy, in which the dominating character is Henry V. Moreover, in spite of the interval of time which separates *1 Henry IV* from *Richard II*, there is a close connection of historic interest between them. The latter play abounds in references to incidents recorded in the earlier play, and the first scene of *1 Henry IV* is as much a continuation of the last scenes of *Richard II* as the first scenes of *2 Henry IV* are of its immediate forerunner. It is therefore possible to group the four plays together and regard them as an historic tetralogy, which traces the fortunes of the House of Lancaster from nadir to zenith—from the banishment of Bolingbroke and the death of John of Gaunt to the triumph of Agincourt.

Yet, in spite of the historic interest which connects *Richard II* with *1 Henry IV* and its successors, the earlier play has little in common with the later ones when regarded in relation to its plot-construction or general style. The early history or chronicle plays, such as *The Famous Victories of Henry V*, or *The Troublesome Reign of King John*, which were written before the star of Marlowe rose to the ascendant, were more epic than dramatic. In these plays the episodes follow one another in chronological order, scarcely any attempt is made at regular plot-construction or unity of theme, and the action is extended over a considerable number of years. In these plays, too, there is a good deal of boisterous low-life comedy, mixed with the more serious and historical episodes; finally, prose scenes and prose speeches appear intermingled with the poetic portions of the play. Marlowe, however, as Professor Schelling points out in his *English Chronicle Play*, created a new type of history-play with his *Edward II* (entered for publication in 1593). In this play much more attempt is made at plot-construction and unity of design, there is no comic relief, and no

prose.   Shakespeare, who was in his youth under Marlowe's influence, follows the Marlowesque or dramatic
type of history-play in his *Richard III*, and less closely
in *Richard II*.   These plays have throughout the characteristics of Marlowe's *Edward II* as regards unity of
design and absence of prose and of comic relief.   They
mark, indeed, the consummation of the dramatic and tragic
type of history-play.[1]

In *1 Henry IV* Shakespeare reverts to the earlier epic
form.   The play, it is true, has much more unity than
2 Henry IV and *Henry V*, yet such a scene as Act iv.
scene 4, together with the king's speech at the very
end of the play, indicate that the victory at Shrewsbury does not mark the close of the Percy rebellion, but
only of an episode in that rebellion.   In *1 Henry IV*,
too, there is abundant comic relief from the serious interests of the play, and also plenty of prose.[2]   In these
respects, then, *1 Henry IV* thus marks a departure from
the type of play represented by *Richard II*, and a reversion
to, or rather a development of, the earlier type of epic play.

The fusion of comic and tragic, or at least serious,
scenes, which is of the very essence of the romantic drama
as opposed to the classic, is nowhere more triumphantly
effected than in *Henry IV*.   The historic plot and the
Falstaffian comedy are outwardly distinct, but neither is
simply embedded in the other.   Prince Henry, and to
a less extent Falstaff himself, have a part as well in the
serious as in the comic scenes; while towards the close
of the play the comic episodes are not allotted to detached
and independent scenes, but introduced into the historical
narrative, so that we pass without a pause from the heroic
tragedy of Hotspur's death to Falstaff's humorous soliloquy
on counterfeits.

There is another and more subtle connection between

---

[1] *King John*, the probable date of which is 1595, stands in most of these respects
midway between the earlier histories and the later Lancastrian trilogy.

[2] In *1 Henry IV* there are 1464 lines of prose out of a total of 3170 lines;
in *2 Henry IV*, 1860 out of 3446; in *Henry V*, 1531 out of 3379.

the serious and comic scenes. Hotspur, and to a less degree many of the other historic characters, give to the play something of an heroic temper. In the place of the tragic woof of such a play as *Richard II*, Shakespeare presents us with an epic theme to which the quest of honour on the part of Hotspur and Prince Henry lends unity of motive. Viewed thus, the battle-field of Shrewsbury is a tourney-ground as well, and is regarded in this light by the two chief combatants; only there can their equally strong, though differently felt, cravings for honour be satisfied. Honour, with its oblique shadow, reputation, is thus the *leitmotiv* of the historic plot. To all this the comic scenes and the person of Falstaff offer a foil which becomes at times almost a parody. The honour which is so ostentatiously pursued by Hotspur, so quietly by the prince, is in Falstaff's eyes a vain shadow. He orders his life without regard to honour; then, when the preparations for the battle force the consideration of honour upon his mind, he devotes to it his famous catechism, and discovers that honour is but a word. A little later, when he sees Sir Walter Blunt lying dead on the plain of Shrewsbury, honour becomes of even less value : it assumes in his eyes the form of vanity.

The comedy of *1 Henry IV* is a new form of Shakespearian comedy, quite distinct from the romantic comedy of gentlemen and gentlewomen in *Love's Labour's Lost*, *The Two Gentlemen of Verona*, or of the Belmont scene at the close of *The Merchant of Venice*, and no less distinct from the clown-play of Launce and Speed, or of Bottom and his fellow-craftsmen, which came to Shakespeare as a heritage from the pre-Elizabethan drama. In *1 Henry IV* we have, instead of romantic comedy and clown-play, the realistic comedy of London life which the Elizabethan dramatists knew so well, and which was to play so great a part in the comedies of Ben Jonson and his school. The *vis comica* and horse-play of the early drama is not absent from *1 Henry IV*, but it is purged of its grossness and buffoonery, and enriched by the superb humour which lights up the person of Falstaff, and gives to the intellectual fabric of his wit-contests its incandescent glow.

A consideration of the diction and verse of *1 Henry IV* reveals the fact that Shakespeare had by 1596 thrown off most of those mannerisms which are traceable in his early works. He still shows a certain fondness for word-play even in the serious portions of the drama, but little is left of the florid diction, the tricks of rhetoric, and the fancifulness of his earliest dramas. Above all, we notice how diction and verse are subjected to the exigencies of his dramatic instinct. We gain insight into the characters of the *dramatis personæ* not only by what they say, but by their mode of saying it. " The style is the man." The dignified but stilted and formal language of Henry IV, set to verse which is peculiarly regular and chary of " light endings " and " double endings ", is as indicative of the king's character as the abrupt, colloquial diction and impetuous verse of Hotspur's speeches is of him.[1] In like manner, the nobly epic style of Vernon in iv. 1. 97–110 and v. 2. 52–69 is made to reflect an heroic element in his character. The dramatic character of the verse of *Henry IV* is seen in yet another way; not only does it indicate the character of different speakers, but also the different moods of the same speaker at different times. Hotspur's diction is, as we have seen, usually colloquial, but when he is stirred by noble indignation or chivalrous ardour it loses its prosaic quality and becomes suddenly impassioned and imaginative. (See i. 3. 93–112, and 201–208.)

Looking at the style of the poetic portions of *1 Henry IV* as a whole, we cannot fail to be struck by its amplitude and massive strength. Occasionally there is epigrammatic point, as in the Prince's dictum on the seemingly dead Falstaff:

" I could have better spared a better man ",

but for the most part Shakespeare seeks to impress rather

---

[1] Compare the king's speeches in i. 1 and iii. 2 with those of Hotspur in iii. 1.

than to dazzle. The style of *Henry IV* (to quote Professor
Herford) "has a breadth and largeness of movement, an
unsought greatness of manner, which marks the consum-
mate artist who no longer dons his singing-robes when
he sings".

When we apply to *1 Henry IV* those metrical tests
which have so often been adduced to furnish evidence as
to the date of composition of Shakespeare's plays, one
striking feature comes into prominence—the infrequency
of double or feminine endings.[1] Referring to the tables
given by Professor Dowden in his *Primer*, and by Professor Herford in his Introduction to *Richard II* (Warwick
Shakespeare), we find that the percentage of double endings in *1 Henry IV* falls as low as 5.1, but rises to 16.3
in *2 Henry IV*, and to 20.5 in *Henry V*. In Shakespeare's
later plays the percentage of double endings steadily rises
till in *The Tempest* it reaches 33. In *Richard III* the
percentage is 19.5, in *Richard II*, 11, and in *King John*, 6.3.
The infrequency of double endings in *1 Henry IV* points
to the fact, as Professor Herford states, that Shakespeare
was here making experiments as to the rhythmical effects
of the different forms of blank verse; it also seems probable
that it is intended to give to the blank verse of *1 Henry
IV* something of an epic character. In epic blank verse,
such as that of Milton, double endings are rare; according
to Professor Masson the occurrence of such endings in
Paradise Lost varies from about 1 per cent in Book i
to about 5 per cent in Book x. Whether this attempt
to give to the blank verse of *1 Henry IV* an epic character,
by reducing to a minimum the number of double endings,
has anything in common with the fact that in this play
he is reverting to the epic type of history-play is a matter
of speculation: certain it is that in *2 Henry IV* and *Henry
V*, the plots of which are more epic in structure than that
of *1 Henry IV*, Shakespeare used double endings with
a greater frequency than he had done in any earlier play
with the exception of *Richard III*.

[1] For the explanation of these terms see Dowden's *Shakespeare Primer*.

Turning in the last place from outward form to inner meaning, we may briefly consider the political significance of the play. Both parts of *Henry IV* present a study in the working of Nemesis. Richard II's deposition was in the interests of the country a necessary act, and the deposer was in every way a man more fit to rule. Yet the stigma of usurpation clings to Bolingbroke, renders his rule insecure, and embitters his life. The prophecy of the aged bishop of Carlisle (see *Richard II*, iv. 1) is fulfilled to the letter, and in the two parts of *Henry IV* we follow the course of those tumultuous wars which "kin with kin and kind with kind confound". Nor is this all: not only is there open warfare in the country and discord within the king's family circle, but there is also the working of remorse in his own soul. This is brought home to us most forcibly in the *Second Part* (see Act iv. scene 5), but it is present already in the *First Part*. The king sees in his son's "wildness" divine vengeance for his own "mistreadings". That this Nemesis should be called into play here may seem paradoxical. Henry IV is the deliverer of his country from the hands of a weak tyrant, and as such merits reward rather than punishment. But Shakespeare seems to have regarded the kingly office as something sacred. It is true that as a patriot he placed the welfare and safety of England high above the welfare and safety of any individual monarch; yet he saw evil in usurpation. Just as in the trilogy of Aeschylus, Orestes, though he does right in slaying his murderess-mother Clytemnestra, is nevertheless pursued by the Furies, so Bolingbroke, though he frees England from extortion and misgovernment, has to expiate the crime of usurpation. Shakespeare even makes Henry V feel a sense of the wrong his father committed when, on the field of Agincourt, he prays:

> " Not to-day, O Lord,
> O, not to-day, think not upon the fault
> My father made in compassing the crown!"
>
> —iv. 1. 277.

A king as king is in Shakespeare's eyes

> " The figure of God's majesty,
> His captain, steward, deputy, elect ";
>   (*Richard II*, iv. 1. 125),

and accordingly Nemesis overtakes the man who de-thrones him.   But though the usurper has to expiate his crime, yet, inasmuch as he too becomes the anointed head of his people, he acquires a sacred nature.   The loyal Blunt, when Hotspur reproaches him that he is his enemy, replies:

> " And God defend but still I should stand so,
> So long as out of limit and true rule
> You stand against *anointed majesty* ".

Blunt's loyalty to Henry IV is not a merely personal matter: he sees in the king, usurper though he be, "anointed majesty", and for this he lays down his life.

4. THE CHARACTERS

Hazlitt was writing of *Henry IV* when he said of Shake-speare : " He appears to have been all the characters, and in all the situations he describes ".   Though the play is deficient in female characters, it is second to none in the rich variety and lifelikeness of its characterization.   We are introduced to a world of full activity; the court, the tavern, and the camp are the scenes of action, and in each of them the pulse of life beats strongly.   Most of the his-torical characters are drawn from the pages of Holinshed, but whereas in the Chronicle they are often devoid of individuality, they receive at Shakespeare's hands full individualization.   Holinshed is content to tell us what his characters did, but Shakespeare lays bare the motives of their action.

The characters fall naturally into two groups, which correspond to the two centres of action—the historic plot and the Falstaffian comedy.   The central figure in the

former group is Hotspur; in the latter, Falstaff: but the
true hero of the play, and the man who unites the two
spheres of action, is the Prince of Wales.

King Henry, though an imposing, is not an attractive
figure, and his character in the play is a natural development of his character as Bolingbroke in *Richard
II*. Holinshed's Henry IV is a martial figure,
who distinguishes himself as much on the field of battle
as in the council - chamber; but Shakespeare, while he
reveals his promptness and decision of action in taking
steps to quell the Percy rebellion, makes little of his prowess
in the fight. He won the crown from Richard by diplomacy, and not by shock of arms, and Hotspur, who scorns
diplomacy, calls him a " vile politician " and a " king of
smiles ". We come into closest contact with the King
when, in his private interview with the Prince of Wales,
he lays bare the devices which he used in winning the
throne:

> " And then I stole all courtesy from heaven,
>   And dress'd myself in such humility
>   That I did pluck allegiance from men's hearts,
>   Loud shouts and salutations from their mouths,
>   Even in the presence of the crowned king ".
>   —iii. 2. 50-54.

There is a singular correspondence between these words
placed on the lips of Henry and those which Richard
uttered years before when Bolingbroke was being driven
into exile:

> " Ourself and Bushy, Bagot here and Green,
>   Observed his courtship to the common people:
>   How he did seem to dive into their hearts,
>   With humble and familiar courtesy,
>   What reverence he did throw away on slaves,
>   Wooing poor craftsmen with the craft of smiles
>   And patient underbearing of his fortune,
>   As 't were to banish their affects with him ".
>   —*Richard II*, Act i. sc. 4.

Henry IV has won the crown by subtle contrivings, and
no man knows better than he the insecurity of his position.
Looked at from one point of view, both parts of *Henry IV*
represent the fulfilment of the aged Bishop of Carlisle's
prophecy:

> " And if you crown him, let me prophesy;
> The blood of English shall manure the ground,
> And future ages groan for this foul act;
> Peace shall go sleep with Turks and infidels,
> And in this seat of peace tumultuous wars
> Shall kin with kin and kind with kind confound ".
> —*Richard II*, Act iv. sc. 1.

The insecurity of his position renders Henry suspicious
and jealous. He is jealous of Hotspur's victory over
Douglas, suspicious of Mortimer, whose right to the
throne is better than his own, and it is this suspicion
and jealousy which foment the Percy rebellion. His
growing sense of suspicion bears its own Nemesis with
it; it dulls his understanding, and renders his life lonely.
He fails to understand the character of his eldest son,
suspects his loyalty, and drives him from the court to the
tavern. The atmosphere of that court is chill and numb-
ing; no gracious womanly figure, like that of Richard's
consort, appears there, and the King looks upon all with
mistrust. The Percy rising brings out what is best in
him, and in his plans for the campaign we see once again
the far-seeing, practical man that won the throne from the
hapless Richard. He forms a plan of action wisely and
swiftly, is generous in his offers of mercy before the battle,
and shows that he has the welfare of his people at heart.
It is in the *Second Part of Henry IV* that we fully see
how hard the kingly crown has pressed upon his brow.
Anxiety and sleeplessness have rendered him prematurely
old, remorse for the evil that he has done in compassing
the crown pricks him, and his life is lonely and loveless.
In every act of Henry we see the success and the failure
which attend upon the calculating, diplomatic nature.

In opposition to Henry IV stands Henry Percy, the

Hotspur of the North. Shakespeare's love of character-contrasts was very great when he wrote *Henry IV*, and in the person of Hotspur he has presented us with a contrast both to the King and to the Prince of Wales. Hotspur is an heroic figure, a representative of the vanishing age of chivalry. His character is composed of apparently antagonistic elements. Rough in speech, and affecting a contempt for "mincing poetry", he is at the same time full of the imaginative power which makes for poetry, and some of the most poetic speeches in the play fall from his lips. Placing the quest of honour above all things, it seems to him

> "an easy leap
> To pluck bright honour from the pale-faced moon",

and then a moment later he talks of having the Prince of Wales "poison'd with a pot of ale". Again, ardent and emotional as his nature is, he opposes a cold scepticism to the superstitious arrogance of Glendower, and adopts towards his wife, Lady Percy, a bantering tone which appears to conceal his deep affection for her. This inconsistency springs from a nature which is, before all things, impulsive. Hotspur is indeed swayed by impulse, as the King is swayed by calculation. In word and in act he expresses the thoughts and feelings of the moment, and by so doing betrays his lack of self-restraint and tact. Thus he offends Glendower by his scornful ridicule of his pretensions, brooks no opposition in the division of the land, and cannot endure the thought of postponing the battle of Shrewsbury until his forces are all on the field and ready for action. Hotspur delights us with his candour, his high spirits and valiant manliness, but we are forced to confess that his nature is not profound. Even his love of honour is superficial when compared with that of the Prince of Wales. He will leap to the moon or dive to the bottom of the sea in quest of honour, provided that he may bear about with him, for all to see, the "dignities" of the honour he has won; but the Prince of Wales, having satisfied his own inward cravings for honour in the moment of his victory over Hotspur, cares little for "the bubble reputation", and is content that the credit of having slain Hotspur shall be Falstaff's. Hotspur's superficiality renders him at times ungenerous. The Prince, though in the presence of Falstaff he parodies with complete success Hotspur's restless activity and absent-mindedness, bears on more than one occasion a high tribute to his manly virtues; but his rival will say nothing good of him, nor listen to the praise of others. In Hotspur's eyes he is simply the "madcap Prince of Wales", and when Vernon ventures to praise the Prince's manly bearing, he impatiently interrupts him:

> "No more, no more; worse than the sun in March,
> This praise doth nourish agues".

Yet with all the defects of his qualities, Hotspur is a great and inspiring figure. His greatness is contagious, and compels admiration and imitation from his associates. Lady Percy makes no idle vaunt when, after his death, she says:

> "He was the mark and glass, copy and book,
> That fashioned others".

If he is scornful of Glendower's pretensions, his scorn springs from his deep love of truth. "Tell truth and shame the devil" is his candid advice to Glendower, while to Douglas he avers:

> "By God, I cannot flatter; I do defy
> The tongues of soothers".

It is his hatred of injustice and hypocrisy that makes him a rebel, his impatience and masterfulness are merely the effervescence of virile force, and his tactlessness flows from his candour. Hotspur's death at the hands of the Prince of Wales indicates something more than inferiority of swordsmanship: in his fall we see the valorous but unthinking heroism of a chivalrous age overcome by one in whom deftness of hand is combined with agility of mind.

critics

The Prince of Wales, though he has had his detractors, has usually, and we think rightly, been regarded as Shakespeare's ideal man of action, and, in the play which bears his name, his ideal king. This is a very different thing from saying that he is Shakespeare's ideal man. Some of the finer graces of manhood, which lie remote from the practical issues of life, find no place in his character. He lacks the poetic charm of Richard II, the intellectual subtlety of Hamlet, the ingenuousness of Brutus, and it is only fair to add that if he had possessed these qualities he would not have been Shakespeare's ideal man of action. For Shakespeare knew, as well as Aristotle and Spenser, that the politic virtues—the virtues of kingship—are different from the private virtues—the virtues of manhood; the qualities of kingliness which Shakespeare saw in Henry are all of a practical nature, and are united in him with a fineness of proportion which establishes a well-balanced character, and gives to that character elasticity and resilience.

Prince Henry.

We are concerned here with the character of Henry only in its earlier stages, before he came to be king. The chroniclers were fond of insisting on the sudden and almost miraculous conversion of the Prince on his father's death. Following a not altogether credible tradition, they represent him in his youth as a dissipated roysterer who is suddenly changed into a model king. Shakespeare accepts this tradition only to a certain degree; he allows the Archbishop of Canterbury and the Bishop of Ely to assert it in the opening scene of *Henry V*, but as we read the three plays in which Henry plays so prominent a part, we realize that the change is less sudden and less complete than the chroniclers represent it. From the Prince's soliloquy at the end of *1 Henry IV*, Act i. scene 2, we see that he is very far from being the slave of riotous pleasure, and that revelry is for him only a pastime with which he will dispense when the hour for strenuous action arrives. In his interview with his father in iii. 2, and in his conduct at the battle of Shrewsbury, we discover that the

the character develops for the letter in the play.

promise made by him in his soliloquy is fulfilled to the letter. The Prince's detractors have seen in this soliloquy, and in the pledges which the Prince makes to his father, a strain of self-consciousness and arrogance. Yet what seems like arrogance is in reality nothing more than that self-knowledge which the Greeks made the highest of all knowledge, and which is assuredly a politic virtue. Self-knowledge meant for him also self-control, and we are made conscious of this latent power of self-control amid the Prince's most riotous scenes. His temporary indulgence in tavern revelry, while it comes as a welcome relief after the strained formality of the court, serves also a diplomatic purpose:

> "And like bright metal on a sullen ground,
> My reformation, glittering o'er my fault,
> Shall show more goodly and attract more eyes
> Than that which hath no foil to set it off.
> I 'll so offend to make offence a skill;
> Redeeming time when men think least I will."

As we read these words of the Prince, we realize that he was not Bolingbroke's son for nothing; there is diplomacy even in his moments of revelry. His association with ostlers and drawers serves yet another purpose. His desire is to gain a fuller knowledge of men in every rank of life, and through fulness of knowledge to win broader sympathies and deeper insight into the duties of one who will one day be king, not only of nobles and prelates, but of tapsters and serving-men as well.

going in different directions

When we look discerningly into the Prince's character we realize that he unites in himself the highest qualities of men so divergent from each other as Henry IV and Hotspur. He has the diplomacy of Bolingbroke, but he tempers it with the martial prowess and chivalry of the great Percy. The latter is no match for him in soldiership, and on the field of Shrewsbury he is forced to "render every glory up" to the man he has so persistently derided. He has, too, the finer graces of the chivalrous nature—generosity and

scorned, made fun of

reverence. He has only praise for Hotspur, alive or dead, while the prowess of his brother, John of Lancaster, wins from him the highest tribute of respect:

> "Before, I loved thee as a brother, John;
> But now, I do respect thee as my soul". *what he deserves*

When the King, in return for his high deserts, gives him the life of Douglas, he graciously bestows the favour upon his younger brother, and contrives that Douglas's ransomless freedom shall come to him as a gift from Prince John. His reverence is seen in his bearing towards his father. In his interview with the King (iii. 2) he receives cruel insult. He is accused of "vassal fear" and "base inclination", and is represented as a traitor who is only too likely to side with the Percies against his own father. His reply to this wanton charge is full of a forbearance which springs from deep filial reverence:

> "Do not think so; you shall not find it so:
> And God forgive them that so much have sway'd
> Your majesty's good thoughts away from me".

balance   We recognize in the Prince a master-spirit. He possesses the highest qualities of kingliness, and holds those qualities in gracious equipoise. There is no littleness in him, and no excess; Shakespeare has granted to him what he withheld from the heroes of his tragedies—a well-balanced nature.

The remaining characters, with the exception of Falstaff, must be treated more summarily. The timorous Northumberland, who presents such a contrast to his audacious

Northumberland.   son, and who, "crafty-sick", leaves that son to fight without him at Shrewsbury, is a contemptible figure; no less contemptible is Hotspur's uncle, Worcester. A schemer by nature, he is the real author of the conspiracy. His refusal to communicate to

Worcester.   his nephew the King's generous offer of pardon on the eve of the battle of Shrewsbury, prompted as that refusal is by cowardly motives, makes us regard the death-sentence passed upon him by Henry IV a just recompense for his treachery.

At the time when Shakespeare was writing *Henry IV* and *Henry V*, it would seem as though the Welsh nature were claiming his attention. In *1 Henry IV* he has given us Glendower, in *Henry V*, Fluellen; and in either character we trace certain national traits Glendower. upon which the individual features are superimposed. Owen Glendower occupies a somewhat heroic position in Welsh history, and Shakespeare, though he subjects the Welshman to a distinctly humorous treatment, is aware of his fine proportions. Mortimer declares him to be

> "valiant as a lion,
> And wondrous affable, and as bountiful
> As mines of India".

Glendower does not, like Fluellen, speak with a Welsh accent, but he betrays his nationality in other and deeper ways. Holinshed tells us that in his youth, spent at the English court, he had studied law; Shakespeare says nothing of this, but endows him with a racial love for music, which accords with his romantic temperament much better than jurisprudence:

> "I framed to the harp
> Many an English ditty lovely well,
> And gave the tongue a helpful ornament".

Racial, too, is his superstition, which in his case is also made to pamper to a childish egoism. In this Shakespeare was building upon the foundations of Holinshed, who invests Glendower with an atmosphere of necromancy, and tells of the strange wonders which attended him on his campaigns. Glendower ostentatiously regards himself as a man set apart for high purposes; "I am not in the roll of common men" is his vain contention, and he persists in asserting his supernatural powers in spite of the wholesome ridicule of Hotspur.

The fascination exercised over us by Hotspur or Prince

2

Henry is quite different from, and less potent [strong] than, that
exercised by Falstaff.   We may apply to him the
words which he whimsically applies to Poins:

Falstaff.

"I am bewitched with the rogue's company.   If the rascal
have not given me medicines to make me love him, I'll be
hanged; it could not be else; I have drunk medicines."

It is a witchery which holds us fast in its toils, which
deadens for the time our moral judgment, and makes us
in love with knavery when that knavery is so full of mirth.
Charles Lamb's ingenious claim for the characters of the
later Restoration Comedy, that they belong to a world of
their own which lies outside of the world of Christendom
and everyday life, appeals to us with added force in contem-
plating the character of Falstaff.   When we soberly analyse
his nature from the ethical [moral] stand-point, we are forced to
confess that he is a liar, a profligate, and a cheat: but
when we are actually reading and entering into the
spirit of the Falstaff scenes, we stubbornly refuse to apply
this moral analysis, and give ourselves up to the pure
enjoyment of humour which is as radiant as sunshine,
and of wit, which, for all its keenness, leaves no sting
behind.

[person leading an evil life]

Falstaff is, beyond all contention, the most humorous
creation in the whole field of literature.   Attempts have
been made to point to certain elements which go to the
formation of his character, and which had taken literary
shape before Shakespeare's time.   Comparisons have been
drawn between Falstaff and the *miles gloriosus* and the
scurra of early Latin comedy, and between Falstaff and
Rabelais' Panurge; but when the most is made of such
points of resemblance, we must allow that the hereditary
influence of literary ancestors nowhere counts for less
than in the case of the man who is "Jack Falstaff with
my familiars, John with my brothers and sisters, and Sir
John with all Europe".

The tap-root of humour runs very far beneath the surface of life, and draws its sustenance from the hidden

springs of human sympathy.   At the same time humour
can only exist by recognizing and utilizing the incon-
gruities which go to the formation of character, and incongruity is the body of the humour of Falstaff.   Maurice
Morgann, the special pleader on behalf of Falstaff against
the many charges of cowardice brought against him,
rightly summed up the incongruous elements in Falstaff's
character in his *Essay on the Character of Falstaff*, written
more than a century since.   Falstaff is, wrote Morgann,
"a man at once young and old, enterprising and fat, a
dupe and a wit, harmless and wicked, weak in principle
and resolute by constitution, cowardly in appearance and
brave in reality; a knave without malice, a liar without
deceit; and a knight, a gentleman, and a soldier, without
either dignity, decency, or honour".   Incongruity is ever
fertile in surprises, and as we follow the career of Falstaff
through the play, we find him creating for us incidents
which are as delightful as they are unforeseen.   How
humorously incongruous are the exclamations which this
grey-beard of seventy summers makes when robbing the
travellers in Act ii. scene 2: "They hate us youth.   What,
ye knaves, young men must live!"   How rich in surprises
is his behaviour on the battle-field of Shrewsbury!   But
perhaps the most incongruous element in his nature is his
wit, the nimbleness of which accords so ill with that tun
of flesh which requires levers to lift it from the ground.
Wit and humour, as Coleridge has taught us, are different things, and we must allow that some of the most
humorous characters in literature—Don Quixote for instance — are seldom consciously witty.   But in Falstaff
humour and wit meet and mingle: his humour makes his
words more witty, and his wit exhibits new facets of his
infinitely humorous and versatile character.   Moreover, as
he himself declares in Part II, he is not only witty himself, "but a cause that wit is in other men"; like the fool
in *As You Like It*, he is a touchstone by which the wit
and humour that are in men are tested.   Only those who,
like Prince John of Lancaster, have no laughter in them,

fail to respond to Falstaff's gaiety, and insist on regarding him seriously.

Coming back to what has already been stated, we repeat that in the *First Part of Henry IV* Falstaff must not be judged ethically, but enjoyed intellectually. We must regard him as the Prince of Wales regarded him when he sought in his companionship a healthful distraction from the cares and intrigues of real life. There will come, it is true, a time of rude awakening, when the newly-crowned king will find escape from the duties of office no longer possible, but in *1 Henry IV* the rejection of Falstaff—

"I know thee not, old man: fall to thy prayers"—

is still far distant, and we are free to enjoy the boon fellowship of his company, taking no thought for the morrow. Falstaff creates for himself an atmosphere of humorous make-believe, through which the serious concerns of life and all questions of morals cannot penetrate. Neither his cowardice nor his lying is to be taken seriously. As Professor Bradley has shown, his lies are told without any serious attempt to deceive. When he makes two men in buckram into eleven, and when he pretends to the Prince that he has slain Hotspur, deception is out of the question. He resorts to these devices out of an irresistible delight in egregious make-believe, and in order to place himself in a situation the escape from which will bring into play the inexhaustible resources of his wit. It is the same delight in make-believe which inspires his sudden and unenduring moods of piety, and which gives zest to such exclamations as—"A plague of sighing and grief! It blows a man up like a bladder"—or, "Company, villanous company, hath been the spoil of me".

If there is any serious purpose in life for Falstaff, it is to amuse the Prince and to provide him with mirthful entertainment. To achieve this purpose, he is prepared to go to any length, and only once, when he hands him a bottle of sack instead of a pistol on the battle-field of

Shrewsbury, does his ready wit fail to win a welcome. In the *Second Part of Henry IV*, Falstaff is as witty as ever, but we are conscious of an estrangement of sympathy between him and the Prince, though Falstaff fails to realize it. Only once do we find them together before the scene comes in which sentence of banishment is passed upon him. This is not the place to consider the justice or injustice of that sentence of banishment, but we may, in concluding, glance at the last scene of all in his career. Broken-hearted by the king's rejection of him, and finding that his atmosphere of make-believe no longer protects him, he has nothing to do but die. The story of his death is told by Dame Quickly, in *Henry V* (Act ii. scene 3), and it is like no other death-bed scene in literature. Infinitely humorous, it is also infinitely pathetic, and laughter and tears lie very near together:

"*Hostess.* Nay, sure, he's not in hell: he's in Arthur's bosom, if ever man went to Arthur's bosom. A' made a finer end, and went away an it had been any christom child; a' parted even just between twelve and one, even at the turning o' the tide: for after I saw him fumble with the sheets and play with flowers, and smile upon his fingers' ends, I knew there was but one way; for his nose was as sharp as a pen, and a' babbled of green fields. 'How now, Sir John!' quoth I: 'What, man! be o' good cheer.' So a' cried out 'God, God, God!' three or four times. Now I, to comfort him, bid him a' should not think of God; I hoped there was no need to trouble himself with any such thoughts yet. So a' bade me lay more clothes on his feet: I put my hand into the bed and felt them, and they were as cold as any stone; then I felt to his knees, and they were as cold as any stone, and so upward and upward, and all was as cold as any stone."

DRAMATIS PERSONÆ

KING HENRY THE FOURTH.

HENRY, Prince of Wales, }
JOHN OF LANCASTER, } sons to the king.

EARL OF WESTMORELAND.

SIR WALTER BLUNT.

THOMAS PERCY, Earl of Worcester.

HENRY PERCY, Earl of Northumberland.

HENRY PERCY, surnamed HOTSPUR, his son.

EDMUND MORTIMER, Earl of March.

RICHARD SCROOP, Archbishop of York.

ARCHIBALD, Earl of Douglas.

OWEN GLENDOWER.

SIR RICHARD VERNON.

SIR JOHN FALSTAFF.

SIR MICHAEL, a friend to the Archbishop of York.

POINS.

GADSHILL.

PETO.

BARDOLPH.

LADY PERCY, wife to Hotspur, and sister to Mortimer.

LADY MORTIMER, daughter to Glendower, and wife to Mortimer.

MISTRESS QUICKLY, hostess of a tavern in Eastcheap.

Lords, Officers, Sheriff, Vintner, Chamberlain, Drawers, two Carriers, Travellers, and Attendants.

SCENE: *England.*

Time of action: Thirteen months—from the defeat of Mortimer by Glendower, June 22, 1402, to the battle of Shrewsbury, July 21, 1403.

xxxviii

THE FIRST PART OF

KING HENRY THE FOURTH

ACT I

SCENE I. *London. The palace*

Enter KING HENRY, LORD JOHN OF LANCASTER, THE EARL
OF WESTMORELAND, SIR WALTER BLUNT, *and others*

King. So shaken as we are, so wan with care,
Find we a time for frighted peace to pant,
And breathe short-winded accents of new broils
To be commenced in stronds afar remote.
No more the thirsty entrance of this soil
Shall daub her lips with her own children's blood;
No more shall trenching war channel her fields,
Nor bruise her flowerets with the armed hoofs
Of hostile paces: those opposed eyes,
Which, like the meteors of a troubled heaven,   10
All of one nature, of one substance bred,
Did lately meet in the intestine shock
And furious close of civil butchery
Shall now, in mutual well-beseeming ranks,
March all one way and be no more opposed
Against acquaintance, kindred and allies:
The edge of war, like an ill-sheathed knife,
No more shall cut his master.   Therefore, friends,
As far as to the sepulchre of Christ,

Whose soldier now, under whose blessed cross   20
We are impressed and engaged to fight,
Forthwith a power of English shall we levy;
Whose arms were moulded in their mother's womb
To chase these pagans in those holy fields
Over whose acres walk'd those blessed feet
Which fourteen hundred years ago were nail'd
For our advantage on the bitter cross.
But this our purpose now is twelve months old,
And bootless 't is to tell you we will go:
Therefore we meet not now.   Then let me hear   30
Of you, my gentle cousin Westmoreland,
What yesternight our council did decree
In forwarding this dear expedience.
    West. My liege, this haste was hot in question,
And many limits of the charge set down
But yesternight: when all athwart there came
A post from Wales loaden with heavy news;
Whose worst was, that the noble Mortimer,
Leading the men of Herefordshire to fight
Against the irregular and wild Glendower,   40
Was by the rude hands of that Welshman taken,
A thousand of his people butchered;
Upon whose dead corpse there was such misuse,
Such beastly shameless transformation,
By those Welshwomen done as may not be
Without much shame retold or spoken of.
    King. It seems then that the tidings of this broil
Brake off our business for the Holy Land.
    West. This match'd with other did, my gracious lord;
For more uneven and unwelcome news   50
Came from the north and thus it did import:
On Holy-rood day, the gallant Hotspur there,
Young Harry Percy and brave Archibald,
That ever-valiant and approved Scot,

At Holmedon met,
Where they did spend a sad and bloody hour;
As by discharge of their artillery,
And shape of likelihood, the news was told;
For he that brought them, in the very heat
And pride of their contention did take horse,   60
Uncertain of the issue any way.

    King. Here is a dear, a true industrious friend,
Sir Walter Blunt, new lighted from his horse,
Stain'd with the variation of each soil
Betwixt that Holmedon and this seat of ours;
And he hath brought us smooth and welcome news.
The Earl of Douglas is discomfited:
Ten thousand bold Scots, two and twenty knights,
Balk'd in their own blood did Sir Walter see
On Holmedon's plains. Of prisoners, Hotspur took   70
Mordake the Earl of Fife, and eldest son
To beaten Douglas; and the Earl of Athol,
Of Murray, Angus, and Menteith:
And is not this an honourable spoil?
A gallant prize? ha, cousin, is it not?

    West. In faith,
It is a conquest for a prince to boast of.

    King. Yea, there thou makest me sad and makest me sin
In envy that my Lord Northumberland
Should be the father to so blest a son,   80
A son who is the theme of honour's tongue;
Amongst a grove, the very straightest plant;
Who is sweet Fortune's minion and her pride:
Whilst I, by looking on the praise of him,
See riot and dishonour stain the brow
Of my young Harry. O that it could be proved
That some night-tripping fairy had exchanged
In cradle-clothes our children where they lay,
And call'd mine Percy, his Plantagenet!

    2*   (B 101)

Then would I have his Harry, and he mine.   90
But let him from my thoughts.   What think you, coz,
Of this young Percy's pride? the prisoners,
Which he in this adventure hath surprised,
To his own use he keeps; and sends me word,
I shall have none but Mordake Earl of Fife.

West. This is his uncle's teaching: this is Worcester,
Malevolent to you in all aspects;
Which makes him prune himself, and bristle up
The crest of youth against your dignity.

King. But I have sent for him to answer this;   100
And for this cause awhile we must neglect
Our holy purpose to Jerusalem.
Cousin, on Wednesday next our council we
Will hold at Windsor; so inform the lords:
But come yourself with speed to us again;
For more is to be said and to be done
Than out of anger can be uttered.

West. I will, my liege.   [*Exeunt*

SCENE II.   *London.   An apartment of the Prince's*

Enter the PRINCE OF WALES *and* FALSTAFF

Fal. Now, Hal, what time of day is it, lad?

Prince. Thou art so fat-witted, with drinking of old
sack and unbuttoning thee after supper and sleeping upon
benches after noon, that thou hast forgotten to demand
that truly which thou wouldst truly know.   What a devil
hast thou to do with the time of the day?   Unless hours
were cups of sack and minutes capons, I see no reason
why thou shouldst be so superfluous to demand the time
of the day.   9

Fal. Indeed, you come near me now, Hal; for we that
take purses go by the moon and the seven stars, and not
by Phœbus he, 'that wandering knight so fair'.   And,

I prithee, sweet wag, when thou art king, as, God save thy grace,—majesty I should say, for grace thou wilt have none,—

Prince. What, none?

Fal. No, by my troth, not so much as will serve to be prologue to an egg and butter.

Prince. Well, how then? come, roundly, roundly.   19

Fal. Marry, then, sweet wag, when thou art king, let not us that are squires of the night's body be called thieves of the day's beauty: let us be Diana's foresters, gentlemen of the shade, minions of the moon; and let men say we be men of good government, being governed, as the sea is, by our noble and chaste mistress the moon, under whose countenance we steal.   26

Prince. Thou sayest well, and it holds well too; for the fortune of us that are the moon's men doth ebb and flow like the sea, being governed, as the sea is, by the moon. As, for proof, now: a purse of gold most resolutely snatched on Monday night and most dissolutely spent on Tuesday morning; got with swearing 'Lay by' and spent with crying 'Bring in'; now in as low an ebb as the foot of the ladder and by and by in as high a flow as the ridge of the gallows.

Fal. By the Lord, thou sayest true, lad. And is not my hostess of the tavern a most sweet wench?

Prince. As the honey of Hybla, my old lad of the castle. And is not a buff jerkin a most sweet robe of durance?   40

Fal. How now, how now, mad wag! what, in thy quips and thy quiddities? what a plague have I to do with a buff jerkin?

Prince. Why, what a plague have I to do with my hostess of the tavern?

Fal. Well, thou hast called her to a reckoning many a time and oft.

Prince. Did I ever call for thee to pay thy part?   48

Fal. No; I 'll give thee thy due, thou hast paid all there.

Prince. Yea, and elsewhere, so far as my coin would stretch; and where it would not, I have used my credit.

Fal. Yea, and so used it that, were it not here apparent that thou art heir apparent—But, I prithee, sweet wag, shall there be gallows standing in England when thou art king? and resolution thus fobbed as it is with the rusty curb of old father antic the law? Do not thou, when thou art king, hang a thief.

Prince. No; thou shalt.

Fal. Shall I? O rare! By the Lord, I 'll be a brave judge.   60

Prince. Thou judgest false already: I mean, thou shalt have the hanging of the thieves and so become a rare hangman.

Fal. Well, Hal, well; and in some sort it jumps with my humour as well as waiting in the court, I can tell you.

Prince. For obtaining of suits?

Fal. Yea, for obtaining of suits, whereof the hangman hath no lean wardrobe. 'S blood, I am as melancholy as a gib cat or a lugged bear.

Prince. Or an old lion, or a lover's lute.   70

Fal. Yea, or the drone of a Lincolnshire bagpipe.

Prince. What sayest thou to a hare, or the melancholy of Moor-ditch?

Fal. Thou hast the most unsavoury similes and art indeed the most comparative, rascalliest, sweet young prince. But, Hal, I prithee, trouble me no more with vanity. I would to God thou and I knew where a commodity of good names were to be bought. An old lord of the council rated me the other day in the street about you, sir, but I marked him not; and yet he talked very wisely, but I regarded him not; and yet he talked wisely, and in the street too.   82

Prince. Thou didst well; for wisdom cries out in the streets, and no man regards it.

Fal. O, thou hast damnable iteration and art indeed able to corrupt a saint. Thou hast done much harm upon me, Hal; God forgive thee for it! Before I knew thee, Hal, I knew nothing; and now am I, if a man should speak truly, little better than one of the wicked. I must give over this life, and I will give it over: by the Lord, an I do not, I am a villain; I'll be damned for never a king's son in Christendom. 92

Prince. Where shall we take a purse to-morrow, Jack?

Fal. 'Zounds, where thou wilt, lad; I'll make one; an I do not, call me villain and baffle me.

Prince. I see a good amendment of life in thee; from praying to purse-taking.

Fal. Why, Hal, 't is my vocation, Hal; 't is no sin for a man to labour in his vocation. 99

Enter POINS

Poins! Now shall we know if Gadshill have set a match. O, if men were to be saved by merit, what hole in hell were hot enough for him? This is the most omnipotent villain that ever cried 'Stand' to a true man.

Prince. Good morrow, Ned.

Poins. Good morrow, sweet Hal. What says Monsieur Remorse? what says Sir John Sack and Sugar? Jack! how agrees the devil and thee about thy soul, that thou soldest him on Good-Friday last for a cup of Madeira and a cold capon's leg? 109

Prince. Sir John stands to his word, the devil shall have his bargain; for he was never yet a breaker of proverbs: he will give the devil his due.

Poins. Then art thou damned for keeping thy word with the devil.

Prince Else he had been damned for cozening the devil.

Poins. But, my lads, my lads, to-morrow morning, by four o'clock, early at Gadshill! there are pilgrims going to Canterbury with rich offerings, and traders riding to London with fat purses: I have vizards for you all; you have horses for yourselves: Gadshill lies to-night in Rochester: I have bespoke supper to-morrow night in Eastcheap: we may do it as secure as sleep. If you will go, I will stuff your purses full of crowns; if you will not, tarry at home and be hanged.   124

Fal. Hear ye, Yedward; if I tarry at home and go not, I'll hang you for going.

Poins. You will, chops?

Fal. Hal, wilt thou make one?

Prince. Who, I rob? I a thief? not I, by my faith.   129

Fal. There's neither honesty, manhood, nor good fellow-ship in thee, nor thou camest not of the blood royal, if thou darest not stand for ten shillings.

Prince. Well then, once in my days I'll be a madcap.

Fal. Why, that's well said.

Prince. Well, come what will, I'll tarry at home.

Fal. By the Lord, I'll be a traitor then, when thou art king.

Prince. I care not.

Poins. Sir John, I prithee, leave the prince and me alone: I will lay him down such reasons for this adventure that he shall go.   141

Fal. Well, God give thee the spirit of persuasion and him the ears of profiting, that what thou speakest may move and what he hears may be believed, that the true prince may, for recreation's sake, prove a false thief; for the poor abuses of the time want countenance. Farewell: you shall find me in Eastcheap.   147

Prince. Farewell, thou latter spring! farewell, All-hall-own summer!   [*Exit Falstaff*

Poins. Now, my good sweet honey lord, ride with us

to-morrow: I have a jest to execute that I cannot manage alone. Falstaff, Bardolph, Peto and Gadshill shall rob those men that we have already waylaid; yourself and I will not be there; and when they have the booty, if you and I do not rob them, cut this head off from my shoulders.

Prince. How shall we part with them in setting forth?

Poins. Why, we will set forth before or after them, and appoint them a place of meeting, wherein it is at our pleasure to fail, and then will they adventure upon the exploit themselves; which they shall have no sooner achieved, but we'll set upon them. 161

Prince. Yea, but 'tis like that they will know us by our horses, by our habits and by every other appointment, to be ourselves.

Poins. Tut! our horses they shall not see; I'll tie them in the wood; our vizards we will change after we leave them: and, sirrah, I have cases of buckram for the nonce, to immask our noted outward garments. 168

Prince. Yea, but I doubt they will be too hard for us.

Poins. Well, for two of them, I know them to be as true-bred cowards as ever turned back; and for the third, if he fight longer than he sees reason, I'll forswear arms. The virtue of this jest will be, the incomprehensible lies that this same fat rogue will tell us when we meet at supper: how thirty, at least, he fought with; what wards, what blows, what extremities he endured; and in the reproof of this lies the jest.

Prince. Well, I'll go with thee: provide us all things necessary and meet me to-morrow night in Eastcheap; there I'll sup. Farewell. 180

Poins. Farewell, my lord. [*Exit*

Prince. I know you all, and will awhile uphold
The unyoked humour of your idleness:
Yet herein will I imitate the sun,
Who doth permit the base contagious clouds

To smother up his beauty from the world,
That, when he please again to be himself,
Being wanted, he may be more wonder'd at,
By breaking through the foul and ugly mists
Of vapours that did seem to strangle him.   190
If all the year were playing holidays,
To sport would be as tedious as to work;
But when they seldom come, they wish'd for come,
And nothing pleaseth but rare accidents.
So, when this loose behaviour I throw off
And pay the debt I never promised,
By how much better than my word I am,
By so much shall I falsify men's hopes;
And like bright metal on a sullen ground,
My reformation, glittering o'er my fault,   200
Shall show more goodly and attract more eyes
Than that which hath no foil to set it off.
I 'll so offend, to make offence a skill;
Redeeming time when men think least I will.   [*Exit*

SCENE III. *London. The palace*

Enter the KING, NORTHUMBERLAND, WORCESTER, HOTSPUR,
SIR WALTER BLUNT, *with others*

King. My blood hath been too cold and temperate,
Unapt to stir at these indignities,
And you have found me so; accordingly
You tread upon my patience: but be sure
I will from henceforth rather be myself,
Mighty and to be fear'd, than my condition;
Which hath been smooth as oil, soft as young down,
And therefore lost that title of respect
Which the proud soul ne'er pays but to the proud.
Wor. Our house, my sovereign liege, little deserves   10
The scourge of greatness to be used on it;

And that same greatness too which our own hands
Have holp to make so portly.

   North. My lord,—

   King. Worcester, get thee gone; for I do see
Danger and disobedience in thine eye:
O, sir, your presence is too bold and peremptory,
And majesty might never yet endure
The moody frontier of a servant brow.
You have good leave to leave us: when we need   20
Your use and counsel, we shall send for you.   [*Exit Wor.*
You were about to speak.   [*To North.*

   North.   Yea, my good lord.
Those prisoners in your highness' name demanded,
Which Harry Percy here at Holmedon took,
Were, as he says, not with such strength denied
As is deliver'd to your majesty:
Either envy, therefore, or misprision
Is guilty of this fault and not my son.

   Hot. My liege, I did deny no prisoners.
But I remember, when the fight was done,   30
When I was dry with rage and extreme toil,
Breathless and faint, leaning upon my sword,
Came there a certain lord, neat, and trimly dress'd,
Fresh as a bridegroom; and his chin new reap'd
Show'd like a stubble-land at harvest-home;
He was perfumed like a milliner;
And 'twixt his finger and his thumb he held
A pouncet-box, which ever and anon
He gave his nose and took 't away again;
Who therewith angry, when it next came there,   40
Took it in snuff; and still he smiled and talk'd,
And as the soldiers bore dead bodies by,
He call'd them untaught knaves, unmannerly,
To bring a slovenly unhandsome corse
Betwixt the wind and his nobility.

With many holiday and lady terms
He question'd me; amongst the rest, demanded
My prisoners in your majesty's behalf.
I then, all smarting with my wounds being cold,
To be so pester'd with a popinjay,   50
Out of my grief and my impatience,
Answer'd neglectingly I know not what,
He should, or he should not; for he made me mad
To see him shine so brisk and smell so sweet
And talk so like a waiting-gentlewoman
Of guns and drums and wounds,—God save the mark —
And telling me the sovereign'st thing on earth
Was parmaceti for an inward bruise;
And that it was great pity, so it was,
This villanous salt-petre should be digg'd   60
Out of the bowels of the harmless earth,
Which many a good tall fellow had destroy'd
So cowardly; and but for these vile guns,
He would himself have been a soldier.
This bald unjointed chat of his, my lord,
I answer'd indirectly, as I said;
And I beseech you, let not his report
Come current for an accusation
Betwixt my love and your high majesty.
    Blunt. The circumstance consider'd, good my lord,   70
Whate'er Lord Harry Percy then had said
To such a person and in such a place,
At such a time, with all the rest retold,
May reasonably die and never rise
To do him wrong or any way impeach
What then he said, so he unsay it now.
    King. Why, yet he doth deny his prisoners,
But with proviso and exception,
That we at our own charge shall ransom straight
His brother-in-law, the foolish Mortimer;   80

proviesol

Who, on my soul, hath wilfully betray'd
The lives of those that he did lead to fight
Against that great magician, damn'd Glendower
Whose daughter, as we hear, the Earl of March
Hath lately married. Shall our coffers, then,
Be emptied to redeem a traitor home?
Shall we buy treason? and indent with fears,
When they have lost and forfeited themselves?
No, on the barren mountains let him starve;
For I shall never hold that man my friend 90
Whose tongue shall ask me for one penny cost
To ransom home revolted Mortimer.

 Hot. Revolted Mortimer!
He never did fall off, my sovereign liege,
But by the chance of war: to prove that true
Needs no more but one tongue for all those wounds,
Those mouthed wounds, which valiantly he took,
When on the gentle Severn's sedgy bank,
In single opposition, hand to hand,
He did confound the best part of an hour 100
In changing hardiment with great Glendower:
Three times they breathed, and three times did they drink,
Upon agreement, of swift Severn's flood;
Who then, affrighted with their bloody looks,
Ran fearfully among the trembling reeds,
And hid his crisp head in the hollow bank
Bloodstained with these valiant combatants.
Never did base and rotten policy
Colour her working with such deadly wounds;
Nor never could the noble Mortimer 110
Receive so many, and all willingly:
Then let not him be slander'd with revolt.

 King. Thou dost belie him, Percy, thou dost belie him;
He never did encounter with Glendower:
I tell thee,

He durst as well have met the devil alone
As Owen Glendower for an enemy.
Art thou not ashamed?   But, sirrah, henceforth
Let me not hear you speak of Mortimer:
Send me your prisoners with the speediest means,   120
Or you shall hear in such a kind from me
As will displease you.   My Lord Northumberland,
We license your departure with your son.
Send us your prisoners, or you will hear of it.
          [*Exeunt King Henry, Blunt, and train*
     Hot. An if the devil come and roar for them,
I will not send them: I will after straight
And tell him so; for I will ease my heart,
Albeit I make a hazard of my head.
     North. What, drunk with choler? stay and pause awhile:
Here comes your uncle.   130

                    Re-enter WORCESTER

     Hot.   Speak of Mortimer!
'Zounds, I will speak of him; and let my soul
Want mercy, if I do not join with him:
Yea, on his part I 'll empty all these veins,
And shed my dear blood drop by drop in the dust,
But I will lift the down-trod Mortimer
As high in the air as this unthankful king,
As this ingrate and canker'd Bolingbroke.
     North. Brother, the king hath made your nephew mad.
     Wor. Who struck this heat up after I was gone?
     Hot. He will, forsooth, have all my prisoners;   140
And when I urged the ransom once again
Of my wife's brother, then his cheek look'd pale,
And on my face he turn'd an eye of death,
Trembling even at the name of Mortimer.
     Wor. I cannot blame him: was not he proclaim'd
By Richard that dead is the next of blood?

North. He was; I heard the proclamation:
And then it was when the unhappy king,—
Whose wrongs in us God pardon!—did set forth
Upon his Irish expedition;   150
From whence he intercepted did return
To be deposed and shortly murdered.

Wor. And for whose death we in the world's wide mouth
Live scandalized and foully spoken of.

Hot. But, soft, I pray you; did King Richard then
Proclaim my brother Edmund Mortimer
Heir to the crown?

North.   He did; myself did hear it.

Hot. Nay, then I cannot blame his cousin king,
That wish'd him on the barren mountains starve.
But shall it be, that you, that set the crown   160
Upon the head of this forgetful man
And for his sake wear the detested blot
Of murderous subornation, shall it be,
That you a world of curses undergo,
Being the agents, or base second means,
The cords, the ladder, or the hangman rather?
O, pardon me that I descend so low,
To show the line and the predicament
Wherein you range under this subtle king;
Shall it for shame be spoken in these days,   170
Or fill up chronicles in time to come,
That men of your nobility and power
Did gage them both in an unjust behalf,
As both of you—God pardon it!—have done,
To put down Richard, that sweet lovely rose,
And plant this thorn, this canker, Bolingbroke?
And shall it in more shame be further spoken,
That you are fool'd, discarded and shook off
By him for whom these shames ye underwent?
No; yet time serves wherein ye may redeem   180

Your banish'd honours and restore yourselves
Into the good thoughts of the world again,
Revenge the jeering and disdain'd contempt
Of this proud king, who studies day and night
To answer all the debt he owes to you
Even with the bloody payment of your deaths:
Therefore, I say,—
  Wor.   Peace, cousin, say no more:
And now I will unclasp a secret book,
And to your quick-conceiving discontents
I 'll read you matter deep and dangerous,   190
As full of peril and adventurous spirit
As to o'er-walk a current roaring loud
On the unsteadfast footing of a spear.
  Hot. If he fall in, good-night! or sink or swim:
Send danger from the east unto the west,
So honour cross it from the north to south,
And let them grapple: O, the blood more stirs
To rouse a lion than to start a hare!
  North. Imagination of some great exploit
Drives him beyond the bounds of patience.   200
  Hot. By heaven, methinks it were an easy leap,
To pluck bright honour from the pale-faced moon,
Or dive into the bottom of the deep,
Where fathom-line could never touch the ground,
And pluck up drowned honour by the locks;
So he that doth redeem her thence might wear
Without corrival all her dignities:
But out upon this half-faced fellowship!
  Wor. He apprehends a world of figures here,
But not the form of what he should attend.   210
Good cousin, give me audience for a while.
  Hot. I cry you mercy.
  Wor.   Those same noble Scots
That are your prisoners,—

Hot.   I 'll keep them all:
By God, he shall not have a Scot of them;
No, if a Scot would save his soul, he shall not:
I 'll keep them, by this hand.

Wor.   You start away
And lend no ear unto my purposes.
Those prisoners you shall keep.

Hot.   Nay, I will; that 's flat.
He said he would not ransom Mortimer;
Forbad my tongue to speak of Mortimer;   220
But I will find him when he lies asleep,
And in his ear I 'll holla ' Mortimer!'
Nay,
I 'll have a starling shall be taught to speak
Nothing but ' Mortimer ', and give it him,
To keep his anger still in motion.

Wor. Hear you, cousin; a word.

Hot. All studies here I solemnly defy,
Save how to gall and pinch this Bolingbroke:
And that same sword-and-buckler Prince of Wales,   230
But that I think his father loves him not
And would be glad he met with some mischance,
I would have him poison'd with a pot of ale.

Wor. Farewell, kinsman: I 'll talk to you
When you are better temper'd to attend.

North. Why, what a wasp-stung and impatient fool
Art thou to break into this woman's mood,
Tying thine ear to no tongue but thine own!

Hot. Why, look you, I am whipp'd and scourged with rods,
Nettled and stung with pismires, when I hear   240
Of this vile politician, Bolingbroke.
In Richard's time,—what do you call the place?—
A plague upon it, it is in Gloucestershire;
'T was where the madcap duke his uncle kept,
His uncle York; where I first bow'd my knee

Unto this king of smiles, this Bolingbroke,—
'S blood!—
When you and he came back from Ravenspurgh.

   North. At Berkley castle.

   Hot. You say true: 250
Why, what a candy deal of courtesy
This fawning greyhound then did proffer me!
Look, ' when his infant fortune came to age ',
And ' gentle Harry Percy ', and ' kind cousin ';
O, the devil take such cozeners!   God forgive me!
Good uncle, tell your tale; I have done.

   Wor. Nay, if you have not, to it again;
We will stay your leisure.

   Hot.   I have done, i' faith.

   Wor. Then once more to your Scottish prisoners.
Deliver them up without their ransom straight,   260
And make the Douglas' son your only mean
For powers in Scotland; which, for divers reasons
Which I shall send you written, be assured,
Will easily be granted.   You, my lord, [*To Northumberland*
Your son in Scotland being thus employ'd,
Shall secretly into the bosom creep
Of that same noble prelate, well beloved,
The archbishop.

   Hot. Of York, is it not?

   Wor. True; who bears hard   270
His brother's death at Bristol, the Lord Scroop.
I speak not this in estimation,
As what I think might be, but what I know
Is ruminated, plotted and set down,
And only stays but to behold the face
Of that occasion that shall bring it on.

   Hot. I smell it: upon my life, it will do well.

   North. Before the game is afoot, thou still let'st slip.

   Hot. Why, it cannot choose but be a noble plot:

And then the power of Scotland and of York,　　　280
To join with Mortimer, ha?
　　Wor.　　　　　　　　And so they shall.
　　Hot. In faith, it is exceedingly well aim'd.
　　Wor. And 't is no little reason bids us speed,
To save our heads by raising of a head;
For, bear ourselves as even as we can,
The king will always think him in our debt,
And think we think ourselves unsatisfied,
Till he hath found a time to pay us home:
And see already how he doth begin
To make us strangers to his looks of love.　　　290
　　Hot. He does, he does: we 'll be revenged on him.
　　Wor. Cousin, farewell: no further go in this
Than I by letters shall direct your course.
When time is ripe, which will be suddenly,
I 'll steal to Glendower and Lord Mortimer;
Where you and Douglas and our powers at once,
As I will fashion it, shall happily meet,
To bear our fortunes in our own strong arms,
Which now we hold at much uncertainty.
　　North. Farewell, good brother: we shall thrive, I trust.
　　Hot. Uncle, adieu: O, let the hours be short　　　301
Till fields and blows and groans applaud our sport!
　　　　　　　　　　　　　　　　　　[Exeunt

ACT II

Scene I. *Rochester. An inn yard*

Enter a Carrier *with a lantern in his hand*

　　First Car. Heigh-ho! an it be not four by the day, I 'll
be hanged: Charles' wain is over the new chimney, and
yet our horse not packed. What, ostler!

Ost. [*Within*] Anon, anon.

First Car. I prithee, Tom, beat Cut's saddle, put a few flocks in the point; poor jade, is wrung in the withers out of all cess.

Enter another Carrier

Sec. Car. Peas and beans are as dank here as a dog, and that is the next way to give poor jades the bots: this house is turned upside down since Robin Ostler died.   10

First Car. Poor fellow, never joyed since the price of oats rose; it was the death of him.

Sec. Car. I think this be the most villanous house in all London road for fleas: I am stung like a tench.

First Car. Like a tench! by the mass, there is ne'er a king christen could be better bit than I have been since the first cock. What, ostler! come away and be hanged! come away.

Sec. Car. I have a gammon of bacon and two razes of ginger, to be delivered as far as Charing-cross.   20

First Car. God's body! the turkeys in my pannier are quite starved. What, ostler! A plague on thee! hast thou never an eye in thy head? canst not hear? An 't were not as good deed as drink, to break the pate on thee, I am a very villain. Come, and be hanged! hast no faith in thee?

Enter GADSHILL

Gads. Good morrow, carriers. What's o'clock?

First Car. I think it be two o'clock.

Gads. I prithee, lend me thy lantern, to see my gelding in the stable.   30

First Car. Nay, by God, soft; I know a trick worth two of that, i' faith.

Gads. I pray thee, lend me thine.

Sec. Car. Ay, when? canst tell? Lend me thy lantern, quoth he? marry, I'll see thee hanged first.

Gads. Sirrah carrier, what time do you mean to come to London?   37

Sec. Car. Time enough to go to bed with a candle, I warrant thee. Come, neighbour Mugs, we'll call up the gentlemen: they will along with company, for they have great charge.   [*Exeunt Carriers*

Gads. What, ho! chamberlain!

Cham. [*Within*] At hand, quoth pick-purse.

Gads. That's even as fair as — at hand, quoth the chamberlain; for thou variest no more from picking of purses than giving direction doth from labouring; thou layest the plot how.   47

Enter Chamberlain

Cham. Good morrow, Master Gadshill. It holds current that I told you yesternight: there's a franklin in the wild of Kent hath brought three hundred marks with him in gold: I heard him tell it to one of his company last night at supper; a kind of auditor; one that hath abundance of charge too, God knows what. They are up already, and call for eggs and butter: they will away presently.

Gads. Sirrah, if they meet not with Saint Nicholas' clerks, I'll give thee this neck.

Cham. No, I'll none of it: I pray thee, keep that for the hangman; for I know thou worshippest Saint Nicholas as truly as a man of falsehood may.   60

Gads. What talkest thou to me of the hangman? if I hang, I'll make a fat pair of gallows; for if I hang, old Sir John hangs with me, and thou knowest he is no starveling. Tut! there are other Trojans that thou dreamest not of, the which for sport sake are content to do the profession some grace; that would, if matters should be looked into, for their own credit sake, make all whole. I am joined with no foot-land rakers, no long-staff sixpenny strikers, none of these mad mustachio purple-hued malt-worms; but with nobility and tranquillity, burgomasters and great oneyers, such as can hold in, such as will strike sooner than speak, and speak sooner than drink, and drink sooner than pray: and yet, 'zounds, I lie; for they pray continually to their saint, the commonwealth; or rather, not pray to her, but prey on her, for they ride up and down on her and make her their boots.   76

Cham. What, the commonwealth their boots? will she hold out water in foul way?

Gads. She will, she will; justice hath liquored her. We steal as in a castle, cock-sure; we have the receipt of fern-seed, we walk invisible.   81

Cham. Nay, by my faith, I think you are more beholding to the night than to fern-seed for your walking invisible.

Gads. Give me thy hand: thou shalt have a share in our purchase, as I am a true man.

Cham. Nay, rather let me have it, as you are a false thief.

Gads. Go to; 'homo' is a common name to all men. Bid the ostler bring my gelding out of the stable.   Farewell, you muddy knave.   [*Exeunt* 90

SCENE II.   *The highway, near Gadshill*

Enter PRINCE HENRY *and* POINS

Poins. Come, shelter, shelter: I have removed Falstaff's horse, and he frets like a gummed velvet.

Prince. Stand close.

Enter FALSTAFF

Fal. Poins! Poins, and be hanged! Poins!

Prince. Peace, ye fat-kidneyed rascal! what a brawling dost thou keep!

Fal. Where's Poins, Hal?

Prince. He is walked up to the top of the hill: I'll go
seek him.   9

Fal. I am accursed to rob in that thief's company: the
rascal hath removed my horse, and tied him I know not
where. If I travel but four foot by the squier further afoot,
I shall break my wind. Well, I doubt not but to die a
fair death for all this, if I 'scape hanging for killing that
rogue. I have forsworn his company hourly any time this
two and twenty years, and yet I am bewitched with the
rogue's company. If the rascal have not given me medicines to make me love him, I'll be hanged; it could not be
else; I have drunk medicines. Poins! Hal! a plague
upon you both! Bardolph! Peto! I'll starve ere I'll rob
a foot further. An 't were not as good a deed as drink, to
turn true man and to leave these rogues, I am the veriest
varlet that ever chewed with a tooth. Eight yards of uneven ground is threescore and ten miles afoot with me;
and the stony-hearted villains know it well enough: a
plague upon it when thieves cannot be true one to another!
[*They whistle.*] Whew! A plague upon you all! Give
me my horse, you rogues; give me my horse, and be
hanged!   29

Prince. Peace, ye fat-guts! lie down; lay thine ear close
to the ground and list if thou canst hear the tread of
travellers.

Fal. Have you any levers to lift me up again, being
down? 'S blood, I'll not bear mine own flesh so far afoot
again for all the coin in thy father's exchequer. What a
plague mean ye to colt me thus?

Prince. Thou liest; thou art not colted, thou art un-
colted.

Fal. I prithee, good Prince Hal, help me to my horse,
good king's son.   40

Prince. Out, ye rogue! shall I be your ostler?

Fal. Go, hang thyself in thine own heir-apparent garters!

If I be ta'en, I'll peach for this. An I have not ballads
made on you all and sung to filthy tunes, let a cup of sack
be my poison: when a jest is so forward, and afoot too!
I hate it.

Enter GADSHILL, BARDOLPH *and* PETO *with him*

Gads. Stand.

Fal. So I do, against my will.

Poins. O, 'tis our setter: I know his voice. Bardolph,
what news?   50

Bard. Case ye, case ye; on with your vizards: there's
money of the king's coming down the hill; 'tis going to
the king's exchequer.

Fal. You lie, you rogue; 'tis going to the king's tavern.

Gads. There's enough to make us all.

Fal. To be hanged.

Prince. Sirs, you four shall front them in the narrow
lane; Ned Poins and I will walk lower: if they 'scape from
your encounter, then they light on us.

Peto. How many be there of them?   60

Gads. Some eight or ten.

Fal. 'Zounds, will they not rob us?

Prince. What, a coward, Sir John Paunch?

Fal. Indeed, I am not John of Gaunt, your grandfather;
but yet no coward, Hal.

Prince. Well, we leave that to the proof.

Poins. Sirrah Jack, thy horse stands behind the hedge:
when thou needest him, there thou shalt find him. Farewell, and stand fast.

Fal. Now cannot I strike him, if I should be hanged. 70

Prince. Ned, where are our disguises?

Poins. Here, hard by: stand close.

[*Exeunt Prince and Poins*

Fal. Now, my masters, happy man be his dole, say I:
every man to his business.

Enter the Travellers

First Trav. Come, neighbour: the boy shall lead our horses down the hill; we'll walk afoot awhile, and ease our legs.

Thieves. Stand!

Travellers. Jesus bless us! 79

Fal. Strike; down with them; cut the villains' throats: ah! plaguey caterpillars! bacon-fed knaves! they hate us youth: down with them: fleece them.

Travellers. O, we are undone, both we and ours for ever!

Fal. Hang ye, gorbellied knaves, are ye undone? No, ye fat chuffs; I would your store were here! On, bacons, on! What, ye knaves! young men must live. You are grandjurors, are ye? we'll jure ye, 'faith.

[*Here they rob them and bind them. Exeunt*

Re-enter PRINCE HENRY *and* POINS

Prince. The thieves have bound the true men. Now could thou and I rob the thieves and go merrily to London, it would be argument for a week, laughter for a month and a good jest for ever. 91

Poins. Stand close; I hear them coming.

Enter the Thieves *again*

Fal. Come, my masters, let us share, and then to horse before day. An the Prince and Poins be not two arrant cowards, there's no equity stirring: there's no more valour in that Poins than in a wild-duck.

Prince. Your money!

Poins. Villains!

[*As they are sharing, the Prince and Poins set upon them; they all run away; and Falstaff, after a blow or two, runs away too, leaving the booty behind them*

Prince. Got with much ease.   Now merrily to horse:
The thieves are all scatter'd and possess'd with fear   100
So strongly that they dare not meet each other;
Each takes his fellow for an officer.
Away, good Ned.   Falstaff sweats to death.
And lards the lean earth as he walks along.
Were 't not for laughing, I should pity him.
     Poins. How the rogue roar'd!   [*Exeunt*

SCENE III.   *Warkworth castle*

Enter HOTSPUR, *solus, reading a letter*

Hot. 'But, for mine own part, my lord, I could be well
contented to be there, in respect of the love I bear your
house.' He could be contented: why is he not, then? In
respect of the love he bears our house: he shows in this,
he loves his own barn better than he loves our house.
Let me see some more.   'The purpose you undertake is
dangerous;'—why, that's certain: 't is dangerous to take
a cold, to sleep, to drink; but I tell you, my lord fool, out
of this nettle, danger, we pluck this flower, safety.   'The
purpose you undertake is dangerous; the friends you have
named uncertain; the time itself unsorted; and your whole
plot too light for the counterpoise of so great an opposition.'
Say you so, say you so? I say unto you again, you are
a shallow cowardly hind, and you lie. What a lack-brain
is this! By the Lord, our plot is a good plot as ever was
laid; our friends true and constant: a good plot, good
friends, and full of expectation; an excellent plot, very good
friends.   What a frosty-spirited rogue is this! Why, my
lord of York commends the plot and the general course of
the action. 'Zounds, an I were now by this rascal, I could
brain him with his lady's fan. Is there not my father, my
uncle and myself? lord Edmund Mortimer, my lord of
York and Owen Glendower? is there not besides the

Douglas? have I not all their letters to meet me in arms
by the ninth of the next month? and are they not some of
them set forward already? What a pagan rascal is this!
an infidel! Ha! you shall see now in very sincerity of
fear and cold heart, will he to the king and lay open all
our proceedings. O, I could divide myself and go to
buffets, for moving such a dish of skim milk with so
honourable an action! Hang him! let him tell the king:
we are prepared. I will set forward to-night.   32

Enter LADY PERCY

How now, Kate! I must leave you within these two hours.
  Lady. O, my good lord, why are you thus alone?
For what offence have I this fortnight been
A banish'd woman from my Harry's bed?
Tell me, sweet lord, what is 't that takes from thee
Thy stomach, pleasure and thy golden sleep?
Why dost thou bend thine eyes upon the earth,
And start so often when thou sitt'st alone?   40
Why hast thou lost the fresh blood in thy cheeks;
And given my treasures and my rights of thee
To thick-eyed musing and cursed melancholy?
In thy faint slumbers I by thee have watch'd,
And heard thee murmur tales of iron wars;
Speak terms of manage to thy bounding steed;
Cry 'Courage! to the field!' And thou hast talk'd
Of sallies and retires, of trenches, tents,
Of palisadoes, frontiers, parapets,
Of basilisks, of cannon, culverin,   50
Of prisoners' ransom and of soldiers slain,
And all the currents of a heady fight.
Thy spirit within thee hath been so at war
And thus hath so bestirr'd thee in thy sleep,
That beads of sweat have stood upon thy brow
Like bubbles in a late-disturbed stream

And in thy face strange motions have appear'd,
Such as we see when men restrain their breath
On some great sudden hest.   O, what portents are these?
Some heavy business hath my lord in hand,   60
And I must know it, else he loves me not.

   Hot. What, ho!

Enter Servant

                Is Gilliams with the packet gone?
   Serv. He is, my lord, an hour ago.
   Hot. Hath Butler brought those horses from the sheriff?
   Serv. One horse, my lord, he brought even now.
   Hot. What horse? a roan, a crop-ear, is it not?
   Serv. It is, my lord.
   Hot.   That roan shall be my throne.
Well, I will back him straight: O Esperance!
Bid Butler lead him forth into the park.   [*Exit servant*
   Lady. But hear you, my lord.   70
   Hot. What say'st thou, my lady?
   Lady. What is it carries you away?
   Hot. Why, my horse, my love, my horse.
   Lady. Out, you mad-headed ape!
A weasel hath not such a deal of spleen
As you are toss'd with.   In faith,
I 'll know your business, Harry, that I will.
I fear my brother Mortimer doth stir
About his title, and hath sent for you
To line his enterprize: but if you go,—   80
   Hot. So far afoot, I shall be weary, love.
   Lady. Come, come, you paraquito, answer me
Directly unto this question that I ask:
In faith, I 'll break thy little finger, Harry,
An if thou wilt not tell me all things true.
   Hot. Away,
Away, you trifler!   Love! I love thee not,

I care not for thee, Kate: this is no world
To play with mammets and to tilt with lips:
We must have bloody noses and crack'd crowns,   90
And pass them current too.   God 's me, my horse!
What say'st thou, Kate? what would'st thou have with me?
    Lady. Do you not love me? do you not, indeed?
Well, do not then; for since you love me not,
I will not love myself.   Do you not love me?
Nay, tell me if you speak in jest or no.
    Hot. Come, wilt thou see me ride?
And when I am o' horseback, I will swear
I love thee infinitely.   But hark you, Kate;
I must not have you henceforth question me   100
Whither I go, nor reason whereabout:
Whither I must, I must; and, to conclude,
This evening must I leave you, gentle Kate.
I know you wise, but yet no farther wise
Than Harry Percy's wife: constant you are,
But yet a woman: and for secrecy,
No lady closer; for I well believe
Thou wilt not utter what thou dost not know;
And so far will I trust thee, gentle Kate.
    Lady. How! so far?   110
    Hot. Not an inch further.   But hark you, Kate:
Whither I go, thither shall you go too;
To-day will I set forth, to-morrow you.
Will this content you, Kate?
    Lady.   It must of force.   [*Exeunt*

SCENE IV.   *The Boar's-Head Tavern, Eastcheap*

Enter the PRINCE *and* POINS

    Prince. Ned, prithee, come out of that fat room, and lend
me thy hand to laugh a little.
    Poins. Where hast been, Hal?

Prince. With three or four loggerheads amongst three or four score hogsheads. I have sounded the very base-string of humility. Sirrah, I am sworn brother to a leash of drawers; and can call them all by their christen names, as Tom, Dick, and Francis. They take it already upon their salvation, that though I be but Prince of Wales, yet I am the king of courtesy; and tell me flatly I am no proud Jack, like Falstaff, but a Corinthian, a lad of mettle, a good boy, by the Lord, so they call me, and when I am king of England I shall command all the good lads in Eastcheap. They call drinking deep, dyeing scarlet; and when you breathe in your watering, they cry 'hem!' and bid you play it off. To conclude, I am so good a proficient in one quarter of an hour, that I can drink with any tinker in his own language during my life. I tell thee, Ned, thou hast lost much honour, that thou wert not with me in this action. But, sweet Ned,—to sweeten which name of Ned I give thee this pennyworth of sugar, clapped even now into my hand by an under-skinker, one that never spoke other English in his life than 'Eight shillings and six-pence', and 'You are welcome', with this shrill addition, 'Anon, anon, sir! Score a pint of bastard in the Half-moon', or so. But, Ned, to drive away the time till Falstaff come, I prithee, do thou stand in some by-room, while I question my puny drawer to what end he gave me the sugar; and do thou never leave calling 'Francis', that his tale to me may be nothing but 'Anon'. Step aside, and I'll show thee a precedent.   31

Poins. Francis!

Prince. Thou art perfect.

Poins. Francis!   [*Exit Poins*

Enter FRANCIS

Fran. Anon, anon, sir. Look down into the Pomgar-net, Ralph.

Prince. Come hither, Francis.

Fran. My lord?

Prince. How long hast thou to serve, Francis?

Fran. Forsooth, five years, and as much as to—　　ᴀᴏ

Poins. [*Within*] Francis!

Fran. Anon, anon, sir.

Prince. Five year! by 'r lady, a long lease for the clink-
ing of pewter. But, Francis, darest thou be so valiant as
to play the coward with thy indenture and show it a fair
pair of heels and run from it?

Fran. O Lord, sir, I 'll be sworn upon all the books in
England, I could find in my heart.

Poins. [*Within*] Francis!

Fran. Anon, sir.　　　　　　　　　　　　　　　50

Prince. How old art thou, Francis?

Fran. Let me see—about Michaelmas next I shall be—

Poins. [*Within*] Francis!

Fran. Anon, sir. Pray stay a little, my lord.

Prince. Nay, but hark you, Francis: for the sugar thou
gavest me, 't was a pennyworth, was 't not?

Fran. O Lord, I would it had been two!

Prince. I will give thee for it a thousand pound: ask
me when thou wilt, and thou shalt have it.

Poins. [*Within*] Francis!　　　　　　　　　　60

Fran. Anon, anon.

Prince. Anon, Francis? No, Francis; but to-morrow,
Francis; or Francis, o' Thursday; or indeed, Francis,
when thou wilt. But, Francis!

Fran. My lord?

Prince. Wilt thou rob this leathern jerkin, crystal-
button, not-pated, agate-ring, puke-stocking, caddis-garter,
smooth-tongue, Spanish-pouch,—

Fran. O Lord, sir, who do you mean?　　　　　69

Prince. Why, then, your brown bastard is your only
drink; for look you, Francis, your white canvas doublet
will sully: in Barbary, sir, it cannot come to so much.

Fran. What, sir?

Poins. [*Within*] Francis!

Prince. Away, you rogue! dost thou not hear them call?
[*Here they both call him; the drawer stands
amazed, not knowing which way to go*

Enter Vintner

Vint. What, standest thou still, and hearest such a calling? Look to the guests within. [*Exit Francis.*] My lord, old Sir John, with half-a-dozen more, are at the door: shall I let them in?   79

Prince. Let them alone awhile, and then open the door. [*Exit Vintner.*]   Poins!

Re-enter POINS

Poins. Anon, anon, sir.

Prince. Sirrah, Falstaff and the rest of the thieves are at the door; shall we be merry?

Poins. As merry as crickets, my lad. But hark ye; what cunning match have you made with this jest of the drawer? come, what's the issue?

Prince. I am now of all humours that have showed themselves humours since the old days of goodman Adam to the pupil age of this present twelve o'clock at midnight.   91

Re-enter FRANCIS

What's o'clock, Francis?

Fran. Anon, anon, sir.   [*Exit*

Prince. That ever this fellow should have fewer words than a parrot, and yet the son of a woman! His industry is up-stairs and down-stairs; his eloquence the parcel of a reckoning. I am not yet of Percy's mind, the Hotspur of the north; he that kills me some six or seven dozen of Scots at a breakfast, washes his hands, and says to his wife 'Fie upon this quiet life! I want work'. 'O my

sweet Harry,' says she, 'how many hast thou killed
to-day?' 'Give my roan horse a drench,' says he; and
answers 'Some fourteen,' an hour after; 'a trifle, a trifle.'
I prithee, call in Falstaff: I'll play Percy, and that damned
brawn shall play Dame Mortimer his wife. 'Rivo!' says
the drunkard. Call in ribs, call in tallow.   106

Enter FALSTAFF, GADSHILL, BARDOLPH, *and* PETO;
FRANCIS *following with wine*

Poins. Welcome, Jack: where hast thou been?

Fal. A plague of all cowards, I say, and a vengeance
too! marry, and amen! Give me a cup of sack, boy. Ere
I lead this life long, I'll sew nether stocks and mend them
and foot them too. A plague of all cowards! Give me a
cup of sack, rogue. Is there no virtue extant? [*He drinks*

Prince. Didst thou ever see Titan kiss a dish of butter?
pitiful-hearted Titan, that melted at the sweet tale of the
sun's! if thou didst, then behold that compound.   115

Fal. You rogue, here's lime in this sack too: there is
nothing but roguery to be found in villanous man: yet a
coward is worse than a cup of sack with lime in it. A
villanous coward! Go thy ways, old Jack; die when thou
wilt, if manhood, good manhood, be not forgot upon the
face of the earth, then am I a shotten herring. There live
not three good men unhanged in England; and one of
them is fat and grows old: God help the while! a bad
world, I say. I would I were a weaver; I could sing
psalms or any thing. A plague of all cowards, I say still.

Prince. How now, wool-sack! what mutter you?   126

Fal. A king's son! If I do not beat thee out of thy
kingdom with a dagger of lath, and drive all thy subjects
afore thee like a flock of wild-geese, I'll never wear hair
on my face more. You Prince of Wales!

Prince. Why, you plaguey round man, what's the
matter?

Fal. Are not you a coward? answer me to that: and
Poins there?

Poins. 'Zounds, ye fat paunch, an ye call me coward, by
the Lord, I'll stab thee.   136

Fal. I call thee coward! I'll see thee damned ere I call
thee coward: but I would give a thousand pound I could
run as fast as thou canst.   You are straight enough in the
shoulders, you care not who sees your back: call you that
backing of your friends? A plague upon such backing!
give me them that will face me. Give me a cup of sack:
I am a rogue, if I drunk to-day.

Prince. O villain! thy lips are scarce wiped since thou
drunkest last.   145

Fal. All's one for that. [*He drinks.*] A plague of all
cowards, still say I.

Prince. What's the matter?

Fal. What's the matter! there be four of us here have
ta'en a thousand pound this day morning.

Prince. Where is it, Jack? where is it?

Fal. Where is it! taken from us it is: a hundred upon
poor four of us.

Prince. What, a hundred, man?   154

Fal. I am a rogue, if I were not at half-sword with a
dozen of them two hours together. I have 'scaped by
miracle. I am eight times thrust through the doublet,
four through the hose; my buckler cut through and
through; my sword hacked like a hand-saw—ecce signum!
I never dealt better since I was a man: all would not do.
A plague of all cowards! Let them speak: if they speak
more or less than truth, they are villains and the sons of
darkness.   163

Prince. Speak, sirs; how was it?

Gads. We four set upon some dozen—

Fal. Sixteen at least, my lord.

Gads. And bound them.

Peto. No, no, they were not bound.

Fal. You rogue, they were bound, every man of them; or I am a Jew else, an Ebrew Jew.   170

Gads. As we were sharing, some six or seven fresh men set upon us—

Fal. And unbound the rest, and then come in the other.

Prince. What, fought you with them all?

Fal. All! I know not what you call all; but if I fought not with fifty of them, I am a bunch of radish: if there were not two or three and fifty upon poor old Jack, then am I no two-legged creature.   178

Prince. Pray God you have not murdered some of them.

Fal. Nay, that's past praying for: I have peppered two of them; two I am sure I have paid, two rogues in buckram suits. I tell thee what, Hal, if I tell thee a lie, spit in my face, call me horse. Thou knowest my old ward; here I lay, and thus I bore my point. Four rogues in buckram let drive at me—

Prince. What, four? thou saidst but two even now.

Fal. Four, Hal; I told thee four.

Poins. Ay, ay, he said four.

Fal. These four came all a-front, and mainly thrust at me. I made me no more ado but took all their seven points in my target, thus.   191

Prince. Seven? why, there were but four even now.

Fal. In buckram?

Poins. Ay, four, in buckram suits.

Fal. Seven, by these hilts, or I am a villain else.

Prince. Prithee, let him alone; we shall have more anon.

Fal. Dost thou hear me, Hal?

Prince. Ay, and mark thee too, Jack.

Fal. Do so, for it is worth the listening to. These nine in buckram that I told thee of—   201

Prince. So, two more already.

Fal. Their points being broken,—

Poins. Down fell their hose.

Fal. Began to give me ground: but I followed me close, came in foot and hand; and with a thought seven of the eleven I paid.

Prince. O monstrous! eleven buckram men grown out of two!   209

Fal. But, as the devil would have it, three misbegotten knaves in Kendal green came at my back and let drive at me; for it was so dark, Hal, that thou couldst not see thy hand.

Prince. These lies are like their father that begets them; gross as a mountain, open, palpable. Why, thou clay-brained guts, thou knotty-pated fool, thou plaguey, obscene, greasy tallow-ketch.

Fal. What, art thou mad? art thou mad? is not the truth the truth?   219

Prince. Why, how couldst thou know these men in Kendal green, when it was so dark thou couldst not see thy hand? come, tell us your reason: what sayest thou to this?

Poins. Come, your reason, Jack, your reason.

Fal. What, upon compulsion? 'Zounds, an I were at the strappado, or all the racks in the world, I would not tell you on compulsion. Give you a reason on compulsion! if reasons were as plentiful as blackberries, I would give no man a reason upon compulsion, I.   229

Prince. I 'll be no longer guilty of this sin; this san-guine coward, this horseback-breaker, this huge hill of flesh,—

Fal. 'S blood, you starveling, you elf-skin, you dried neat's tongue, you stock-fish! O for breath to utter what is like thee! you tailor's-yard, you sheath, you bow-case, you vile standing-tuck,—

Prince. Well, breathe awhile, and then to it again: and

when thou hast tired thyself in base comparisons, hear me speak but this.

Poins. Mark, Jack.   240

Prince. We two saw you four set on four and bound them, and were masters of their wealth. Mark now, how a plain tale shall put you down. Then did we two set on you four; and, with a word, out-faced you from your prize, and have it; yea, and can show it you here in the house: and, Falstaff, you carried your guts away as nimbly, with as quick dexterity, and roared for mercy and still run and roared, as ever I heard bull-calf. What a slave art thou, to hack thy sword as thou hast done, and then say it was in fight! What trick, what device, what starting-hole, canst thou now find out to hide thee from this open and apparent shame?   252

Poins. Come, let's hear, Jack; what trick hast thou now?

Fal. By the Lord, I knew ye as well as he that made ye. Why, hear you, my masters: was it for me to kill the heir-apparent? should I turn upon the true prince? why, thou knowest I am as valiant as Hercules: but beware instinct; the lion will not touch the true prince. Instinct is a great matter; I was now a coward on instinct. I shall think the better of myself and thee during my life; I for a valiant lion, and thou for a true prince. But, by the Lord, lads, I am glad you have the money. Hostess, clap to the doors: watch to-night, pray to-morrow. Gallants, lads, boys, hearts of gold, all the titles of good fellowship come to you! What, shall we be merry? shall we have a play extempore?   266

Prince. Content; and the argument shall be thy running away.

Fal. Ah, no more of that, Hal, an thou lovest me!

Enter Hostess

Host. O Jesu, my lord the prince!   270

Prince. How now, my lady the hostess! what sayest thou to me?

Host. Marry, my lord, there is a nobleman of the court at door would speak with you: he says he comes from your father.

Prince. Give him as much as will make him a royal man, and send him back again to my mother.

Fal. What manner of man is he?

Host. An old man.

Fal. What doth gravity out of his bed at midnight? Shall I give him his answer?   281

Prince. Prithee, do, Jack.

Fal. 'Faith, and I'll send him packing.   [*Exit*

Prince. Now, sirs: by'r lady, you fought fair; so did you, Peto; so did you, Bardolph: you are lions too, you ran away upon instinct, you will not touch the true prince; no, fie!

Bard. 'Faith, I ran when I saw others run.

Prince. 'Faith, tell me now in earnest, how came Falstaff's sword so hacked?   290

Peto. Why, he hacked it with his dagger, and said he would swear truth out of England but he would make you believe it was done in fight, and persuaded us to do the like.

Bard. Yea, and to tickle our noses with spear-grass to make them bleed, and then to beslubber our garments with it and swear it was the blood of true men. I did that I did not this seven year before, I blushed to hear his monstrous devices.   299

Prince. O villain, thou stolest a cup of sack eighteen years ago, and wert taken with the manner, and ever since thou hast blushed extempore. Thou hadst fire and sword on thy side, and yet thou rannest away: what instinct hadst thou for it?

Bard. My lord, do you see these meteors? do you behold these exhalations?

Prince. I do.

Bard. What think you they portend?

Prince. Hot livers and cold purses.

Bard. Choler, my lord, if rightly taken.　　310

Prince. No, if rightly taken, halter.

Re-enter FALSTAFF

Here comes lean Jack, here comes bare-bone. How now, my sweet creature of bombast! How long is 't ago, Jack, since thou sawest thine own knee?

Fal. My own knee! when I was about thy years, Hal, I was not an eagle's talon in the waist; I could have crept into any alderman's thumb-ring: a plague of sighing and grief! it blows a man up like a bladder. There's villanous news abroad: here was Sir John Bracy from your father; you must to the court in the morning. That same mad fellow of the north, Percy, and he of Wales, that gave Amamon the bastinado and made game of Lucifer and swore the devil his true liegeman upon the cross of a Welsh hook—what a plague call you him?　　324

Poins. O, Glendower.

Fal. Owen, Owen, the same; and his son-in-law Mortimer, and old Northumberland, and that sprightly Scot of Scots, Douglas, that runs o' horseback up a hill perpendicular,—

Prince. He that rides at high speed and with his pistol kills a sparrow flying.　　331

Fal. You have hit it.

Prince. So did he never the sparrow.

Fal. Well, that rascal hath good mettle in him; he will not run.

Prince. Why, what a rascal art thou then, to praise him so for running!

Fal. O' horseback, ye cuckoo; but afoot he will not budge a foot.

Prince. Yes, Jack, upon instinct.   340

Fal. I grant ye, upon instinct. Well, he is there too, and one Mordake, and a thousand blue-caps more: Worcester is stolen away to-night; thy father's beard is turned white with the news: you may buy land now as cheap as stinking-mackerel. But tell me, Hal, art not thou horrible afeard? thou being heir-apparent, could the world pick thee out three such enemies again as that fiend Douglas, that spirit Percy, and that devil Glendower? Art thou not horribly afraid? doth not thy blood thrill at it?   349

Prince. Not a whit, i' faith; I lack some of thy instinct.

Fal. Well, thou wilt be horribly chid to-morrow when thou comest to thy father: if thou love me, practise an answer.

Prince. Do thou stand for my father, and examine me upon the particulars of my life.

Fal. Shall I? content: this chair shall be my state, this dagger my sceptre, and this cushion my crown.

Prince. Thy state is taken for a joined-stool, thy golden sceptre for a leaden dagger, and thy precious rich crown for a pitiful bald crown!   360

Fal. Well, an the fire of grace be not quite out of thee, now shalt thou be moved. Give me a cup of sack to make my eyes look red, that it may be thought I have wept; for I must speak in passion, and I will do it in King Cambyses' vein.

Prince. Well, here is my leg.

Fal. And here is my speech. Stand aside, nobility.

Host. O Jesu, this is excellent sport, i' faith!

Fal. Weep not, sweet queen; for trickling tears are vain.

Host. O, the father, how he holds his countenance!   370

Fal. For God's sake, lords, convey my tristful queen;
For tears do stop the flood-gates of her eyes.

Host. O Jesu, he doth it as like one of these harlotry
players as ever I see!

Fal. Peace, good pint-pot; peace, good tickle-brain.
Harry, I do not only marvel where thou spendest thy time,
but also how thou art accompanied: for though the camomile, the more it is trodden on the faster it grows, yet youth,
the more it is wasted the sooner it wears. That thou art
my son, I have partly thy mother's word, partly my own
opinion, but chiefly a villanous trick of thine eye and a
foolish hanging of thy nether lip, that doth warrant me.
If then thou be son to me, here lies the point; why, being
son to me, art thou so pointed at? Shall the blessed sun
of heaven prove a micher and eat blackberries? a question
not to be asked. Shall the son of England prove a thief
and take purses? a question to be asked. There is a thing,
Harry, which thou hast often heard of and it is known to
many in our land by the name of pitch: this pitch, as
ancient writers do report, doth defile; so doth the company
thou keepest: for, Harry, now I do not speak to thee in
drink but in tears, not in pleasure but in passion, not in
words only, but in woes also: and yet there is a virtuous
man whom I have often noted in thy company, but I know
not his name.   395

Prince. What manner of man, an it like your majesty?

Fal. A goodly portly man, i' faith, and a corpulent; of
a cheerful look, a pleasing eye and a most noble carriage;
and, as I think, his age some fifty, or, by 'r lady, inclining
to three score; and now I remember me, his name is Falstaff: if that man should be lewdly given, he deceiveth me;
for, Harry, I see virtue in his looks. If then the tree may
be known by the fruit, as the fruit by the tree, then, per-
emptorily I speak it, there is virtue in that Falstaff: him
keep with, the rest banish. And tell me now, thou

naughty varlet, tell me, where hast thou been this
month?

Prince. Dost thou speak like a king? Do thou stand
for me, and I'll play my father. 409

Fal. Depose me? if thou dost it half so gravely, so
majestically, both in word and matter, hang me up by the
heels for a rabbit-sucker or a poulter's hare.

Prince. Well, here I am set.

Fal. And here I stand: judge, my masters.

Prince. Now, Harry, whence come you?

Fal. My noble lord, from Eastcheap.

Prince. The complaints I hear of thee are grievous.

Fal. 'S blood, my lord, they are false: nay, I'll tickle ye
for a young prince, i' faith. 419

Prince. Swearest thou, ungracious boy? henceforth ne'er
look on me. Thou art violently carried away from grace:
there is a devil haunts thee in the likeness of an old fat
man; a tun of man is thy companion. Why dost thou
converse with that trunk of humours, that bolting-hutch
of beastliness, that swollen parcel of dropsies, that huge
bombard of sack, that stuffed cloak-bag of guts, that
roasted Manningtree ox with the pudding in his belly,
that reverend vice, that grey iniquity, that father ruffian,
that vanity in years? Wherein is he good, but to taste
sack and drink it? wherein neat and cleanly, but to carve
a capon and eat it? wherein cunning, but in craft? wherein
crafty, but in villany? wherein villanous, but in all things?
wherein worthy, but in nothing? 433

Fal. I would your grace would take me with you: whom
means your grace?

Prince. That villanous abominable misleader of youth,
Falstaff, that old white-bearded Satan.

Fal. My lord, the man I know.

Prince. I know thou dost. 439

Fal. But to say I know more harm in him than in my

self, were to say more than I know. That he is old, the
more the pity, his white hairs do witness it; but that he is,
saving your reverence, an old Satan, that I utterly deny.
If sack and sugar be a fault, God help the wicked! if to be
old and merry be a sin, then many an old host that I know
is damned: if to be fat be to be hated, then Pharaoh's lean
kine are to be loved. No, my good lord; banish Peto,
banish Bardolph, banish Poins: but for sweet Jack Falstaff,
kind Jack Falstaff, true Jack Falstaff, valiant Jack Falstaff,
and therefore more valiant, being, as he is, old Jack Falstaff, banish not him thy Harry's company, banish not him
thy Harry's company: banish plump Jack, and banish all
the world.   453

Prince. I do, I will.   [*A knocking heard*
                          [*Exeunt Hostess, Francis, and Bardolph*

Re-enter BARDOLPH, *running*

Bard. O, my lord, my lord! the sheriff with a most
monstrous watch is at the door.

Fal. Out, ye rogue! Play out the play: I have much to
say in the behalf of that Falstaff.

Re-enter the Hostess

Host. O Jesu, my lord, my lord!   459

Prince. Heigh, heigh! the devil rides upon a fiddlestick:
what's the matter?

Host. The sheriff and all the watch are at the door: they
are come to search the house. Shall I let them in?

Fal. Dost thou hear, Hal? never call a true piece of
gold a counterfeit: thou art essentially mad, without
seeming so.

Prince. And thou a natural coward, without instinct.

Fal. I deny your major: if you will deny the sheriff, so;
if not, let him enter: if I become not a cart as well as

another man, a plague on my bringing up! I hope I shall
as soon be strangled with a halter as another.   471

Prince. Go, hide thee behind the arras: the rest walk up
above. Now, my masters, for a true face and good con-
science.

Fal. Both which I have had: but their date is out, and
therefore I 'll hide me.

Prince. Call in the sheriff.

[*Exeunt all except the Prince and Peto*

Enter Sheriff *and the* Carrier

Now, master sheriff, what is your will with me?

Sher. First, pardon me, my lord.   A hue and cry
Hath follow'd certain men unto this house.   480

Prince. What men?

Sher. One of them is well known, my gracious lord,
A gross fat man.

Car.   As fat as butter.

Prince. The man, I do assure you, is not here;
For I myself at this time have employ'd him.
And, sheriff, I will engage my word to thee
That I will, by to-morrow dinner-time,
Send him to answer thee, or any man,
For any thing he shall be charged withal:
And so let me entreat you leave the house.   490

Sher. I will, my lord.   There are two gentlemen
Have in this robbery lost three hundred marks.

Prince. It may be so: if he have robb'd these men,
He shall be answerable; and so farewell.

Sher. Good night, my noble lord.

Prince. I think it is good morrow, is it not?

Sher. Indeed, my lord, I think it be two o'clock.

[*Exeunt Sheriff and Carrier*

Prince. This oily rascal is known as well as Paul's.
Go, call him forth.

Peto. Falstaff!—Fast asleep behind the arras, and snorting like a horse.   501

Prince. Hark, how hard he fetches breath. Search his pockets. [*He searcheth his pockets and findeth certain papers.*] What hast thou found?

Peto. Nothing but papers, my lord.

Prince. Let's see what they be: read them.

Peto. [*Reads*] Item, A capon, ... 2s. 2d.
                Item, Sauce, ... 4d.
                Item, Sack, two gallons, . . 5s. 8d.
                Item, Anchovies and sack after
                    supper, ... 2s. 6d.
                Item, Bread, ... ob.

Prince. O monstrous! but one half-pennyworth of bread to this intolerable deal of sack! What there is else, keep close: we'll read it at more advantage: there let him sleep till day. I'll to the court in the morning. We must all to the wars, and thy place shall be honourable. I'll procure this fat rogue a charge of foot; and I know his death will be a march of twelve-score. The money shall be paid back again with advantage. Be with me betimes in the morning; and so, good morrow, Peto.   520

                                                [*Exeunt*

Peto. Good morrow, good my lord.

ACT III

SCENE I. *Bangor. The Archdeacon's house*

Enter HOTSPUR, WORCESTER, MORTIMER, *and* GLENDOWER

Mort. These promises are fair, the parties sure,
And our induction full of prosperous hope.

Hot. Lord Mortimer, and cousin Glendower,
Will you sit down?

And uncle Worcester: a plague upon it!
I have forgot the map.

    Glend.   No, here it is.
Sit, cousin Percy; sit, good cousin Hotspur,
For by that name as oft as Lancaster
Doth speak of you, his cheek looks pale and with
A rising sigh he wisheth you in heaven.   10

    Hot. And you in hell as often as he hears
Owen Glendower spoke of.

    Glend. I cannot blame him: at my nativity
The front of heaven was full of fiery shapes,
Of burning cressets: and at my birth
The frame and huge foundation of the earth
Shaked like a coward.

    Hot. Why, so it would have done at the same season,
if your mother's cat had but kittened, though yourself had
never been born.   20

    Glend. I say the earth did shake when I was born.

    Hot. And I say the earth was not of my mind,
If you suppose as fearing you it shook.

    Glend. The heavens were all on fire, the earth did tremble.

    Hot. O, then the earth shook to see the heavens on fire,
And not in fear of your nativity.
Diseased nature oftentimes breaks forth
In strange eruptions; oft the teeming earth
Is with a kind of colic pinch'd and vex'd
By the imprisoning of unruly wind   30
Within her womb; which, for enlargement striving,
Shakes the old beldam earth and topples down
Steeples and moss-grown towers.   At your birth
Our grandam earth, having this distemperature,
In passion shook.

    Glend.   Cousin, of many men
I do not bear these crossings.   Give me leave
To tell you once again that at my birth

The front of heaven was full of fiery shapes,
The goats ran from the mountains, and the herds
Were strangely clamorous to the frighted fields.   40
These signs have mark'd me extraordinary;
And all the courses of my life do show
I am not in the roll of common men.
Where is he living, clipp'd in with the sea
That chides the banks of England, Scotland, Wales,
Which calls me pupil, or hath read to me?
And bring him out that is but woman's son
Can trace me in the tedious ways of art
And hold me pace in deep experiments.

   Hot. I think there's no man speaks better Welsh.   50
I'll to dinner.

   Mort. Peace, cousin Percy; you will make him mad.

   Glend. I can call spirits from the vasty deep.

   Hot. Why, so can I, or so can any man;
But will they come when you do call for them?

   Glend. Why, I can teach you, cousin, to command
The devil.

   Hot. And I can teach thee, coz, to shame the devil
By telling truth: tell truth and shame the devil.
If thou have power to raise him, bring him hither,   60
And I'll be sworn I have power to shame him hence.
O, while you live, tell truth and shame the devil!

   Mort. Come, come, no more of this unprofitable chat.

   Glend. Three times hath Henry Bolingbroke made head
Against my power; thrice from the banks of Wye
And sandy-bottom'd Severn have I sent him
Bootless home and weather-beaten back.

   Hot. Home without boots, and in foul weather too!
How 'scapes he agues, in the devil's name?

   Glend. Come, here's the map: shall we divide our right
According to our threefold order ta'en?   71

   Mort. The archdeacon hath divided it

Into three limits very equally:
England, from Trent and Severn hitherto,
By south and east is to my part assign'd:
All westward, Wales beyond the Severn shore,
And all the fertile land within that bound,
To Owen Glendower: and, dear coz, to you
The remnant northward, lying off from Trent.
And our indentures tripartite are drawn;   80
Which being sealed interchangeably,
A business that this night may execute,
To-morrow, cousin Percy, you and I
And my good Lord of Worcester will set forth
To meet your father and the Scottish power,
As is appointed us, at Shrewsbury.
My father Glendower is not ready yet,
Nor shall we need his help these fourteen days.
Within that space you may have drawn together
Your tenants, friends and neighbouring gentlemen.   90
    Glend. A shorter time shall send me to you, lords:
And in my conduct shall your ladies come;
From whom you now must steal and take no leave,
For there will be a world of water shed
Upon the parting of your wives and you.
    Hot. Methinks my moiety, north from Burton here,
In quantity equals not one of yours:
See how this river comes me cranking in,
And cuts me from the best of all my land
A huge half-moon, a monstrous cantle out.   100
I 'll have the current in this place damm'd up;
And here the smug and silver Trent shall run
In a new channel, fair and evenly;
It shall not wind with such a deep indent,
To rob me of so rich a bottom here.
    Glend. Not wind? it shall, it must; you see it doth.
    Mort. Yea, but

Mark how he bears his course, and runs me up
With like advantage on the other side;
Gelding the opposed continent as much   110
As on the other side it takes from you.

   Wor. Yea, but a little charge will trench him here
And on this north side win this cape of land;
And then he runs straight and even.

    Hot. I 'll have it so: a little charge will do it.

    Glend. I 'll not have it alter'd.

    Hot.   Will not you?

    Glend. No, nor you shall not.

    Hot.   Who shall say me nay?

    Glend. Why, that will I.

    Hot. Let me not understand you, then; speak it in Weish.

    Glend. I can speak English, lord, as well as you;   210
For I was train'd up in the English court;
Where, being but young, I framed to the harp
Many an English ditty lovely well
And gave the tongue a helpful ornament,
A virtue that was never seen in you.

    Hot. Marry,
And I am glad of it with all my heart:
I had rather be a kitten and cry mew
Than one of these same metre ballad-mongers;
I had rather hear a brazen canstick turn'd,   130
Or a dry wheel grate on the axle-tree;
And that would set my teeth nothing on edge,
Nothing so much as mincing poetry:
'T is like the forced gait of a shuffling nag.

    Glend. Come, you shall have Trent turn'd.

    Hot. I do not care: I 'll give thrice so much land
To any well-deserving friend;
But in the way of bargain, mark ye me,
I 'll cavil on the ninth part of a hair.
Are the indentures drawn? shall we be gone?   140

Glend. The moon shines fair; you may away by night:
I 'll haste the writer and withal
Break with your wives of your departure hence:
I am afraid my daughter will run mad,
So much she doteth on her Mortimer.   *[Exit*

Mort. Fie, cousin Percy! how you cross my father!

Hot. I cannot choose: sometime he angers me
With telling me of the moldwarp and the ant,
Of the dreamer Merlin and his prophecies,
And of a dragon and a finless fish,   150
A clip-wing'd griffin and a moulten raven,
A couching lion and a ramping cat,
And such a deal of skimble-skamble stuff
As puts me from my faith.   I tell you what;
He held me last night at least nine hours
In reckoning up the several devils' names
That were his lackeys: I cried 'hum', and 'well, go **to**',
But mark'd him not a word.   O, he is as tedious
As a tired horse, a railing wife;
Worse than a smoky house: I had rather live   160
With cheese and garlic in a windmill, far,
Than feed on cates and have him talk to me
In any summer-house in Christendom.

Mort. In faith, he is a worthy gentleman,
Exceedingly well read, and profited
In strange concealments, valiant as a lion
And wondrous affable and as bountiful
As mines of India.   Shall I tell you, cousin?
He holds your temper in a high respect
And curbs himself even of his natural scope   170
When you come 'cross his humour; faith, he does:
I warrant you, that man is not alive
Might so have tempted him as you have done,
Without the taste of danger and reproof:
But do not use it oft, let me entreat you.

Wor. In faith, my lord, you are too wilful-blame;
And since your coming hither have done enough
To put him quite beside his patience.
You must needs learn, lord, to amend this fault:
Though sometimes it show greatness, courage, blood,— 180
And that's the dearest grace it renders you,—
Yet oftentimes it doth present harsh rage,
Defect of manners, want of government,
Pride, haughtiness, opinion and disdain:
The least of which haunting a nobleman
Loseth men's hearts and leaves behind a stain
Upon the beauty of all parts besides,
Beguiling them of commendation.

Hot. Well, I am school'd: good manners be your speed!
Here come our wives, and let us take our leave. 190

Re-enter GLENDOWER *with the* Ladies

Mort. This is the deadly spite that angers me;
My wife can speak no English, I no Welsh.

Glend. My daughter weeps: she will not part with you;
She'll be a soldier too, she'll to the wars.

Mort. Good father, tell her that she and my Aunt Percy
Shall follow in your conduct speedily.

[*Glendower speaks to her in Welsh, and she answers
him in the same*

Glend. She is desperate here; a peevish self-willed harlotry, one that no persuasion can do good upon.

[*The lady speaks in Welsh*

Mort. I understand thy looks: that pretty Welsh
Which thou pour'st down from these swelling heavens 200
I am too perfect in; and, but for shame,
In such a parley should I answer thee.

[*The lady speaks again in Welsh*

I understand thy kisses and thou mine,
And that's a feeling disputation:

But I will never be a truant, love,
Till I have learn'd thy language; for thy tongue
Makes Welsh as sweet as ditties highly penn'd,
Sung by a fair queen in a summer's bower,
With ravishing division, to her lute.

    Glend. Nay, if you melt, then will she run mad.   210
                              [The lady speaks again in Welsh
    Mort. O, I am ignorance itself in this!
    Glend. She bids you on the wanton rushes lay you down
And rest your gentle head upon her lap,
And she will sing the song that pleaseth you
And on your eyelids crown the god of sleep,
Charming your blood with pleasing heaviness,
Making such difference 'twixt wake and sleep
As is the difference betwixt day and night
The hour before the heavenly-harness'd team
Begins his golden progress in the east.   220
    Mort. With all my heart I'll sit and hear her sing:
By that time will our book, I think, be drawn.
    Glend. Do so;
And those musicians that shall play to you
Hang in the air a thousand leagues from hence,
And straight they shall be here: sit, and attend.
    Hot. Come, Kate, thou art perfect in lying down: come,
quick, quick, that I may lay my head in thy lap.
    Lady P. Go, ye giddy goose.
                                 [The music plays
    Hot. Now I perceive the devil understands Welsh;   230
And 't is no marvel he is so humorous.
By 'r lady, he is a good musician.
    Lady P. Then should you be nothing but musical, for
you are altogether governed by humours. Lie still, ye
thief, and hear the lady sing in Welsh.
    Hot. I had rather hear Lady, my brach, howl in Irish.
    Lady P. Wouldst thou have thy head broken?

Hot. No.

Lady P. Then be still.

Hot. Neither; 't is a woman's fault.　　　240

Lady P. Now God help thee! What 's that?

Hot. Peace! she sings.

　　　　　　　[*Here the lady sings a Welsh song*

Hot. Come, Kate, I 'll have your song too.

Lady P. Not mine, in good sooth.

Hot. Not yours, in good sooth! Heart! you swear like
a comfit-maker's wife. 'Not you, in good sooth', and
'as true as I live', and 'as God shall mend me', and
'as sure as day',

And givest such sarcenet surety for thy oaths,

As if thou never walk'st further than Finsbury.　　　250

Swear me, Kate, like a lady as thou art,

A good mouth-filling oath, and leave 'in sooth',

And such protest of pepper-gingerbread,

To velvet-guards and Sunday-citizens.

Come, sing.

Lady P. I will not sing.

Hot. 'T is the next way to turn tailor, or be red-breast
teacher. An the indentures be drawn, I 'll away within
these two hours; and so, come in when ye will. [*Exit*

Glend. Come, come, Lord Mortimer; you are as slow

As hot Lord Percy is on fire to go.　　　261

By this our book is drawn; we 'll but seal,

And then to horse immediately.

Mort.　　　　　　　With all my heart. [*Exeunt*

SCENE II. *London.　The palace*

Enter the KING, PRINCE OF WALES, *and others*

King. Lords, give us leave; the Prince of Wales and I
Must have some private conference: but be near at hand,
For we shall presently have need of you. [*Exeunt Lords*

I know not whether God will have it so,
For some displeasing service I have done,
That, in his secret doom, out of my blood
He 'll breed revengement and a scourge for me;
But thou dost in thy passages of life
Make me believe that thou art only mark'd
For the hot vengeance and the rod of heaven   10
To punish my mistreadings.   Tell me else,
Could such inordinate and low desires,
Such poor, such bare, such lewd, such mean attempts,
Such barren pleasures, rude society,
As thou art match'd withal and grafted to,
Accompany the greatness of thy blood
And hold their level with thy princely heart?
     Prince. So please your majesty, I would I could
Quit all offences with as clear excuse
As well as I am doubtless I can purge   20
Myself of many I am charged withal:
Yet such extenuation let me beg,
As, in reproof of many tales devised,
Which oft the ear of greatness needs must hear,
By smiling pick-thanks and base newsmongers,
I may, for some things true, wherein my youth
Hath faulty wander'd and irregular,
Find pardon on my true submission.
     King. God pardon thee! yet let me wonder, Harry,
At thy affections, which do hold a wing   30
Quite from the flight of all thy ancestors.
Thy place in council thou hast rudely lost,
Which by thy younger brother is supplied,
And art almost an alien to the hearts
Of all the court and princes of my blood:
The hope and expectation of thy time
Is ruin'd, and the soul of every man
Prophetically do forethink thy fall.

Had I so lavish of my presence been,
So common-hackney'd in the eyes of men,   40
So stale and cheap to vulgar company,
Opinion, that did help me to the crown,
Had still kept loyal to possession
And left me in reputeless banishment,
A fellow of no mark nor likelihood.
By being seldom seen, I could not stir
But like a comet I was wonder'd at;
That men would tell their children 'This is he';
Others would say 'Where, which is Bolingbroke?'
And then I stole all courtesy from heaven,   50
And dress'd myself in such humility
That I did pluck allegiance from men's hearts,
Loud shouts and salutations from their mouths,
Even in the presence of the crowned king.
Thus did I keep my person fresh and new;
My presence, like a robe pontifical,
Ne'er seen but wonder'd at: and so my state,
Seldom but sumptuous, showed like a feast
And wan by rareness such solemnity.
The skipping king, he ambled up and down   60
With shallow jesters and rash bavin wits,
Soon kindled and soon burnt; carded his state,
Mingled his royalty with capering fools,
Had his great name profaned with their scorns
And gave his countenance, against his name,
To laugh at gibing boys and stand the push
Of every beardless vain comparative,
Grew a companion to the common streets,
Enfeoff'd himself to popularity;
That, being daily swallow'd by men's eyes,   70
They surfeited with honey and began
To loathe the taste of sweetness, whereof a little
More than a little is by much too much.

So when he had occasion to be seen,
He was but as the cuckoo is in June,
Heard, not regarded; seen, but with such eyes
As, sick and blunted with community,
Afford no extraordinary gaze,
Such as is bent on sun-like majesty
When it shines seldom in admiring eyes;   80
But rather drowsed and hung their eyelids down,
Slept in his face and render'd such aspect
As cloudy men use to their adversaries,
Being with his presence glutted, gorged and full.
And in that very line, Harry, standest thou;
For thou hast lost thy princely privilege
With vile participation: not an eye
But is a-weary of thy common sight,
Save mine, which hath desired to see thee more;
Which now doth that I would not have it do,   90
Make blind itself with foolish tenderness.
    Prince. I shall hereafter, my thrice gracious lord.
Be more myself.
    King.   For all the world
As thou art to this hour was Richard then
When I from France set foot at Ravenspurgh,
And even as I was then is Percy now.
Now, by my sceptre and my soul to boot,
He hath more worthy interest to the state
Than thou the shadow of succession;
For of no right, nor colour like to right,   100
He doth fill fields with harness in the realm,
Turns head against the lion's armed jaws,
And, being no more in debt to years than thou,
Leads ancient lords and reverend bishops on
To bloody battles and to bruising arms.
What never-dying honour hath he got
Against renowned Douglas! whose high deeds,

Whose hot incursions and great name in arms
Holds from all soldiers chief majority
And military title capital   110
Through all the kingdoms that acknowledge Christ:
Thrice hath this Hotspur, Mars in swathling clothes,
This infant warrior, in his enterprizes
Discomfited great Douglas, ta'en him once,
Enlarged him and made a friend of him,
To fill the mouth of deep defiance up
And shake the peace and safety of our throne.
And what say you to this?   Percy, Northumberland
The Archbishop's grace of York, Douglas, Mortimer,
Capitulate against us and are up.   120
But wherefore do I tell these news to thee?
Why, Harry, do I tell thee of my foes,
Which art my near'st and dearest enemy?
Thou that art like enough, through vassal fear,
Base inclination and the start of spleen,
To fight against me under Percy's pay,
To dog his heels and curtsy at his frowns,
To show how much thou art degenerate.
    Prince. Do not think so; you shall not find it so:
And God forgive them that so much have sway'd   130
Your majesty's good thoughts away from me!
I will redeem all this on Percy's head
And in the closing of some glorious day
Be bold to tell you that I am your son;
When I will wear a garment all of blood
And stain my favours in a bloody mask,
Which, wash'd away, shall scour my shame with it:
And that shall be the day, whene'er it lights,
That this same child of honour and renown,
This gallant Hotspur, this all-praised knight,   140
And your unthought-of Harry chance to meet.
For every honour sitting on his helm,

Would they were multitudes, and on my head
My shames redoubled! for the time will come,
That I shall make this northern youth exchange
His glorious deeds for my indignities.
Percy is but my factor, good my lord,
To engross up glorious deeds on my behalf;
And I will call him to so strict account,
That he shall render every glory up,   150
Yea, even the slightest worship of his time,
Or I will tear the reckoning from his heart.
This, in the name of God, I promise here:
The which if He be pleased I shall perform,
I do beseech your majesty may salve
The long-grown wounds of my intemperance:
If not, the end of life cancels all bands;
And I will die a hundred thousand deaths
Ere break the smallest parcel of this vow.

   King. A hundred thousand rebels die in this: 160
Thou shalt have charge and sovereign trust herein.

Enter BLUNT

How now, good Blunt? thy looks are full of speed.
   Blunt. So hath the business that I come to speak of.
Lord Mortimer of Scotland hath sent word
That Douglas and the English rebels met
The eleventh of this month at Shrewsbury:
A mighty and a fearful head they are,
If promises be kept on every hand,
As ever offer'd foul play in a state.

   King. The Earl of Westmoreland set forth to-day;   170
With him my son, Lord John of Lancaster;
For this advertisement is five days old:
On Wednesday next, Harry, you shall set forward;
On Thursday we ourselves will march: our meeting
Is Bridgenorth: and, Harry, you shall march

Through Gloucestershire; by which account,
Our business valued, some twelve days hence
Our general forces at Bridgenorth shall meet.
Our hands are full of business: let's away;
Advantage feeds him fat while men delay.   [*Exeunt* 180

SCENE III. *Eastcheap. The Boar's-Head Tavern*

Enter FALSTAFF *and* BARDOLPH

Fal. Bardolph, am I not fallen away vilely since this
last action? do I not bate? do I not dwindle? Why, my
skin hangs about me like an old lady's loose gown; I am
withered like an old apple-john. Well, I'll repent, and
that suddenly, while I am in some liking; I shall be out of
heart shortly, and then I shall have no strength to repent.
An I have not forgotten what the inside of a church is made
of, I am a peppercorn, a brewer's horse: the inside of a
church! Company, villanous company, hath been the spoil
of me.   10

Bard. Sir John, you are so fretful, you cannot live long.

Fal. Why, there is it: come sing me a song; make me
merry. I was as virtuously given as a gentleman need
to be; virtuous enough; swore little; diced not above seven
times a week; payed money that I borrowed, three or four
times; lived well and in good compass: and now I live out
of all order, out of all compass.

Bard. Why, you are so fat, Sir John, that you must
needs be out of all compass, out of all reasonable compass,
Sir John.   20

Fal. Do thou amend thy face, and I'll amend my life:
thou art our admiral, thou bearest the lantern in the poop,
but 'tis in the nose of thee; thou art the Knight of the
Burning Lamp.

Bard. Why, Sir John, my face does you no harm.   25

Fal. No, I'll be sworn; I make as good use of it as

4   (B 101)

many a man doth of a Death's-head or a memento mori:
I never see thy face but I think upon hell-fire and Dives
that lived in purple; for there he is in his robes, burning,
burning. If thou wert any way given to virtue, I would
swear by thy face; my oath should be 'By this fire, that's
God's angel': but thou art altogether given over; and wert
indeed, but for the light in thy face, the son of utter darkness. When thou rannest up Gadshill in the night to
catch my horse, if I did not think thou hadst been an ignis
fatuus or a ball of wildfire, there's no purchase in money.
O, thou art a perpetual triumph, an everlasting bonfire-
light! Thou hast saved me a thousand marks in links
and torches, walking with thee in the night betwixt tavern
and tavern: but the sack that thou hast drunk me would
have bought me lights as good cheap at the dearest chandler's in Europe. I have maintained that salamander of
yours with fire any time this two and thirty years; God
reward me for it!   44

   Bard. 'S blood, I would my face were in your belly!

   Fal. God-a-mercy! so should I be sure to be heart-
burned.

Enter Hostess

How now, Dame Partlet the hen! have you inquired yet
who picked my pocket?

   Host. Why, Sir John, what do you think, Sir John? do
you think I keep thieves in my house? I have searched,
I have inquired, so has my husband, man by man, boy by
boy, servant by servant: the tithe of a hair was never lost
in my house before.   54

   Fal. Ye lie, hostess: Bardolph was shaved and lost many
a hair; and I'll be sworn my pocket was picked. Go to,
you are a woman, go.

   Host. Who, I? no; I defy thee: God's light, I was never
called so in mine own house before.

   Fal. Go to, I know you well enough.   60

Host. No, Sir John; you do not know me, Sir John. I
know you, Sir John: you owe me money, Sir John; and
now you pick a quarrel to beguile me of it: I bought you a
dozen of shirts to your back.

Fal. Dowlas, filthy dowlas: I have given them away to
bakers' wives, and they have made bolters of them.

Host. Now, as I am a true woman, holland of eight
shillings an ell. You owe money here besides, Sir John,
for your diet and by-drinkings, and money lent you, four
and twenty pound.   70

Fal. He had his part of it; let him pay.

Host. He? alas, he is poor; he hath nothing.

Fal. How! poor? look upon his face; what call you
rich? let them coin his nose, let them coin his cheeks: I'll
not pay a denier. What, will you make a younker of me?
shall I not take mine ease in mine inn but I shall have my
pocket picked? I have lost a seal-ring of my grandfather's
worth forty mark.

Host. O Jesu, I have heard the prince tell him, I know
not how oft, that that ring was copper!   80

Fal. How! the prince is a Jack, a sneak-cup: 's blood,
an he were here, I would cudgel him like a dog, if he
would say so.

Enter the PRINCE *and* PETO, *marching, and* FALSTAFF
meets them playing on his truncheon like a fife

How now, lad! is the wind in that door, i' faith? must we
all march?

Bard. Yea, two and two, Newgate fashion.

Host. My lord, I pray you, hear me.

Prince. What sayest thou, Mistress Quickly? How
doth thy husband? I love him well; he is an honest
man.   90

Host. Good my lord, hear me

Fal. Prithee, let her alone, and list to me.

Prince. What sayest thou, Jack?

Fal. The other night I fell asleep here behind the arras and had my pocket picked.

Prince. What didst thou lose, Jack?

Fal. Wilt thou believe me, Hal? three or four bonds of forty pound a-piece, and a seal-ring of my grandfather's.

Prince. A trifle, some eight-penny matter.   99

Host. So I told him, my lord; and I said I heard your grace say so: and, my lord, he speaks most vilely of you, like a foul-mouthed man as he is; and said he would cudgel you.

Prince. What! he did not?

Host. There's neither faith, truth, nor womanhood in me else.

Fal. There's no more faith in thee than in a stewed prune; nor no more truth in thee than in a drawn fox; and for womanhood, Maid Marian may be the deputy's wife of the ward to thee. Go, you thing, go.   110

Host. Say, what thing? what thing?

Fal. What thing! why, a thing to thank God on.

Host. I am no thing to thank God on, I would thou shouldst know it; I am an honest man's wife: and, setting thy knighthood aside, thou art a knave to call me so.

Fal. Setting thy womanhood aside, thou art a beast to say otherwise.

Host. Say, what beast, thou knave, thou?

Fal. What beast! why, an otter.

Prince. An otter, Sir John! why an otter?   120

Fal. Why, she's neither fish nor flesh; a man knows not where to have her.

Host. Thou art an unjust man in saying so: thou or any man knows where to have me, thou knave, thou!

Prince. Thou sayest true, hostess; and he slanders thee most grossly.

Host. So he doth you, my lord; and said this other day you ought him a thousand pound.

Prince. Sirrah, do I owe you a thousand pound?

Fal. A thousand pound, Hal! a million: thy love is worth a million: thou owest me thy love.   131

Host. Nay, my lord, he called you Jack, and said he would cudgel you.

Fal. Did I, Bardolph?

Bard. Indeed, Sir John, you said so.

Fal. Yea, if he said my ring was copper.

Prince. I say 't is copper: darest thou be as good as thy word now?

Fal. Why, Hal, thou knowest, as thou art but man, I dare: but as thou art prince, I fear thee as I fear the roaring of the lion's whelp.   141

Prince. And why not as the lion?

Fal. The king himself is to be feared as the lion: dost thou think I 'll fear thee as I fear thy father? nay, an I do, I pray God my girdle break.

Prince. O, if it should, how would thy guts fall about thy knees! But, sirrah, there's no room for faith, truth, nor honesty in this bosom of thine; it is filled up with guts and midriff. Charge an honest woman with picking thy pocket! why, thou impudent, embossed rascal, if there were anything in thy pocket but tavern-reckonings, and one poor penny-worth of sugar-candy to make thee long-winded, if thy pocket were enriched with any other in-juries but these, I am a villain: and yet you will stand to it; you will not pocket up wrong: art thou not ashamed?

Fal. Dost thou hear, Hal? thou knowest in the state of innocency Adam fell; and what should poor Jack Falstaff do in the days of villany? Thou seest I have more flesh than another man, and therefore more frailty. You con-fess then, you picked my pocket?   160

Prince. It appears so by the story.

Fal. Hostess, I forgive thee: go, make ready breakfast; love thy husband, look to thy servants, cherish thy guests: thou shalt find me tractable to any honest reason: thou seest I am pacified still. Nay, prithee, begone. [*Exit Hostess.*] Now, Hal, to the news at court: for the robbery, lad, how is that answered?

Prince. O, my sweet beef, I must still be good angel to thee: the money is paid back again.   169

Fal. O, I do not like that paying back; 'tis a double labour.

Prince. I am good friends with my father and may do any thing.

Fal. Rob me the exchequer the first thing thou doest, and do it with unwashed hands too.

Bard. Do, my lord.

Prince. I have procured thee, Jack, a charge of foot.

Fal. I would it had been of horse. Where shall I find one that can steal well? O for a fine thief, of the age of two and twenty or thereabouts! I am heinously unprovided. Well, God be thanked for these rebels, they offend none but the virtuous: I laud them, I praise them.   182

Prince. Bardolph!

Bard. My lord?

Prince. Go bear this letter to Lord John of Lancaster, to my brother John; this to my Lord of Westmoreland. [*Exit Bardolph.*] Go, Peto, to horse, to horse; for thou and I have thirty miles to ride yet ere dinner time. [*Exit Peto.*] Jack, meet me to-morrow in the temple hall at two o'clock in the afternoon.   190

There shalt thou know thy charge; and there receive
Money and order for their furniture.
The land is burning; Percy stands on high;
And either we or they must lower lie.   [*Exit*

Fal. Rare words! brave world! Hostess, my breakfast, come!
O, I could wish this tavern were my drum!   [*Exit*

ACT IV

SCENE I. *The rebel camp near Shrewsbury*

Enter HOTSPUR, WORCESTER, *and* DOUGLAS

Hot. Well said, my noble Scot: if speaking truth
In this fine age were not thought flattery,
Such attribution should the Douglas have,
As not a soldier of this season's stamp
Should go so general current through the world.
By God, I cannot flatter; I do defy
The tongues of soothers; but a braver place
In my heart's love hath no man than yourself:
Nay, task me to my word; approve me, lord.
 Doug. Thou art the king of honour:
No man so potent breathes upon the ground
But I will beard him.
 Hot.   Do so, and 't is well.

Enter a Messenger *with letters*

What letters hast thou there?—I can but thank you.
 Mess. These letters come from your father.
 Hot. Letters from him! why comes he not himself?
 Mess. He cannot come, my lord; he is grievous sick.
 Hot. 'Zounds! how has he the leisure to be sick
In such a justling time? Who leads his power?
Under whose government come they along?
 Mess. His letters bear his mind, not I, my lord.
 Wor. I prithee, tell me, doth he keep his bed?
 Mess. He did, my lord, four days ere I set forth;
And at the time of my departure thence
He was much fear'd by his physicians.
 Wor. I would the state of time had first been whole

Ere he by sickness had been visited:
His health was never better worth than now.

    Hot. Sick now! droop now! this sickness doth infect
The very life-blood of our enterprise;
'T is catching hither, even to our camp.   30
He writes me here, that inward sickness—
And that his friends by deputation could not
So soon be drawn, nor did he think it meet
To lay so dangerous and dear a trust
On any soul removed but on his own.
Yet doth he give us bold advertisement,
That with our small conjunction we should on,
To see how fortune is disposed to us;
For, as he writes, there is no quailing now,
Because the king is certainly possess'd   40
Of all our purposes.   What say you to it?

    Wor. Your father's sickness is a maim to us.

    Hot. A perilous gash, a very limb lopp'd off:
And yet, in faith, it is not; his present want
Seems more than we shall find it: were it good
To set the exact wealth of all our states
All at one cast? to set so rich a main
On the nice hazard of one doubtful hour?
It were not good; for therein should we read
The very bottom and the soul of hope,   50
The very list, the very utmost bound
Of all our fortunes.

    Doug.   'Faith, and so we should;
Where now remains a sweet reversion:
We may boldly spend upon the hope of what
Is to come in:
A comfort of retirement lives in this.

    Hot. A rendezvous, a home to fly unto,
If that the devil and mischance look big
Upon the maidenhead of our affairs.

Wor. But yet I would your father had been here.   60
The quality and hair of our attempt
Brooks no division: it will be thought
By some, that know not why he is away,
That wisdom, loyalty and mere dislike
Of our proceedings kept the earl from hence:
And think how such an apprehension
May turn the tide of fearful faction
And breed a kind of question in our cause;
For well you know we of the offering side
Must keep aloof from strict arbitrement,   70
And stop all sight-holes, every loop from whence
The eye of reason may pry in upon us:
This absence of your father's draws a curtain,
That shows the ignorant a kind of fear
Before not dreamt of.

    Hot.   You strain too far.
I rather of his absence make this use:
It lends a lustre and more great opinion,
A larger dare to our great enterprise,
Than if the earl were here; for men must think,
If we without his help can make a head   80
To push against a kingdom, with his help
We shall o'erturn it topsy-turvy down.
Yet all goes well, yet all our joints are whole.

    Doug. As heart can think: there is not such a word
Spoke of in Scotland as this term of fear.

Enter SIR RICHARD VERNON

    Hot. My cousin Vernon! welcome, by my soul.
    Ver. Pray God my news be worth a welcome, lord.
The Earl of Westmoreland, seven thousand strong,
Is marching hitherwards; with him Prince John.
    Hot. No harm: what more?
    Ver   And further, I have learn'd,

The king himself in person is set forth,   91
Or hitherwards intended speedily,
With strong and mighty preparation.
   Hot. He shall be welcome too.   Where is his son,
The nimble-footed, madcap Prince of Wales,
And his comrades, that daff'd the world aside,
And bid it pass?
   Ver.   All furnish'd, all in arms;
All plumed like estridges that with the wind
Bated, like eagles having lately bathed;
Glittering in golden coats, like images;   100
As full of spirit as the month of May,
And gorgeous as the sun at midsummer;
Wanton as youthful goats, wild as young bulls.
I saw young Harry, with his beaver on,
His cuisses on his thighs, gallantly arm'd,
Rise from the ground like feather'd Mercury,
And vaulted with such ease into his seat,
As if an angel dropp'd down from the clouds,
To turn and wind a fiery Pegasus
And witch the world with noble horsemanship.   110
   Hot. No more, no more: worse than the sun in March,
This praise doth nourish agues.   Let them come;
They come like sacrifices in their trim,
And to the fire-eyed maid of smoky war
All hot and bleeding will we offer them:
The mailed Mars shall on his altar sit
Up to the ears in blood.   I am on fire
To hear this rich reprisal is so nigh
And yet not ours.   Come, let me taste my horse,
Who is to bear me like a thunderbolt   120
Against the bosom of the Prince of Wales:
Harry to Harry shall, hot horse to horse,
Meet and ne'er part till one drop down a corse.
O that Glendower were come'

Ver.   There is more news:
I learn'd in Worcester, as I rode along,
He cannot draw his power this fourteen days.
   Doug. That's the worst tidings that I hear of yet.
   Wor. Ay, by my faith, that bears a frosty sound.
   Hot. What may the king's whole battle reach unto?
   Ver. To thirty thousand.
   Hot.   Forty let it be: 130
My father and Glendower being both away,
The powers of us may serve so great a day.
Come, let us take a muster speedily:
Doomsday is near; die all, die merrily.
   Doug. Talk not of dying: I am out of fear
Of death or death's hand for this one half-year.   [*Exeunt*

SCENE II. *A public road near Coventry*

Enter FALSTAFF *and* BARDOLPH

   Fal. Bardolph, get thee before to Coventry; fill me a
bottle of sack: our soldiers shall march through; we'll to
Sutton Co'fil' to-night.
   Bard. Will you give me money, captain?
   Fal. Lay out, lay out.
   Bard. This bottle makes an angel.
   Fal. An if it do, take it for thy labour; and if it make
twenty, take them all; I'll answer the coinage. Bid my
lieutenant Peto meet me at town's end.
   Bard. I will, captain: farewell.   [*Exit* 10
   Fal. If I be not ashamed of my soldiers, I am a soused
gurnet. I have misused the king's press damnably. I
have got, in exchange of a hundred and fifty soldiers,
three hundred and odd pounds. I press me none but good
householders, yeomen's sons; inquire me out contracted
bachelors, such as had been asked twice on the banns;
such a commodity of warm slaves, as had as lieve hear the

devil as a drum; such as fear the report of a caliver worse
than a struck fowl or a hurt wild-duck. I pressed me none
but such toasts-and-butter, with hearts in their bellies no
bigger than pins' heads, and they have bought out their
services; and now my whole charge consists of ancients,
corporals, lieutenants, gentlemen of companies, slaves as
ragged as Lazarus in the painted cloth, where the glutton's
dogs licked his sores; and such as indeed were never
soldiers, but discarded unjust serving-men, younger sons
to younger brothers, revolted tapsters and ostlers trade-
fallen, the cankers of a calm world and a long peace, ten
times more dishonourable ragged than an old faced ancient: and such have I, to fill up the rooms of them that
have bought out their services, that you would think that
I had a hundred and fifty tattered prodigals lately come
from swine-keeping, from eating draff and husks. A mad
fellow met me on the way and told me I had unloaded
all the gibbets and pressed the dead bodies. No eye hath
seen such scarecrows. I'll not march through Coventry
with them, that's flat: nay, and the villains march wide
betwixt the legs, as if they had gyves on; for indeed I had
the most of them out of prison. There's but a shirt and a
half in all my company; and the half shirt is two napkins
tacked together and thrown over the shoulders like an
herald's coat without sleeves; and the shirt, to say the
truth, stolen from my host at St. Alban's, or the red-nose
inn-keeper of Daventry. But that's all one; they'll find
linen enough on every hedge.   45

Enter the PRINCE *and* WESTMORELAND

Prince. How now, blown Jack! how now, quilt!

Fal. What, Hal! how now, mad wag! what a devil
dost thou in Warwickshire? My good Lord of Westmoreland, I cry you mercy: I thought your honour had already
been at Shrewsbury.   50

West. Faith, Sir John, 't is more than time that I were there, and you too; but my powers are there already. The king, I can tell you, looks for us all: we must away all night.

Fal. Tut, never fear me: I am as vigilant as a cat to steal cream.

Prince. I think, to steal cream indeed, for thy theft hath already made thee butter. But tell me, Jack, whose fellows are these that come after?

Fal. Mine, Hal, mine. 60

Prince. I did never see such pitiful rascals.

Fal. Tut, tut; good enough to toss; food for powder, food for powder; they 'll fill a pit as well as better: tush, man, mortal men, mortal men.

West. Ay, but, Sir John, methinks they are exceeding poor and bare, too beggarly.

Fal. 'Faith, for their poverty, I know not where they had that; and for their bareness, I am sure they never learned that of me.

Prince. No, I 'll be sworn; unless you call three fingers on the ribs bare. But, sirrah, make haste: Percy is already in the field. 72

Fal. What, is the king encamped?

West. He is, Sir John: I fear we shall stay too long.

Fal. Well,
To the latter end of a fray and the beginning of a feast
Fits a dull fighter and a keen guest. [*Exeunt*

SCENE III. *The rebel camp near Shrewsbury*

Enter HOTSPUR, WORCESTER, DOUGLAS, *and* VERNON

Hot. We 'll fight with him to-night.

Wor. It may not be.

Doug. You give him then advantage.

Ver. Not a whit.

Hot. Why say you so? looks he not for supply?

Ver. So do we.

Hot.   His is certain, ours is doubtful.

Wor. Good cousin, be advised; stir not to-night.

Ver. Do not, my lord.

Doug.   You do not counsel well:
You speak it out of fear and cold heart.

Ver. Do me no slander, Douglas: by my life,
And I dare well maintain it with my life,
If well-respected honour bid me on,   10
I hold as little counsel with weak fear
As you, my lord, or any Scot that this day lives:
Let it be seen to-morrow in the battle
Which of us fears.

Doug.   Yea, or to-night.

Ver.   Content.

Hot. To-night, say I.

Ver. Come, come, it may not be. I wonder much,
Being men of such great leading as you are,
That you foresee not what impediments
Drag back our expedition: certain horse
Of my cousin Vernon's are not yet come up: 20
Your uncle Worcester's horse came but to-day;
And now their pride and mettle is asleep,
Their courage with hard labour tame and dull,
That not a horse is half the half of himself.

Hot. So are the horses of the enemy
In general, journey-bated and brought low:
The better part of ours are full of rest.

Wor. The number of the king exceedeth ours:
For God's sake, cousin, stay till all come in.

                              [*The trumpet sounds a parley*

Enter SIR WALTER BLUNT

Blunt. I come with gracious offers from the king,　　30
If you vouchsafe me hearing and respect.

Hot. Welcome, Sir Walter Blunt; and would to God
You were of our determination!
Some of us love you well; and even those some
Envy your great deservings and good name,
Because you are not of our quality,
But stand against us like an enemy.

Blunt. And God defend but still I should stand so,
So long as out of limit and true rule
You stand against anointed majesty.　　40
But to my charge.　The king hath sent to know
The nature of your griefs, and whereupon
You conjure from the breast of civil peace
Such bold hostility, teaching his duteous land
Audacious cruelty.　If that the king
Have any way your good deserts forgot,
Which he confesseth to be manifold,
He bids you name your griefs; and with all speed
You shall have your desires with interest
And pardon absolute for yourself and these　　50
Herein misled by your suggestion.

Hot. The king is kind; and well we know the king
Knows at what time to promise, when to pay.
My father and my uncle and myself
Did give him that same royalty he wears;
And when he was not six and twenty strong,
Sick in the world's regard, wretched and low,
A poor unminded outlaw sneaking home,
My father gave him welcome to the shore;
And when he heard him swear and vow to God　　60
He came but to be Duke of Lancaster,
To sue his livery and beg his peace,

With tears of innocency and terms of zeal,
My father, in kind heart and pity moved,
Swore him assistance and perform'd it too.
Now when the lords and barons of the realm
Perceived Northumberland did lean to him,
The more and less came in with cap and knee;
Met him in boroughs, cities, villages,
Attended him on bridges, stood in lanes,   70
Laid gifts before him, proffer'd him their oaths,
Gave him their heirs, as pages follow'd him
Even at the heels in golden multitudes.
He presently, as greatness knows itself,
Steps me a little higher than his vow
Made to my father, while his blood was poor,
Upon the naked shore at Ravenspurgh;
And now, forsooth, takes on him to reform
Some certain edicts and some strait decrees
That lie too heavy on the commonwealth,   80
Cries out upon abuses, seems to weep
Over his country's wrongs; and by this face,
This seeming brow of justice, did he win
The hearts of all that he did angle for;
Proceeded further; cut me off the heads
Of all the favourites that the absent king
In deputation left behind him here,
When he was personal in the Irish war.
    Blunt. Tut, I came not to hear this.
    Hot.   Then to the point.
In short time after, he deposed the king;   90
Soon after that, deprived him of his life;
And in the neck of that, task'd the whole state;
To make that worse, suffer'd his kinsman March,
Who is, if every owner were well placed,
Indeed his king, to be engaged in Wales,
There without ransom to lie forfeited;

Disgraced me in my happy victories,
Sought to entrap me by intelligence;
Rated mine uncle from the council-board;
In rage dismiss'd my father from the court;   100
Broke oath on oath, committed wrong on wrong,
And in conclusion drove us to seek out
This head of safety; and withal to pry
Into his title, the which we find
Too indirect for long continuance.

Blunt. Shall I return this answer to the king?

Hot. Not so, Sir Walter: we'll withdraw awhile.
Go to the king; and let there be impawn'd
Some surety for a safe return again,
And in the morning early shall my uncle   110
Bring him our purposes; and so farewell.

Blunt. I would you would accept of grace and love.

Hot. And may be so we shall.

Blunt.   Pray God you do. [*Exeunt*

Scene IV. *York. The Archbishop's palace*

Enter the Archbishop of York *and* Sir Michael

Arch. Hie, good Sir Michael; bear this sealed brief
With winged haste to the lord marshal;
This to my cousin Scroop, and all the rest
To whom they are directed. If you knew
How much they do import, you would make haste.

Sir M. My good lord,
I guess their tenour.

Arch.   Like enough you do.
To-morrow, good Sir Michael, is a day
Wherein the fortune of ten thousand men
Must bide the touch; for, sir, at Shrewsbury,   10
As I am truly given to understand,
The king with mighty and quick-raised power

Meets with Lord Harry: and, I fear, Sir Michael,
What with the sickness of Northumberland,
Whose power was in the first proportion,
And what with Owen Glendower's absence thence,
Who with them was a rated sinew too
And comes not in, o'er-ruled by prophecies,
I fear the power of Percy is too weak
To wage an instant trial with the king.   20

Sir M. Why, my good lord, you need not fear;
There is Douglas and Lord Mortimer.

Arch. No, Mortimer is not there.

Sir M. But there is Mordake, Vernon, Lord Harry Percy,
And there is my Lord of Worcester and a head
Of gallant warriors, noble gentlemen.

Arch. And so there is: but yet the king hath drawn
The special head of all the land together:
The Prince of Wales, Lord John of Lancaster,
The noble Westmoreland and warlike Blunt;   30
And many moe corrivals and dear men
Of estimation and command in arms.

Sir M. Doubt not, my lord, they shall be well opposed.

Arch. I hope no less, yet needful 't is to fear;
And, to prevent the worst, Sir Michael, speed:
For if Lord Percy thrive not, ere the king
Dismiss his power, he means to visit us,
For he hath heard of our confederacy,
And 't is but wisdom to make strong against him:
Therefore make haste. I must go write again   40
To other friends; and so farewell, Sir Michael.   [*Exeunt*

ACT V

SCENE I.   *The King's camp near Shrewsbury*

Enter the KING, PRINCE OF WALES, LORD JOHN OF LAN-
    CASTER, EARL OF WESTMORELAND, SIR WALTER
    BLUNT, *and* FALSTAFF

King. How bloodily the sun begins to peer
Above yon busky hill! the day looks pale
At his distemperature.
    Prince.   The southern wind
Doth play the trumpet to his purposes,
And by his hollow whistling in the leaves
Foretells a tempest and a blustering day.
    King. Then with the losers let it sympathise,
For nothing can seem foul to those that win.

                              [*The trumpet sounds*

Enter WORCESTER *and* VERNON

How now, my lord of Worcester! 't is not well
That you and I should meet upon such terms   10
As now we meet.   You have deceived our trust
And made us doff our easy robes of peace,
To crush our old limbs in ungentle steel:
This is not well, my lord, this is not well.
What say you to it? will you again unknit
This churlish knot of all-abhorred war?
And move in that obedient orb again
Where you did give a fair and natural light,
And be no more an exhaled meteor,
A prodigy of fear and a portent   20
Of broached mischief to the unborn times?
    Wor. Hear me, my liege:
For mine own part, I could be well content

To entertain the lag-end of my life
With quiet hours; for I do protest,
I have not sought the day of this dislike.

 King. You have not sought it! how comes it, then?

 Fal. Rebellion lay in his way, and he found it.

 Prince. Peace, chewet, peace!

 Wor. It pleased your majesty to turn your looks 30
Of favour from myself and all our house;
And yet I must remember you, my lord,
We were the first and dearest of your friends.
For you my staff of office did I break
In Richard's time; and posted day and night
To meet you on the way, and kiss your hand,
When yet you were in place and in account
Nothing so strong and fortunate as I.
It was myself, my brother and his son,
That brought you home and boldly did outdare 40
The dangers of the time. You swore to us,
And you did swear that oath at Doncaster,
That you did nothing purpose 'gainst the state;
Nor claim no further than your new-fall'n right,
The seat of Gaunt, dukedom of Lancaster:
To this we swore our aid. But in short space
It rain'd down fortune showering on your head;
And such a flood of greatness fell on you,
What with our help, what with the absent king,
What with the injuries of a wanton time, 50
The seeming sufferances that you had borne,
And the contrarious winds that held the king
So long in his unlucky Irish wars
That all in England did repute him dead:
And from this swarm of fair advantages
You took occasion to be quickly woo'd
To gripe the general sway into your hand;
Forgot your oath to us at Doncaster;

And being fed by us you used us so
As that ungentle gull, the cuckoo's bird,   60
Useth the sparrow; did oppress our nest;
Grew by our feeding to so great a bulk
That even our love durst not come near your sight
For fear of swallowing; but with nimble wing
We were enforced, for safety sake, to fly
Out of your sight and raise this present head;
Whereby we stand opposed by such means
As you yourself have forged against yourself
By unkind usage, dangerous countenance,
And violation of all faith and troth   70
Sworn to us in your younger enterprise.
   King. These things indeed you have articulate,
Proclaim'd at market-crosses, read in churches,
To face the garment of rebellion
With some fine colour that may please the eye
Of fickle changelings and poor discontents,
Which gape and rub the elbow at the news
Of hurlyburly innovation:
And never yet did insurrection want
Such water-colours to impaint his cause;   80
Nor moody beggars, starving for a time
Of pellmell havoc and confusion.
   Prince. In both your armies there is many a soul
Shall pay full dearly for this encounter,
If once they join in trial.   Tell your nephew,
The Prince of Wales doth join with all the world
In praise of Henry Percy: by my hopes,
This present enterprise set off his head,
I do not think a braver gentleman,
More active-valiant or more valiant-young,   90
More daring or more bold, is now alive
To grace this latter age with noble deeds.
For my part, I may speak it to my shame,

I have a truant been to chivalry;
And so I hear he doth account me too;
Yet this before my father's majesty—
I am content that he shall take the odds
Of his great name and estimation,
And will, to save the blood on either side,
Try fortune with him in a single fight.   100

   King. And, Prince of Wales, so dare we venture thee,
Albeit considerations infinite
Do make against it.   No, good Worcester, no,
We love our people well; even those we love
That are misled upon your cousin's part;
And, will they take the offer of our grace,
Both he and they and you, yea, every man
Shall be my friend again and I 'll be his:
So tell your cousin, and bring me word
What he will do: but if he will not yield,   110
Rebuke and dread correction wait on us
And they shall do their office.   So, be gone;
We will not now be troubled with reply:
We offer fair; take it advisedly.
                  [Exeunt Worcester and Vernon

   Prince. It will not be accepted, on my life:
The Douglas and the Hotspur both together
Are confident against the world in arms.

   King. Hence, therefore, every leader to his charge;
For, on their answer, will we set on them:
And God befriend us, as our cause is just!   120
        [Exeunt all but the Prince of Wales and Falstaff

   Fal. Hal, if thou see me down in the battle and bestride
me, so; 't is a point of friendship.

   Prince. Nothing but a colossus can do thee that friendship.   Say thy prayers, and farewell.

   Fal. I would 't were bed-time, Hal, and all well.

   Prince. Why, thou owest God a death.   *[Exit*

Fal. 'T is not due yet; I would be loath to pay him before his day. What need I be so forward with him that calls not on me? Well, 't is no matter; honour pricks me on. Yea, but how if honour prick me off when I come on? how then? Can honour set to a leg? no: or an arm? no: or take away the grief of a wound? no. Honour hath no skill in surgery, then? no. What is honour? a word. What is in that word honour? what is that honour? air. A trim reckoning! Who hath it? he that died o' Wednesday. Doth he feel it? no. Doth he hear it? no. 'T is insensible, then. Yes, to the dead. But will it not live with the living? no. Why? detraction will not suffer it Therefore I 'll none of it. Honour is a mere scutcheon: and so ends my catechism.   [*Exit* 140

SCENE II.   *The rebel camp*

Enter WORCESTER *and* VERNON

Wor. O, no, my nephew must now know, Sir Richard
The liberal and kind offer of the king.

Ver. 'T were best he did.

Wor.   Then are we all undone.
It is not possible, it cannot be,
The king should keep his word in loving us;
He will suspect us still and find a time
To punish this offence in other faults:
Suspicion all our lives shall be stuck full of eyes;
For treason is but trusted like the fox,
Who, ne'er so tame, so cherish'd and lock'd up,   10
Will have a wild trick of his ancestors.
Look how we can, or sad or merrily,
Interpretation will misquote our looks,
And we shall feed like oxen at a stall,
The better cherish'd, still the nearer death
My nephew's trespass may be well forgot;

It hath the excuse of youth and heat of blood,
And an adopted name of privilege,
A hare-brain'd Hotspur, govern'd by a spleen:
All his offences live upon my head   20
And on his father's; we did train him on,
And, his corruption being ta'en from us,
We, as the spring of all, shall pay for all.
Therefore, good cousin, let not Harry know,
In any case, the offer of the king.

    Ver. Deliver what you will; I 'll say 't is so.
Here comes your cousin.

Enter HOTSPUR *and* DOUGLAS

    Hot. My uncle is return'd:
Deliver up my Lord of Westmoreland.
Uncle, what news?   30
    Wor. The king will bid you battle presently.
    Doug. Defy him by the Lord of Westmoreland.
    Hot. Lord Douglas, go you and tell him so.
    Doug. Marry, and shall, and very willingly.   [*Exit*
    Wor. There is no seeming mercy in the king.
    Hot. Did you beg any?   God forbid!
    Wor. I told him gently of our grievances,
Of his oath-breaking; which he mended thus,
By now forswearing that he is forsworn:
He calls us rebels, traitors; and will scourge   40
With haughty arms this hateful name in us.

Re-enter DOUGLAS

    Doug. Arm, gentlemen; to arms! for I have thrown
A brave defiance in King Henry's teeth,
And Westmoreland, that was engaged, did bear it;
Which cannot choose but bring him quickly on.
    Wor. The Prince of Wales stepp'd forth before the king,
And, nephew, challenged you to single fight.

Hot. O, would the quarrel lay upon our heads,
And that no man might draw short breath to-day
But I and Harry Monmouth!   Tell me, tell me,   50
How show'd his tasking? seem'd it in contempt?
    Ver. No, by my soul; I never in my life
Did hear a challenge urged more modestly,
Unless a brother should a brother dare
To gentle exercise and proof of arms.
He gave you all the duties of a man:
Trimm'd up your praises with a princely tongue,
Spoke your deservings like a chronicle,
Making you ever better than his praise
By still dispraising praise valued with you;   60
And, which became him like a prince indeed,
He made a blushing cital of himself;
And chid his truant youth with such a grace
As if he master'd there a double spirit
Of teaching and of learning instantly.
There did he pause: but let me tell the world,
If he outlive the envy of this day,
England did never owe so sweet a hope,
So much misconstrued in his wantonness.
    Hot. Cousin, I think thou art enamoured   70
On his follies: never did I hear
Of any prince so wild a libertine.
But be he as he will, yet once ere night
I will embrace him with a soldier's arm,
That he shall shrink under my courtesy.
Arm, arm with speed: and, fellows, soldiers, friends,
Better consider what you have to do
Than I, that have not well the gift of tongue,
Can lift your blood up with persuasion.

Enter a Messenger

Mess. My lord, here are letters for you.   80
Hot. I cannot read them now.
O gentlemen, the time of life is short!
To spend that shortness basely were too long,
If life did ride upon a dial's point,
Still ending at the arrival of an hour.
An if we live, we live to tread on kings;
If die, brave death, when princes die with us!
Now, for our consciences, the arms are fair,
When the intent of bearing them is just.

Enter another Messenger

Mess. My lord, prepare; the king comes on apace.   90
Hot. I thank him, that he cuts me from my tale,
For I profess not talking; only this—
Let each man do his best: and here draw I
A sword, whose temper I intend to stain
With the best blood that I can meet withal
In the adventure of this perilous day.
Now, Esperance! Percy! and set on.
Sound all the lofty instruments of war,
And by that music let us all embrace;
For, heaven to earth, some of us never shall   100
A second time do such a courtesy.

[*The trumpets sound. They embrace, and exeunt*

SCENE III. *Plain between the camps*

The KING *enters with his power. Alarum to the battle.
Then enter* DOUGLAS *and* SIR WALTER BLUNT

Blunt. What is thy name, that in the battle thus
Thou crossest me? what honour dost thou seek
Upon my head?

Doug.   Know then, my name is Douglas;
And I do haunt thee in the battle thus
Because some tell me that thou art a king.

Blunt. They tell thee true.

Doug. The Lord of Stafford dear to-day hath bought
Thy likeness, for instead of thee, King Harry,
This sword hath ended him: so shall it thee,
Unless thou yield thee as my prisoner.   10

Blunt. I was not born a yielder, thou proud Scot;
And thou shalt find a king that will revenge
Lord Stafford's death.   [*They fight. Douglas kills Blunt*

Enter HOTSPUR

Hot. O Douglas, hadst thou fought at Holmedon thus,
I never had triumph'd upon a Scot.

Doug. All 's done, all 's won; here breathless lies the
     king.

Hot. Where?

Doug. Here.

Hot. This, Douglas? no: I know this face full well:
A gallant knight he was, his name was Blunt;   20
Semblably furnish'd like the king himself.

Doug. A fool go with thy soul, whither it goes!
A borrow'd title hast thou bought too dear:
Why didst thou tell me that thou wert a king?

Hot. The king hath many marching in his coats.

Doug. Now, by my sword, I will kill all his coats;
I 'll murder all his wardrobe, piece by piece,
Until I meet the king.

Hot.   Up, and away!
Our soldiers stand full fairly for the day.   [*Exeunt* 29

Alarum. Enter FALSTAFF, *solus*

Fal. Though I could 'scape shot-free at London, I fear
the shot here; here 's no scoring but upon the pate. Soft!

who are you? Sir Walter Blunt: there's honour for you!
here's no vanity! I am as hot as molten lead, and as
heavy too: God keep lead out of me! I need no more
weight than mine own bowels. I have led my ragamuffins
where they are peppered: there's not three of my hundred
and fifty left alive; and they are for the town's end, to beg
during life. But who comes here?

Enter the PRINCE

Prince. What, stand'st thou idle here? lend me thy
    sword:
Many a nobleman lies stark and stiff   40
Under the hoofs of vaunting enemies,
Whose deaths are yet unrevenged: I prithee, lend me thy
    sword.

Fal. O Hal, I prithee, give me leave to breathe awhile.
Turk Gregory never did such deeds in arms as I have done
this day. I have paid Percy, I have made him sure.

Prince. He is, indeed; and living to kill thee. I prithee,
lend me thy sword.

Fal. Nay, before God, Hal, if Percy be alive, thou get'st
not my sword; but take my pistol, if thou wilt.

Prince. Give it me: what, is it in the case?   50

Fal. Ay, Hal; 't is hot, 't is hot; there's that will sack a
city.

    [*The Prince draws it out, and finds it to be a bottle of sack*

Prince. What, is it a time to jest and dally now?

               [*He throws the bottle at him. Exit*

Fal. Well, if Percy be alive, I'll pierce him. If he do
come in my way, so: if he do not, if I come in his
willingly, let him make a carbonado of me. I like not
such grinning honour as Sir Walter hath: give me life:
which if I can save, so; if not, honour comes unlooked
for, and there's an end.   [*Exit*

SCENE IV. *Another part of the field*

Alarum. Excursions. Enter the KING, *the* PRINCE, LORD
JOHN OF LANCASTER, *and* EARL OF WESTMORELAND

King. I prithee,
Harry, withdraw thyself; thou bleed'st too much.
Lord John of Lancaster, go you with him.

Lan. Not I, my lord, unless I did bleed too.

Prince. I beseech your majesty, make up,
Lest your retirement do amaze your friends.

King. I will do so.
My Lord of Westmoreland, lead him to his tent.

West. Come, my lord, I 'll lead you to your tent.

Prince. Lead me, my lord? I do not need your help: 10
And God forbid a shallow scratch should drive
The Prince of Wales from such a field as this,
Where stain'd nobility lies trodden on,
And rebels' arms triumph in massacres!

Lan. We breathe too long: come, cousin Westmoreland,
Our duty this way lies; for God's sake, come.
         [*Exeunt Prince John and Westmoreland*

Prince. By God, thou hast deceived me, Lancaster;
I did not think thee lord of such a spirit:
Before, I loved thee as a brother, John;
But now, I do respect thee as my soul.   20

King. I saw him hold Lord Percy at the point
With lustier maintenance than I did look for
Of such an ungrown warrior.

Prince.   O, this boy
Lends mettle to us all!   [*Exit*

Enter DOUGLAS

Doug. Another king! they grow like Hydra's heads:
I am the Douglas, fatal to all those

That wear those colours on them: what art thou,
That counterfeit'st the person of a king?

King. The king himself; who, Douglas, grieves at heart
So many of his shadows thou hast met   30
And not the very king.   I have two boys
Seek Percy and thyself about the field:
But, seeing thou fall'st on me so luckily,
I will assay thee: so, defend thyself.

Doug. I fear thou art another counterfeit;
And yet, in faith, thou bear'st thee like a king:
But mine I am sure thou art, whoe'er thou be,
And thus I win thee. [*They fight; the King being in danger,
                              re-enter Prince of Wales*

Prince. Hold up thy head, vile Scot, or thou art like
Never to hold it up again! the spirits   40
Of valiant Shirley, Stafford, Blunt, are in my arms:
It is the Prince of Wales that threatens thee;
Who never promiseth but he means to pay.
                              [*They fight; Douglas flies*
Cheerly, my lord: how fares your grace?
Sir Nicholas Gawsey hath for succour sent,
And so hath Clifton: I 'll to Clifton straight.

King. Stay, and breathe awhile:
Thou hast redeem'd thy lost opinion,
And show'd thou makest some tender of my life,
In this fair rescue thou hast brought to me.   50

Prince. O God! they did me too much injury
That ever said I hearken'd for your death.
If it were so, I might have let alone
The insulting hand of Douglas over you,
Which would have been as speedy in your end
As all the poisonous potions in the world
And save the treacherous labour of your son.

King. Make up to Clifton: I 'll to Sir Nicholas Gawsey.
                                        [*Exit*

Enter HOTSPUR

Hot. If I mistake not, thou art Harry Monmouth.
Prince. Thou speak'st as if I would deny my name.   60
Hot. My name is Harry Percy.
Prince.   Why, then I see
A very valiant rebel of the name.
I am the Prince of Wales; and think not, Percy,
To share with me in glory any more:
Two stars keep not their motion in one sphere;
Nor can one England brook a double reign,
Of Harry Percy and the Prince of Wales.
Hot. Nor shall it, Harry; for the hour is come
To end the one of us; and would to God
Thy name in arms were now as great as mine!   70
Prince. I 'll make it greater ere I part from thee;
And all the budding honours on thy crest
I 'll crop, to make a garland for my head.
Hot. I can no longer brook thy vanities.   [*They fight*

Enter FALSTAFF

Fal. Well said, Hal! to it, Hal! Nay, you shall find no
boy's play here, I can tell you.

Re-enter DOUGLAS; *he fights with* FALSTAFF, *who falls down
as if he were dead, and exit* DOUGLAS. HOTSPUR *is
wounded, and falls*

Hot. O, Harry, thou hast robb'd me of my youth!
I better brook the loss of brittle life
Than those proud titles thou hast won of me;
They wound my thoughts worse than thy sword my flesh: 80
But thought 's the slave of life, and life time 's fool;
And time, that takes survey of all the world,
Must have a stop. O, I could prophesy,
But that the earthy and cold hand of death

Lies on my tongue: no, Percy, thou art dust,
And food for—   [*Dies*
    Prince. For worms, brave Percy: fare thee well, great
    heart!
Ill-weaved ambition, how much art thou shrunk!
When that this body did contain a spirit,
A kingdom for it was too small a bound;   90
But now two paces of the vilest earth
Is room enough: this earth that bears thee dead
Bears not alive so stout a gentleman.
If thou wert sensible of courtesy,
I should not make so dear a show of zeal:
But let my favours hide thy mangled face;
And, even in thy behalf, I 'll thank myself
For doing these fair rites of tenderness.
Adieu, and take thy praise with thee to heaven!
Thy ignominy sleep with thee in the grave,   100
But not remember'd in thy epitaph!
           [*He spieth Falstaff on the ground*
What, old acquaintance! could not all this flesh
Keep in a little life? Poor Jack, farewell!
I could have better spared a better man:
O, I should have a heavy miss of thee,
If I were much in love with vanity!
Death hath not struck so fat a deer to-day,
Though many dearer, in this bloody fray.
Embowell'd will I see thee by and by:
Till then in blood by noble Percy lie.   [*Exit* 110
    Fal. [*Rising up*] Embowelled! if thou embowel me
to-day, I 'll give you leave to powder me and eat me to-
morrow. 'S blood, 't was time to counterfeit, or that hot
termagant Scot had paid me scot and lot too. Counterfeit?
I lie, I am no counterfeit: to die, is to be a counterfeit; for
he is but the counterfeit of a man who hath not the life
of a man: but to counterfeit dying, when a man thereby

liveth, is to be no counterfeit, but the true and perfect
image of life indeed. The better part of valour is discretion; in the which better part I have saved my life. 'Zounds,
I am afraid of this gunpowder Percy, though he be dead:
how, if he should counterfeit too and rise? by my faith, I
am afraid he would prove the better counterfeit. Therefore I 'll make him sure; yea, and I 'll swear I killed him.
Why may not he rise as well as I? Nothing confutes me
but eyes, and nobody sees me. Therefore, sirrah [*stabbing
him*], with a new wound in your thigh, come you along
with me.　　　　　　　　　　[*Takes up Hotspur on his back*

Re-enter the PRINCE OF WALES, *and* LORD JOHN OF
LANCASTER

Prince. Come, brother John; full bravely hast thou flesh'd
Thy maiden sword.

Lan.　　　　　　But, soft! whom have we here?　　130
Did you not tell me this fat man was dead?

Prince. I did; I saw him dead,
Breathless and bleeding on the ground. Art thou alive?
Or is it fantasy that plays upon our eyesight?
I prithee, speak; we will not trust our eyes
Without our ears: thou art not what thou seem'st.

Fal. No, that 's certain; I am not a double man: but if
I be not Jack Falstaff, then am I a Jack. There is Percy
[*throwing the body down*]: if your father will do me any
honour, so; if not, let him kill the next Percy himself. I
look to be either earl or duke, I can assure you.　　141

Prince. Why, Percy I killed myself and saw thee dead.

Fal. Didst thou? Lord, Lord, how this world is given
to lying! I grant you I was down and out of breath; and
so was he: but we rose both at an instant and fought a
long hour by Shrewsbury clock. If I may be believed, so;
if not, let them that should reward valour bear the sin upon

their own heads. I 'll take it upon my death, I gave him
this wound in the thigh: if the man were alive and would
deny it, 'zounds, I would make him eat a piece of my
sword.   151

Lan. This is the strangest tale that ever I heard.

Prince. This is the strangest fellow, brother John.
Come, bring your luggage nobly on your back:
For my part, if a lie may do thee grace,
I 'll gild it with the happiest terms I have.

                                    [*A retreat is sounded*

The trumpet sounds retreat; the day is ours.
Come, brother, let us to the highest of the field,
To see what friends are living, who are dead.

                    [*Exeunt Prince of Wales and Lancaster*

Fal. I 'll follow, as they say, for reward. He that re-
wards me, God reward him! If I do grow great, I 'll grow
less; for I 'll purge, and leave sack, and live cleanly as a
nobleman should do.   [*Exit* 163

Scene V.   *Another part of the field*

The trumpets sound.   Enter the King, Prince of Wales,
Lord John of Lancaster, Earl of Westmoreland,
with Worcester *and* Vernon *prisoners*

King. Thus ever did rebellion find rebuke.
Ill-spirited Worcester! did not we send grace,
Pardon and terms of love to all of you?
And wouldst thou turn our offers contrary?
Misuse the tenour of thy kinsman's trust?
Three knights upon our party slain to-day,
A noble earl and many a creature else
Had been alive this hour,
If like a Christian thou hadst truly borne
Betwixt our armies true intelligence.   10

Wor. What I have done my safety urged me to;

And I embrace this fortune patiently,
Since not to be avoided it falls on me.

    King. Bear Worcester to the death and Vernon too:
Other offenders we will pause upon.

                      [Exeunt Worcester and Vernon guarded
How goes the field?

    Prince. The noble Scot, Lord Douglas, when he saw
The fortune of the day quite turn'd from him,
The noble Percy slain, and all his men
Upon the foot of fear, fled with the rest;   20
And falling from a hill, he was so bruised
That the pursuers took him. At my tent
The Douglas is; and I beseech your grace
I may dispose of him.

    King.   With all my heart.

    Prince. Then, brother John of Lancaster, to you
This honourable bounty shall belong:
Go to the Douglas, and deliver him
Up to his pleasure, ransomless and free:
His valour shown upon our crests to-day
Hath taught us how to cherish such high deeds   30
Even in the bosom of our adversaries.

    Lan. I thank your grace for this high courtesy,
Which I shall give away immediately.

    King. Then this remains, that we divide our power.
You, son John, and my cousin Westmoreland
Towards York shall bend you with your dearest speed,
To meet Northumberland and the prelate Scroop,
Who, as we hear, are busily in arms:
Myself and you, son Harry, will towards Wales,
To fight with Glendower and the Earl of March.   40
Rebellion in this land shall lose his sway,
Meeting the check of such another day:
And since this business so fair is done,
Let us not leave till all our own be won.   *[Exeunt*

NOTES

Dramatis Personæ. The following brief sketches of the historical characters of the play are intended to indicate how far Shakespeare abides by, and how far he departs from, historic truth as viewed in the light of modern historical criticism. The chief authorities consulted are J. H. Wylie's *History of England under Henry IV* and the *Dictionary of National Biography.*

King Henry IV (1367–1413). Reference has already been made in the Introduction (p. xiv) to the changes made by Shakespeare in King Henry's age at the time of the Percy rising, while the king's earlier career may be traced in *Richard II.* After his accession to the throne in the October of 1399, and the death of Richard in January, 1400, Henry was chiefly occupied in restoring order to the kingdom. The Welsh expedition against Owen Glendower, undertaken in the autumn of 1400, ended disastrously, and subsequent expeditions were scarcely more satisfactory. The contrast between his own failure to subdue Glendower and the success of the Percies against the Scots at Humbledon (Holmedon) Hill in September, 1402, was very striking. In the three years which elapsed between the death of Richard II and the opening scene of our play the king had grown very unpopular. He had little money at his disposal, and the attempts of his officers to obtain supplies without paying for them had aroused the ill-will of the people. Riots broke out in 1402, and rumours were circulated that Richard was still alive. On February 7, 1403, the king married a second wife, Joan, the daughter of Charles the Bad of Navarre, and widow of John, fourth Duke of Brittany. Shakespeare, perhaps in order to accentuate Henry's position of loneliness, does not introduce Joan into his play, but it is probably to her that the prince refers when he says in ii. 4: " Give him as much as will make him a royal man, and send him back again to my mother ". The outbreak of the Percy rebellion followed within a month of his marriage. Shakespeare keeps fairly closely to historic truth in stating the causes of that rebellion, though he makes little of Holinshed's references to " taxes and tallages ", the imposition of which by the king had

133

incensed both the Percies and the people. Shakespeare, as stated elsewhere, has somewhat depreciated the king's personal prowess in the battle of Shrewsbury, but his account of Henry's preparations for the battle and of the attempts made by him to settle the dispute without bloodshed is substantially correct.

Henry, Prince of Wales. Born in 1387, Henry was only sixteen at the time of the battle of Shrewsbury. He had remained in England during the time of his father's banishment, King Richard taking him under his charge. On his father's coronation he was knighted and created Prince of Wales and Earl of Chester. He was with his father in his unsuccessful attempt to overthrow Glendower in the autumn of 1400, and remained behind at Chester. In April, 1401, we find him advancing into Wales in the company of Hotspur, and securing the submission of Merioneth and Carnarvon. A little later, Henry Percy, Earl of Worcester, was appointed his tutor —a fact of which Shakespeare makes no mention. At the time when Shakespeare represents him as frequenting the Eastcheap tavern, he seems to have been campaigning in Wales, having been appointed as commander of the king's forces against the Welsh insurgents on March 7, 1403. Shrewsbury was his headquarters, and here his father joined him on the eve of the battle. He fought bravely on that occasion, but there is no evidence that Hotspur fell by his hand.

With regard to the excesses of the prince's youth, upon which the later chroniclers insist, and which became indeed an accepted tradition, little definite information is obtainable. That these excesses and his subsequent conversion were exaggerated is certain, but there is sufficient evidence to show that the tradition was not entirely unsupported by fact. Elmham, the contemporary biographer and panegyrist of Henry V, confesses in his *Vita et Gesta Henrici Quinti* that "when not engaged with Mars he found time for the service of Venus"; and frequent references are made by other contemporaries to the change that came over him at his accession. Mr. J. H. Wylie, in his *History of England under Henry IV* (vol. iv, p. 91), summarizes the matter in the following words:—"For though he had his serious and superstitious moods, in which he would hear nothing that sounded to vice, yet there is evidence enough that the traditional stories of the wildness of his youth are not without some basis of fact, and that there were times when he was a truant to chivalry, losing his princely privilege in barren pleasures and rude society".

John of Lancaster (1389–1435) was the third son of Henry IV. Knighted at his father's coronation in 1399, he was made Constable of England in 1403. We have no knowledge that he was present at the battle of Shrewsbury, nor does

Holinshed mention him in this connection. On the outbreak of hostilities in 1405 he joined the Earl of Westmoreland in the campaign which ended in the capture of Archbishop Scroop on Shipton Moor. (See *2 Henry IV*.) Soon after the accession of Henry V he was created Duke of Bedford, and on the king's departure for the campaign in France was appointed lieutenant of the kingdom. On the death of Henry V he was left in charge of the realm, and bore an active and resolute part in the civil and military transactions which occupied the period of Henry VI's minority. (See *1 Henry VI*.) It was a troublous and in many ways a disastrous period in English history, but Bedford's policy was singularly sound, and his character courageous and unselfish. He died at Rouen in 1435.

Ralph Neville, first Earl of Westmoreland (1364-1425), was one of the most important of the north-country barons of the time of Henry IV. Richard II created him Earl of Westmoreland in 1397, but he joined the banner of Bolingbroke on his landing at Ravenspurgh in 1399, and on the accession of the new king he was appointed Marshal of England. Shakespeare's account of the part he played in the Percy rebellion is fairly accurate, as is also the later account (*2 Henry IV*) of his capture of Mowbray and Scroop on Shipton Moor in 1405. On the accession of Henry V he joined that king in his French campaigns, and every reader of the play of *Henry V* will remember that it was in reply to Westmoreland's wish before the battle of Agincourt—

> O that we now had here
> But one ten thousand of those men in England
> That do no work to-day!

—that the king delivered his famous Crispian speech.

Sir Walter Blunt, or Blount, who appears in our play as the loyal supporter of Henry IV, had in early manhood accompanied the Black Prince and John of Gaunt on the Spanish expedition of 1367. He married a Spanish lady after the campaign was over, and was somewhat closely bound up with the English relations with Spain in the succeeding years. In 1398 John of Gaunt granted to Sir Walter and his wife an annuity of 100 marks as a reward for their labours in his service. Sir Walter represented Derbyshire, where he had an estate, in the first parliament of Henry IV, and held the post of standard-bearer at the battle of Shrewsbury. Shakespeare's account of his death at the hands of Douglas, who mistook him for the king because of the resemblance of his armour to that worn by Henry, is in accordance with the accounts given by contemporary chroniclers.

Thomas Percy, Earl of Worcester (circ. 1344-1403), was the younger brother of the Earl of Northumberland. He took part in the French campaigns of Edward III and in John of Gaunt's Spanish expedition of 1386. Before this he had been made a knight of the garter, and after his return to England in 1389 was appointed vice-chamberlain to the king. He accompanied King Richard to Ireland on his two Irish expeditions, and on the landing of Bolingbroke at Ravenspurgh he returned with the king to Wales. Some of the chroniclers state that he deserted Richard on his landing at Milford, but the matter is not certain. Whatever was his attitude towards Bolingbroke, he was present at his coronation, and took office as admiral of the fleet under him. In 1402 he was appointed tutor to the Prince of Wales, a fact mentioned by Holinshed, but ignored by Shakespeare. Shakespeare is probably right in making him a prime mover in the Percy rebellion, and also in the story of his misrepresentation to Hotspur of the king's offer of pardon. Shakespeare follows Holinshed in representing Worcester as factious and intriguing; but Froissart, who met him in 1595, speaks of him as "gentle, reasonable, and gracious".

Henry Percy, first Earl of Northumberland (1342-1408), who appears in *1 Henry IV* as a hesitating and rather cowardly leader, holds an important position in the history of the reigns of Richard II and Henry IV. He succeeded to the Percy estates on his father's death in 1368, and in the following years served in the French campaigns. He espoused the side of the people in the Good Parliament of 1376, but was won over to the Court party by the promise of the office of Marshal of England, which he received in 1377. Thanks to the favour of John of Gaunt he was created Earl of Northumberland by Richard II in 1377, and during the next year was chiefly occupied in contests and negotiations with the Scots. In 1398 he quarrelled with Richard, and because of his refusal to obey the king's summons to attend him in Ireland, sentence of banishment was passed on him and his son, Henry Hotspur. Northumberland at once joined the standard of Bolingbroke, and was chiefly instrumental in securing him the crown. Shakespeare's account of Northumberland's subsequent defection from the side of Henry is correct in its main points. The story of his life after the battle of Shrewsbury is told by Shakespeare in *2 Henry IV*. Historians are agreed in characterizing Northumberland as selfish and crafty.

Henry Percy, surnamed Hotspur (1364-1403), was the eldest son of the Earl of Northumberland. Shakespeare represents him as being of the same age as Prince Henry, but in reality he was his senior by twenty-three years. He was knighted by Edward III in the last year of his reign, and early won a high military reputation. As governor of Berwick he found himself, in 1388, in open hostility with the Scotch under

Earl Douglas, and in the following year took part in the famous battle of Otterburn, which Froissart describes as "the best fought and severest of all the battles I have related in my history", and of which the fame still lives in the well-known ballad. In the dethronement of Richard, Henry Percy acted in company with his father, and did much to quell the risings in Cheshire and North Wales which occupied Henry IV during the first year of his reign. For these services Percy received little or no reward, and a disaffection towards the new king arose which assumed a more acute form after the battle of Humbledon Hill. Shakespeare's account of the origin of the Percy rebellion is substantially correct, as is also his account of the events which led up to the battle of Shrewsbury and the death of Hotspur. He fell, however, by an unknown hand and not by that of the Prince of Wales. Mr. Tait's characterization of Hotspur (see *Dictionary of National Biography*, vol. xliv) is singularly in keeping with Shakespeare's heroic portraiture: "Hotspur is the last and not the least in the long roll of chivalrous figures whose prowess fills the pages of Froissart. He had the virtues and the defects of his class and time. A doughty fighter rather than a skilful soldier, he was instinct with stormy energy, passionate, and 'intolerant of the shadow of a slight'."

Edmund de Mortimer (1376-1409?) was the youngest son of Edmund de Mortimer, third earl of March, and tradition relates that portents attended his birth. He joined Bolingbroke on his return to England in 1399, and on the outbreak of the Glendower rebellion in 1402 Mortimer raised the men of Herefordshire and marched against him. A battle ensued in which Glendower was victorious, and Mortimer became his prisoner. He was carried off to the mountains by his captor, and the Percies immediately took steps to procure his ransom. King Henry, however, believing a current rumour that Mortimer had sought captivity, forbade the Percies to take steps in the matter. A little later, Mortimer gave colour to this rumour by making peace with Glendower and marrying his daughter. Thenceforward he was Glendower's ally, and in December, 1402, he issued a circular to the people of Herefordshire declaring that he had joined Glendower in his desire either to restore the crown to Richard, or, in case of Richard's death, to bestow it upon his own nephew, Edmund Mortimer, son of Roger Mortimer, fourth earl of March, whom he declared to be the true heir to Richard. Shakespeare, as pointed out in the Notes, has followed Holinshed in confusing the two Edmund Mortimers and in making of them one and the same person. Mortimer was in sympathy with the Percies in their rebellion, but was not present at the battle of Shrewsbury.

Archibald Douglas, fourth earl of Douglas (1369?-1424),

5*

was the head of the Douglas family during the reign of Henry
IV, having succeeded to the earldom in 1400. He was the
nephew of James, second earl of Douglas, who fell so glori-
ously in the great battle of Otterburn. His defeat at the
hands of Hotspur on Humbledon Hill, on September 24, 1402,
forms, together with the preceding defeat of Mortimer by
Glendower, the starting-point of the play. On the outbreak of
the Percy rebellion, Douglas was won over to the side of the
rebels on the promise that Berwick and a part of Northumberland should be given to him. His valour at the battle of
Shrewsbury is attested by contemporary historians. Shakespeare, in order to emphasize the generosity of his hero, the
Prince of Wales, represents him as receiving his freedom at
the Prince's petition after the battle: in reality he remained the
king's prisoner till 1408.

Sir Richard Vernon. Little is known of this knight except
that he fought on the Percy side at Shrewsbury, and was captured and beheaded by Henry IV. He was probably of the
same family as the Sir Richard Vernon who was Speaker of
the House of Commons under Henry VI.

Richard Scroop, or Richard le Scrope (1350?–1405), holds
a very insignificant place in *1 Henry IV*, but appears much
more prominently in *2 Henry IV*, where he is one of the leaders
of the rebels. Falling into the king's hands at Shipton Moor,
he was beheaded at York. He was made archbishop of York
by Richard II in 1398, acquiesced in the revolution of 1399,
but joined the Percies when the rebellion was raised.

Owen Glendower (1359?–1416?) was the head of an old
Welsh family whose seat was at Glyndyvrdwy in Merioneth-
shire. In his youth he had studied English law at Westminster, and had served as squire to the Earl of Arundel, and
as such had sided with the Lancastrian party. It was his old
family quarrel with Lord Grey of Ruthin which led him to take
up arms against Henry IV. Between 1400 and 1402 he won
several victories over the English, the king himself fitting out
no less than three expeditions to overthrow him, all of which
were unsuccessful. His capture of Mortimer on June 22,
1402, materially strengthened his prestige, and at one time he
was master of a large portion of Wales. He at once sided
with the Percies on the outbreak of the rebellion, but did not
reach Shrewsbury in time for the battle, though he committed
great ravages in Shropshire and Herefordshire after the king's
forces had withdrawn from that town. He remained a rebel
during the rest of the king's reign, though his power waned
after 1406. He was included in the general pardon granted by
Henry V on his accession in 1413; nothing is heard of him
after February, 1416, and popular report in the next century
represented him as dying of starvation among the mountains.

Act I—Scene 1

The opening scene of the play stands in the closest relation with the last act of *Richard II*, and thus serves to bind the two plays together as closely as the *First Part of Henry IV* is bound to the *Second Part*, or the *Second Part* to *Henry V*. In reality three years had elapsed (1399–1402) since the deposition of Richard and the battle of Holmedon, but the impression which we receive from the king's opening speech is of an almost immediate continuation of the historic narrative. Bolingbroke ends the play of *Richard II* by announcing his intention of a crusade to the Holy Land, and he opens the new play with a declaration of the same purpose. It must be borne in mind, however, that there is an interval of several years between the composition of the two plays. There gathers round this opening speech, the florid diction of which savours of insincerity, an element of deep irony. Civil war, the king assures us, has passed away for ever, but before the scene is at an end the seeds of discord which will shortly produce another civil war are sown. The projected crusade was a pious—and also a politic—wish to which King Henry tenaciously clung during the rest of his life, but which never grew nearer realization. When at the end of the speech he bids Westmoreland relate what took place in Council, we pass forthwith from visionary longings to the grim actuality of the butchery in Wales.

In making the king himself the first speaker in the play, Shakespeare follows the practice established by him in his earlier Histories. In *King John*, *Richard III*, and *Richard II* the opening speech is in each case delivered by the character whose name gives the title to the play; in *Henry V* he departs from this practice, and does not introduce the king until the second scene. In the great series of tragedies which followed the history-plays, the protagonists rarely appear until some of the minor characters have spoken and paved the way for them. This opening scene is throughout introductory in its scope. All the chief historic characters not actually present are mentioned by name, and from what is said concerning them we are able to form a primitive conception of their character; thus we hear mention made of "the noble Mortimer", "the irregular and wild Glendower", "gallant Hotspur", "brave Archibald", and "malevolent Worcester". Finally, we see how two characters—Hotspur and Prince Henry—are singled out from among the rest, made equal in years, and placed over against each other in bold antagonism. The one is "Fortune's minion and her pride"; the other, to all appearances, a ne'er-do-weel who costs his father bitter hours of repining. The difference between real and seeming worth is a favourite text of Shakespeare's.

Stage Direction. **The palace.** The royal palace at Westminster.

2, 3. Find we a time . . . new broils. 'Let us give a breathing space to harassed Peace, and then, while recovering her breath, she will tell of new encounters.' The figure is probably that of a doe pursued by the hounds.

4. stronds, strands, shores. Chaucer spells the word in the same way. The remote strand is, of course, the shore of the Holy Land.

5. entrance. "Entrants" and "Erinnys" have been suggested as emendations for *entrance*, but the Quarto reading is probably right, the abstract term being used for the concrete. The figure is a bold one, but is in keeping with the high-flown rhetorical character of the whole of the king's speech. The following verses from the old play of *King John* (1591) introduce a similar figure:—

> "Is all the blood y-spilt on either part,
>   Closing the crannies of the thirsty earth,
>   Grown to a love-game and a bridal-feast?"

Still nearer to the figure of Shakespeare is that found in *Genesis*, iv. 11: "And now art thou cursed from the earth, which hath opened her mouth to receive thy brother's blood".

7. trenching, cutting up the ground into trenches.

9. those opposed eyes, the eyes of the opposing forces.

11. All of one nature . . . bred. The reference is to the fact that in the war which led to the dethronement of Richard, and the accession of Henry IV, the combatants were all Englishmen.

13. close, encounter.

14. mutual, united.

18. his. The form *its*, which never occurs in the Authorized Version of the Bible, is rarely used by Shakespeare.

   master, owner.

21. impressed, enlisted. See Glossary.

22. levy. This use of *levy* in the sense of *conduct*, or rather with the double meaning of *raise and conduct*, occurs also in Gosson's *School of Abuse* (1587): "Scipio before he levied his force to the walles of Carthage, gave his soldiers the fruit of the city in a cake to be devoured".

30. Therefore . . . now. 'This is not the reason for our meeting.'

31. cousin. Deighton states that it was Henry IV who first introduced the monarchical custom of using the term 'cousin' in addressing the nobility.

33. **expedience.** The word is used by Shakespeare, as we now use the word *expedition*, in the twofold sense of *enterprise* and *haste*. The first verse of Westmoreland's speech suggests that the meaning here is *haste*, or perhaps *hasty enterprise*.

34. **hot in question,** hotly debated.

35. **limits,** estimates.

charge, expense. Prof. Herford explains *limits of the charge* as "express and definite instructions".

36. **all athwart,** all to cross purposes.

38. **the noble Mortimer . . . &c.** Shakespeare's information is drawn from Holinshed, who writes: "Owen Glendouer, according to his accustomed manner, robbing and spoiling within the English borders, caused all the forces of the shire of Hereford to assemble togither against them, under the conduct of Edmund Mortimer, earle of March. But coming to trie the matter by battell, whether by treason or otherwise, so it fortuned, that the English power was discomfited, the earle taken prisoner, and above a thousand of his people slaine in the place. The shamefull villanie used by the Welsh women towards the dead carcasses was such as honest eares would be ashamed to heare, and continent toongs to speake thereof."

39. **Herefordshire,** three syllables.

43. **corpse,** corpses.

44. **transformation,** mutilation.

49. **did.** This is the reading of the first two Quartos. The later Quartos and the Folios read *like*.

52. **Holyrood day,** or Holy-cross day, was instituted as a church festival in memory of the recovery of a portion of the cross of Christ by the Emperor Heraclius. The cross had been carried away to Persia when the Persian king, Cosroes, plundered Jerusalem, *circ*. 615. The date of the festival is September 14.

53. **Archibald,** Earl of Douglas.

54. **approved,** well-tried.

55. **Holmedon.** The modern Humbleton in Northumberland.

56. **sad,** serious.

58. **shape of likelihood,** according to our conjectures of what was probable.

61. **any way,** either way.

62. **a dear, a true industrious friend.** Sir Walter Blunt's character is here summed up in a single verse. He plays the part of "true industrious friend" to the king throughout the drama.

63. new lighted, newly alighted.

64. the variation of each soil, the various kinds of soil.

66. smooth and welcome news. The adjectives are in direct antithesis to the *uneven and unwelcome news* mentioned before.

69. Balk'd, piled up in *balks* or ridges. Grey would read *bak'd* for *balk'd*, and such a reading is supported by the following quotation from *Hamlet*:

"... horrible, trick'd
With blood of fathers, mothers, daughters, sons,
Bak'd and impasted".

71. Mordake. Murdach Stewart, son of the Duke of Albany, Regent of Scotland. Shakespeare, following Holinshed, makes him the son of Douglas. Holinshed's account of the battle and the capture is as follows:—"For at a place called Homildon, they [the Scots] were so fiercely assailed by the Englishmen, under the leading of the lord Persie, surnamed Henrie Hotspur, and George earle of March, that with violence of the English shot they were quite vanquished and put to flight, on the Rood day in harvest, with a great slaughter made by the Englishmen. There were slaine of men of estimation sir John Swinton, sir Adam Gordon, sir John Leviston, sir Alexander Ramsie of Dalhousie, and three and twentie knights, besides ten thousand of the commons; and of prisoners among other were these— Mordacke earle of Fife, son to the governour Archembald earle Dowglas, which in the fight lost one of his eies, Thomas erle of Murrey, Robert earle of Angus, and (as some writers have) the earles of Atholl and Menteith, with five hundred other of meaner degrees."

76, 77. In faith It is. This is the reading of the Cambridge editors. The first and second Quarto editions read as follows:

"A gallant prize? ha, cousin, is it not? In faith it is."
Westmoreland. A conquest for a prince to boast of."

83. minion, darling (Fr. *mignon*).

84–86. Whilst I ... my young Harry. With this reference to Prince Henry may be compared the following verses uttered by Henry IV as Bolingbroke in the play of *Richard II*, v. 3. 1:

"Can no man tell me of my unthrifty son?
'T is full three months since I did see him last:
If any plague hang over us, 't is he."

87. some night-tripping fairy ... Shakespeare, as noticed elsewhere, makes the Prince of Wales and Hotspur equal in years, whereas in reality Hotspur was three years older than the king.

95. **I shall have none . . . Fife.** "Percy had an exclusive right to these prisoners, except the Earl of Fife. By the law of arms, every man who had taken any captive, whose redemption did not exceed ten thousand crowns, had him clearly for himself, either to acquit or ransom, at his pleasure" (Tollet). The Earl of Fife, being a prince of the blood royal, fell to the share of the king.

97. **aspects**, respects. The word has here as elsewhere an astrological meaning. Cf. *Troilus and Cressida*, i. 3. 92: "Corrects the ill aspects of planets evil".

98. **prune**, preen; as a bird preens its feathers. Cf. *Cymbeline*, v. 4:

> "His royal bird
> Prunes the immortal wing, and cloys his beak".

101, 102. **we must neglect . . . Jerusalem.** The projected crusade is thus postponed *sine die*. Considered in the light of the scene as a whole, it seems as though the project, as set forth in the king's opening speech, was a mere pretence on his part. When he asks Westmoreland what has been done to forward "this dear experience", he knows of the battle of Holmedon and of Percy's refusal to deliver up his prisoners. He has sent for Percy, and foresees that trouble is in store, and knows that the crusade will have to be postponed until the matter is settled.

107. **Than out of anger . . . uttered.** The scene begins with thoughts of peace, but ends in anger.

Scene 2

The passage from Act i, Scene 1 to Act i, Scene 2 is a passage from poetry to prose, and the change of diction is significant of the change in the character of the surroundings. The constrained and formal bearing of the king's court, from which Prince Henry's exuberant nature instinctively revolts, is exchanged for the free society of the prince's apartments, where, as afterwards at the Boar's Head Tavern in Eastcheap, Falstaff reigns as unconquerable king of wit. The whimsical moods of Falstaff as he turns from praying to purse-taking, the rallies of wit and the word-play which pass between him and the prince, offer a striking contrast to the preceding scene. The plot of the highway robbery, and the second plot of Poins to rob the robbers, together with the foreshadowing of the tavern scene and Falstaff's "incomprehensible lies", promise us full relief from the serious interests of the play. The final soliloquy of the prince, with the return to verse-diction, enables us to judge how far the king's estimate of his son's real character is just. We learn that beneath the light-heartedness of "madcap

Hal" there is a self-command and a hidden strength of which the prince himself is alone aware.

Stage Direction. The stage direction: "London. An apartment of the prince's" was first filled in by Theobald.

2. **fat-witted.** Cf. fat-brained (*Henry V*, iii. 7. 143).

4-6. **that thou hast forgotten . . . day.** Prince Henry takes objection to Falstaff's use of the word "day". The prince contends that Falstaff's concern is with the night and not with the day, and Falstaff himself acknowledges this when he says immediately afterwards: " For we that take purses go by the moon and the seven stars, and not by Phœbus". We may accordingly render the prince's words as follows: ' Your concern is with the night, but in the dulness of your wit you have forgotten this, and ask what is the time of the day '.

8. **why thou shouldst be so superfluous,** why you should give yourself the unnecessary trouble.

10. **you come near me,** your words strike home.

11. **the seven stars,** the Pleiades.

12. **'that wandering knight so fair'.** Steevens conjectures that this is a quotation from "some forgotten ballad ", based on the Spanish romance *El Donzel del Febo* (the Knight of the Sun), which was translated into English in Shakespeare's time under the title of *The Mirror of Princely Deeds and Knighthood.*

14. **grace.** The word is punningly used in a threefold sense: (1) a term of respect used in addressing monarchs and the highest nobles, (2) piety, (3) thanksgiving, grace before meat.

19. **roundly,** plainly, without ceremony.

21, 22. **body . . . beauty.** Prof. Herford interprets, "Let not us who play the squire to Sir Night (Knight) be slandered as mere thieves to Lady Day, *i.e.* as blots upon daylight". Theobald would read *booty* for *beauty.*

26. **countenance,** favour.

32. **' Lay by ',** lay aside your arms, stand and deliver.

33. **' Bring in '.** A summons to the innkeeper to bring in more sack, &c.

33, 34. **the ladder.** The reference is to the ladder by which the criminal mounted the gallows. The ridge is the cross-beam of the same.

38. **As the honey of Hybla.** There are three towns of this name in Sicily. Cf. *Julius Cæsar*, v. i. 13:

> " But for your words, they rob the Hybla bees,
> And leave them honeyless ".

38, 39. **my old lad of the castle.** See Introduction.

39. a buff jerkin, a leather jacket. The word *buff*, which has given its name to a colour, means properly leather prepared from the hide of the ox or buffalo. The buff jerkin was chiefly worn by the sheriff's officers.

39, 40. robe of durance. The quip lies in the double meaning of the word, (1) a dress which will last a long time, (2) a prison dress. The same thought occurs in the description of the catchpole in *A Comedy of Errors*, iv. 2. 32:

"A devil in an everlasting garment has him,
A wolf; nay worse, a fellow all in buff".

42. quiddities, frivolous distinctions. The word *quiddity*, from the late Latin *quiditas*, was much in use among the mediæval schoolmen. Its scholastic use is ridiculed by Butler in his *Hudibras*, Part I, Canto I:

"Where entity and quiddity
The ghosts of defunct bodies fly ".

53. heir. The h was pronounced in Shakespeare's time.

55, 56. and resolution . . . the law? 'And shall a brave purpose be thwarted as is now the case by the restraints of old-fashioned and decrepit laws?'

59, 60. I'll be a brave judge. Steevens has pointed out the resemblance of this thought to the following conversation in *The Famous Victories of Henry V*:—

Henry V. Ned, so soon as I am king, the first thing I will do shall be to put my *lord chief justice* out of office; and thou shalt be my *lord chief justice* of England.

Ned. Shall I be *lord chief justice?* By gogs wounds. I'll be the bravest lord chief justice that ever was in England.

64. jumps with, suits, fits in with.

66. suits. The play on words is still kept up, the double meaning being, (1) favours obtained by court solicitations, (2) suits of clothes.

68. 'Sblood, by God's (*i.e.* Christ's) blood.

69. a gib cat, a tom-cat; gib is a contraction of Gilbert, and the phrase 'gib cat' is used as we still use robin redbreast or tom-tit. The phrase "melancholy as a cat" occurs in Lyly's *Midas*.

a lugged bear, a performing bear dragged about from place to place.

71. drone, the drone is the largest tube of the bagpipe, which emits a hoarse sound like that of a drone bee.

a Lincolnshire bagpipe. The bagpipe, which we now regard as a peculiarly Scottish instrument, was formerly in favour in England also. There is a reference to the "sweete baliade of the Lincolnshire Bagpipes" in *The Pleasant and Stately Morall of three Lordes and three Ladies of London*, 1590.

72. a hare. Cf. Drayton's *Polyolbion*:

"The melancholy hare is form'd in brakes and briers".

It was probably from the fact that the hare crouches alone in its form that it was called melancholy.

73. Moor-ditch, a foul and stagnant ditch in Moor-fields on the outskirts of the city of London. Dekker compares the "scouring of Moor-ditch" to the cleansing of the Augean stables.

75. most comparative, most apt to find comparisons.

77. commodity, store.

83, 84. for wisdom . . . regards it. The prince's words are based on those of the *Book of Proverbs*, i. 20-24. "Wisdom crieth without; she uttereth her voice in the streets. She crieth . . . saying, 'I have stretched out my hand, and no man regarded'." A statute was passed in the reign of James I forbidding the use of scriptural language on the stage, and accordingly in the Folio editions the words "wisdom cries out in the streets" were omitted, and the text read: "Thou didst well, for no man regards it", which is quite meaningless.

85. damnable iteration, a damnable habit of repeating Scripture.

94. 'Zounds, by God's wounds.

95. baffle, disgrace, unknight. The term is a technical one drawn from the ritual of chivalry. The baffled knight was suspended by the heels.

100. set a match, made an appointment.

103. true, honest.

107. agrees . . . thee. Pope, with too keen an eye for modern usage, changed *agrees* to *agree* and *thee* to *thou*. But the use of *thee* for *thou* and of the singular form of the verb for the plural is not unusual in Shakespeare.

112. his due, *i.e.* his soul.

115. cozening, cheating. See Glossary.

117. Gadshill. Besides being the name of a character in the play, it is also the name of a hill near Rochester, on the road to Canterbury. It was a notorious spot for highway robberies.

118. rich offerings. These were probably for the shrine of Thomas à Becket. The traders would probably be returning to London from the Continent.

121, 122. in Eastcheap, *i.e.* at the tavern of Dame Quickly.

125. Yedward, for Edward, Poins' Christian name.

126. I'll hang you. I'll have you hanged.

131, 132. if thou . . . stand for ten shillings. 'If you will not take your place with the rest of us and rob these travellers, . . .' There is also a secondary meaning implied: 'If you are not good for a paltry ten shillings robbery'.

146. want countenance, need patronage.

148, 149. thou latter spring . . . summer. Falstaff is thus addressed because of the youthful sprightliness and sunshine of his nature, which he has preserved with advancing years. All Hallows or All Saints' Day is the first of November. It was Pope who suggested the reading *thou* for the *thee* of the Quartos and Folios.

150. my good . . . lord; cf. *Love's Labour's Lost*, v. 2: "My fair, sweet honey monarch".

152. Falstaff, Bardolph, Peto and Gadshill. This is Theobald's emendation for the reading of the Qq. and Ff.: "Falstaff, Harvey, Rossill, and Gadshill". There is no mention of Harvey and Rossill elsewhere in the play, whereas in the account of the robbery in Act II the robbers are Falstaff, Bardolph, Peto, and Gadshill. Harvey and Rossill are probably the names of the actors who took the parts of Bardolph and Peto.

153. waylaid, set an ambush.

162. like, likely.

163. habits, dress.

appointment, piece of armour, equipment.

167. cases, suits.

buckram, coarse linen, stiffened with gum.

nonce. See Glossary.

169. doubt, fear.

173. incomprehensible. The word does not mean 'unintelligible', but 'boundless'.

175. wards, guards in fencing.

176. reproof, refutation.

183. unyoked, unrestrained.

185. contagious, injurious. The image is similar to that of Shakespeare's thirty-third Sonnet:
"Full many a glorious morning have I seen
Flatter the mountain-tops with sovereign eye.—
Anon permit the basest clouds to ride
With ugly rack on his celestial face".

188. **wanted**, needed.

194. **accidents**, occurrences, incidents.

198. **falsify men's hopes**, deceive men's expectations. This purpose of the prince is continually before his mind, and by making him insist on it, Shakespeare prepares us for the reformation which comes with his accession to the throne. In *2 Henry IV*, v. 2, when the prince is at last king, he once more utters in his address to the nobles the thought set forth in these verses:

> " I survive,
> To mock the expectation of the world,
> To frustrate prophecies, and to raze out
> Rotten opinion, which hath writ me down
> After my seeming ".

203. **I 'll so offend . . . skill.** ' I will offend in such a way as to make my offence seem a piece of good policy.' Note the use of the couplet rounding off the scene, and indicating its close to the spectators.

Scene 3

In this scene the action advances rapidly. The seeds of discord which we have discovered in Scene 1 have now germinated, and as the scene comes to an end we find that the conspiracy, the working out of which is the theme of the play, is fully planned. The arch-conspirator is not the hesitating Northumberland, nor yet the impetuous Hotspur, but Worcester, who, dismissed from the king's presence early in the scene, rejoins his brother and nephew after the audience is over, and inoculates them with the virus of rebellion. While Hotspur blusters, Worcester schemes and calculates, and finds no difficulty in winning Hotspur's approval for all his designs.

All the important characters of the play are now before us, and in this scene we are permitted to gain a very deep insight into the personality of the famous Hotspur. It is in keeping with the deeper character of Prince Henry that his individuality becomes only very gradually revealed, whereas his rival, Hotspur, comes swiftly into full view. Most of the outstanding traits in his character are set forth in this scene: we realize his impetuousness, his impatience of all opposition, his chivalrous worship of honour, and his romanticism. How vivid a presentation of the man is set before us in his own account of the conversation which took place between him and King Henry's carpet-knight! The splendid contempt of the bluff man of action for the effeminate fopperies of the courtier enables us to see the high qualities from which this contempt springs. The incident is Shakespeare's own invention. Holinshed's foundation for this highly dramatic scene is as follows:—

" Henrie earle of Northumberland, with his brother Thomas earle of Worcester, and his sonne the lord Henrie Persie, sur-named Hotspur, which were to king Henrie in the beginning of his reigne both faithfull freends, and earnest aiders, began now to envie his wealth and felicitie; and especiallie they were greeved, because the king demanded of the earle and his sonne such Scotish prisoners as were taken at Homeldon and Nesbit: for of all the captives which were taken in the conflicts foughten in those two places, there was delivered to the kings possession onlie Mordake earle of Fife, the duke of Albanies sonne, though the king did divers and sundrie times require deliverance of the residue, and that with great threatnings: wherewith the Persies being sore offended, for that they claimed them as their owne proper prisoners, and their pecu-liar preies, by the counsell of the lord Thomas Persie earle of Worcester, whose studie was ever (as some write) to procure malice, and set things in a broile, came to the king unto Windsore (upon a purpose to proove him) and there required of him, that either by ransome or otherwise, he would cause to be delivered out of prison Edmund Mortimer, earle of March, their cousine germane, whome (as they reported) Owen Glen-dower kept in filthie prison, shakled with irons, onlie for that he tooke his part, and was to him faithfull and true.

" The king began not a little to muse at this request, and not without cause: for indeed it touched him somewhat neere, sith this Edmund was sonne to Roger earle of March, sonne to the ladie Philip, daughter of Lionell duke of Clarence, the third sonne of King Edward the third; which Edmund at King Richards going into Ireland, was proclamed heire apparant to the crowne and realme . . . ; and therefore King Henrie could not well heare that anie man should be earnest about the advancement of that linage. The king when he had studied on the matter, made answer that the earle of March was not taken prisoner for his cause, nor in his service, but willinglie suffered himselfe to be taken, bicause he would not withstand the attempts of Owen Glendouer and his complices, and there-fore he would neither ransome him nor releeve him.

" The Persies with this answer and fraudulent excuse were not a little fumed, insomuch that Henrie Hotspur said openlie: ' Behold the heire of the relme is robbed of his right, and yet the robber with his owne will not redeeme him '. So in this furie the Persies departed, minding nothing more than to depose King Henrie from the high type of his roialtie, and to place in his seat their cousine Edmund, earle of March, whom they did not onlie deliver out of captivitie, but also (to the high displeasure of King Henrie) entered in league with the fore-said Owen Glendouer."

Stage Direction. London. The palace. In Holinshed's narrative this scene between the king and the Percies takes place at Windsor.

3. **And you have found me so.** I accept this emendation of Prof. Littledale's. The early editions read: "And you have found me; for accordingly . . . "; 'for' would be an easy misprint for '*soe*', written *foe*.

6. **my condition,** my natural self.

10-13. **Our house, my liege . . . so portly.** Worcester's speech is deliberately intended to rouse the king to anger. Worcester, as we learn later, has formed his conspiracy, and is in correspondence with Archbishop Scroop. What he desires is to stir up a quarrel between the king and Hotspur, and by so doing to win the whole-hearted support of Hotspur and his father for the plans which he has formed. Nothing could irritate Henry so much as a bold reminder of his indebtedness to the house of Percy. The king knows the scheming nature of Worcester and dismisses him from his presence.

13. **portly,** important, imposing.

15. **Worcester.** The word is here a trisyllable.

17. **peremptory,** audacious. The word must here be read as a dissyllable. See Metrical Notes.

18, 19. **And majesty . . . brow.** 'Kings have never been willing to endure sullen opposition from their subjects'; *frontier* is not *forehead*, for that would cause redundance with *brow*; it is a term borrowed from military science, and denotes an outwork or line of fortification. Cf. *1 Henry IV*, ii. 3: "Of palisadoes, frontiers, parapets". From this literal meaning is derived the abstract idea of opposition.

20. **good leave,** full permission.

21. **use,** assistance.

25, 26. **not with such strength . . . majesty,** were not so resolutely refused as report has told you.

27. **envy,** ill-will, malice.

     misprision, misapprehension.

36. **milliner.** In Shakespeare's day the milliners were men; cf. *Winter's Tale*, iv. 4. 192:

> "No milliner can
> So fit *his* customers with gloves".

The word means originally one who dealt in wares of Milan.

38. **pouncet-box,** a perfume-box, which was perforated at the top with small holes.

41. **Took it in snuff.** The *double entendre* is (1) snuffed it up, and (2) took offence at it.

46. With many . . . terms, using an extravagant and mincing style of speech. *Holiday terms* would mean words not in everyday use, but employed only on special occasions. Cf. *Winter's Tale*, iii, 2. 69: "He speaks holiday".

49. with my wounds being cold, because my wounds had begun to grow cold and to smart. Cf. Drayton's *Mortimeriados*, 1596: "As when the blood is cold, we feel the wound".

50. popinjay, parrot.

51. grief, pain of body. See Glossary.

56. God save the mark! This expression is literally a prayer that physical blemishes may be averted.

58. Was parmaceti . . . bruise. "Why this spermaceti? Why this dwelling upon so trivial and ludicrous a detail? Because it is a touch of reality and begets illusion. Precisely because we cannot at first see the reason why Percy should recall so trifling a circumstance, it seems impossible that the thing should be a mere invention. And from this insignificant word all the rest of the speech hangs as by a chain. If this be real, then all the rest is real, and Henry Percy stands before our eyes, covered with dust and blood, as on the field of Holmedon. We see the courtier at his side, holding his nose as the bodies are carried past, and we hear him giving the young commander his medical advice and irritating him to the verge of frenzy" (Brandes).

parmaceti, spermaceti. This form of the word is found elsewhere in Elizabethan English, *e.g.* Sir R. Hawkins' *Voyage into the South Sea*, 1593.

62. tall, valiant. Cf. Beaumont and Fletcher's *Humorous Lieutenant*, i. 4: "We fought like honest and tall men". See Glossary.

66. indirectly, vaguely.

68, 69. Come current . . . majesty. 'Be made an accusation against me, and weaken the good-will which exists between myself and your majesty.'

76. so, so that, provided that.

78. But with proviso and exception, unless suitable terms are agreed to.

80. His brother-in-law, Mortimer. It has been pointed out by Steevens that Shakespeare here confuses Edmund, Earl of March, nephew to Lady Percy, with Sir Edmund Mortimer, who was Lady Percy's brother, and brother-in-law to Hotspur.

83. that great magician, damn'd Glendower. The king, in spite of his astuteness, is not proof against superstition, and his superstitious fear of Glendower is in contrast to the

bold scepticism with which Hotspur meets Glendower's claims
to supernatural power in iii. 1. A little later (113–117) he
denies that Mortimer has fought Glendower, and the grounds
of his denial disclose his own dread of the Welsh chieftain:

> " He durst as well have met the devil alone
> As Owen Glendower for an enemy ".

87. indent with, sign indentures with, make a bargain with.

fears. Various emendations, such as *foes, peers, fools,*
have been suggested; but there is no need to change the
word. Just as *treason* is used for traitors, *fears* stands for
objects of fear. Cf. Part II, iv. 5:

> " All these bold fears
> Thou see'st with peril I have answered ".

91. one penny cost, the expenditure of a single penny.

95. But by the chance of war. Mortimer had been captured
by Glendower in pitched battle, and had then come to terms
with his conqueror and married his daughter. See quotation
from Holinshed.

97. mouthed, gaping.

100. confound, spend. This rather curious use of *confound*
is supported by a verse in *Coriolanus,* i. 6:

> " How could'st thou in a mile confound an hour?"

101. In changing hardiment, in doughty exchange of
blows.

102. Three times they breathed . . . Hotspur's language,
when he is deeply stirred, acquires an epic and deeply imaginative character which contrasts very strikingly with the
abrupt unrhythmical diction which he uses at other times. His
imagination becomes mythopœic, and he personifies the Severn,
just as a little later he personifies honour and danger.

106. crisp head, curled head, rippling surface. The word
head suggests that Shakespeare is personifying the river
Severn, as Drayton personified all the rivers of England in
his *Polyolbion.*

108. base. This is the reading of the Ff.; the Qq. read
bare.

policy, craft. The word is used here in a bad sense.

109. Colour, disguise.

113. belie him, give a false account of his conduct.

121. kind, manner.

127. ease my heart, let loose my feelings.

128. make a hazard of, risk.

137. ingrate, ungrateful.

canker'd, corrupted. The canker is the caterpillar. A second meaning of the word, which is found in line 176, is the dog-rose.

139. heat, quarrel.

143. an eye of death, an eye which threatens death.

145, 146. was not he proclaim'd . . . blood? This was not true of the Edmund Mortimer who was defeated by Owen Glendower, but of his nephew, also called Edmund Mortimer, the son of Roger Mortimer. Richard II had proclaimed Edmund Mortimer his heir, previous to his last voyage to Ireland in 1398: he was then a boy of seven. Shakespeare's confusion is due to Holinshed.

149. in us, received at our hands.

155. soft, gently, not so quickly.

163. murderous subornation, perjury which has brought about murder.

165. second means, auxiliaries.

166. the ladder; this is the gallows' ladder alluded to by Prince Henry in i. 2. 34.

168. the predicament; this is another instance of Shakespeare's use of the terminology of the Schoolmen. The *predicaments* or *categories*, which were ten in number, were the subdivisions under which all Being was ranged by Aristotle for purposes of predication. In Milton's *Vacation Exercise* he quaintly personifies the ten Predicaments — which include, amongst others, Substance, Quantity, and Quality—as sons of Ens or Being. Put briefly, Hotspur's words mean ' to show the position in which you stand, &c. '

173. gage, engage, pledge. Shakespeare seems to imply that Hotspur had little part in the dethronement of Richard. He does not feel that he is included in the shame, and is unaware of Richard's proclamation of Edmund Mortimer as his heir.

176. canker, dog-rose: cf. *Sonnet* 54:
" The canker blooms have full as deep a dye,
As the perfumed tincture of the roses ".

183. disdain'd, disdainful.

185. answer, repay.

189. your quick-conceiving discontents, your minds which discontent has made quick to grasp a plan of action.

194. If he . . . or swim. If such a man fall into the current it is all over with him unless he can swim. The saying was proverbial, and something very like it occurs in Chaucer's *Knight's Tale*: " Ne reccheth never, wher I synke or fleete ".

195-197. Send danger . . . grapple. Though a whole world of dangers assail a man, yet will there be nothing to fear if honour, proceeding from an opposite direction, can meet them in bold encounter. " Danger, rush from east to west, hurtles against Honour, crossing it from north to south—two northern Valkyries in full career " (Brandes).

201-208. By heaven, methinks, . . . fellowship! There is a characteristic element of over-strain in this famous speech of Hotspur's, which Beaumont and Fletcher have very happily parodied in the high-falutin' speech of Ralph, the grocer's apprentice, in *The Knight of the Burning Pestle* (*Induction*):

" By Heaven, methinks, it were an easy leap
To pluck bright honour from the pale-faced moon ;
Or dive into the bottom of the sea,
Where never fathom-line touched any ground,
And pluck up drowned honour from the lake of hell ".

206. So, provided that

208. half-fac'd, miserable, venturing to present only half a face to danger. Cf. *2 Henry IV*, iii. 1: " This same half-fac'd fellow Shadow—he presents no mark to the enemy ". The *half-fac'd fellowship* is probably the alliance with Henry IV.

209. figures. The word is used either in the sense of 'figures of speech', such as the personification of Honour, or more probably, in the sense of 'fancies', as in the following verses of *Julius Cæsar*, ii. 1. 231:

" Thou hast no figures, nor no fantasies,
Which busy care draws in the brains of men ".

210. form, the actual shape, the substance.

attend, attend to.

212. I cry you mercy. I pray you forgive my want of attention.

214. a Scot of them. A pun is no doubt intended. See Glossary under *scot*.

216. start away, quit the subject.

218. flat, certain.

228. All studies . . . defy. I herewith renounce all other occupations.

230. sword - and - buckler. The word which is here used adjectivally is similar in meaning to our modern ' swashbuckler'. For the use of the word cf. Beaumont and Fletcher's *Bonduca*, iv. 2:

> " The boy speaks sword and buckler".

233. I would have . . . ale. The man who utters these words is he who has just declared it easy " to pluck bright honour from the pale-fac'd moon ".

236. wasp-stung; this is the reading of the first Quarto, and is certainly preferable to the *waspe-tongue* of the other Qq. or the *waspe-tongu'd* of the Ff. Shakespeare was too exact an observer of nature to place the wasp's sting in its mouth.

240. pismires, ants.

241. politician. Like 'policy', this word has often an evil signification in Shakespeare.

242. what do you call the place? Hotspur's forgetfulness is in keeping with his impulsiveness and impatience. Compare iii. 1. 5, 6:

> "a plague upon it!
> I have forgot the map ".

It is by slight yet telling touches such as this that Shakespeare makes his characters so vividly real.

244. 'T was where . . . kept. The reference is to Edmund, Duke of York, uncle of Henry IV, who plays a part in *Richard II*. Kept, resided.

248. Ravenspurgh. This is the name of the seaport at which Henry IV, then Bolinbroke, landed on his return to England. (See *Richard II*, ii. 3.) It lay at the mouth of the Humber, close to Spurn Head, but the encroachments of the North Sea swept it away soon after Henry landed there.

251. what a candy deal of courtesy, what an amount of sugared language. The position of *candy* before *deal* instead of before *courtesy* is a bold use of the poetical license.

253. "when his infant fortune", &c. The words within inverted commas are very much like those which Shakespeare places in Bolingbroke's mouth in *Richard II*, ii. 3:

> " And as my fortune ripens with thy love,
> It shall be still thy true love's recompense ".

255. cozeners. A play on the words *cousin* and *cozeners* is probably intended.

261, 262. And make . . . in Scotland. ' And make Mordake, Earl of Fife, your sole agent for obtaining a force of men in Scotland.'

266. bosom, confidence.

272. in estimation, on mere conjecture.

278. still, always.

let'st slip, lettest loose the greyhounds.   Cf. *Julius Cæsar*, iii. 2. 273:
  " Cry 'havoc', and let slip the dogs of war ".

284. a head, an armed force.

285. For, bear . . . can.   " However straightforward a course we pursue . . . "   With the thought here expressed may be compared the following passage of *Richard II*, spoken by the king to Northumberland and referring to his [Northumberland's] future relations with Henry IV:
          " Thou shalt think,
Though he divide the realm, and give thee half,
It is too little, helping him to all;
And he shall think that thou, which know'st the way
To plant unrightful kings, wilt know again,
Being ne'er so little urged, another way
To pluck him headlong from the usurped throne '' (v. 1. 59).

288. pay us home, pay us back.

292. Cousin, used as a title of courtesy.   The real relation was that of uncle to nephew.

292, 293. no further go . . . your course.   From directions such as this we realize how completely Worcester is the guiding spirit of the conspiracy.   The ardent, unreflecting nature of Hotspur is not that which plots a conspiracy.   Worcester, however, finding him in a mood for action, panders to his desire for revenge, and easily enrolls him among the band of conspirators.

294. suddenly, very shortly.

300. Farewell . . . we shall thrive, I trust.   Northumberland, it will be noticed, plays a very minor part in hatching the conspiracy.   He is a weak character, and in his words here, as in those in verse 278, we recognize a timorousness which prepares us for his subsequent defection.

302. fields, battle-fields.

Act II—Scene 1

This scene, with its vivid presentation of the bustle of an Elizabethan inn-yard in the early hours of the morning, serves as a prelude to what follows.   It is the aim of Shakespeare, and of the Elizabethan dramatists generally, to impress upon the spectator the reality of the life they set forth, and nowhere is this aim better realized than in scenes such as the present. Brandes well says of this scene: "The night sky, with Charles s Wain 'over the new chimney', the flickering gleam of the lanterns in the dirty yard, the fresh air of the early dawn, the misty atmosphere, the mingled odour of damp peas and beans, of bacon and ginger, all comes straight home to our senses. The situation takes hold of us with all the irresistible force of reality."

2. **Charles' wain**, the Great Bear.

5. **beat Cut's saddle.** The meaning is, as the following words indicate, 'beat the horse's saddle until it is soft'. Cut is the name of a horse in the play, *The Lancashire Witches*. The point is the pommel of the saddle.

6, 7. **out of all cess**, beyond all measure. See Glossary.

9. **bots**, maggots found in the intestines of horses.

10. **Ostler.** The Ff. read *the Ostler*.

11. **joyed**, was cheerful.

14. **tench.** The comparison hardly seems apposite, but in Philemon Holland's translation of the ninth book of Pliny's *Natural History* we read: "In summer what is there not bred within the sea? Even the very fleas that skip so merrily in summer time . . . are there engendered and to be found . . . and this vermin is thought to trouble the poor fishes in their sleep by night within the sea."

16. **christen.** Ff. read *in Christendom*.

17. **cock**, cock-crowing.

19. **razes**, roots tied in a bundle. In *The Famous Victories of Henry V* there is a reference to the "great rase of ginger" of which Dericke the carrier is robbed at Gadshill.

25, 26. **hast no faith in thee?** can no reliance be placed in thee?

34. **Ay, when? canst tell?** This is a colloquial phrase of the time which Mr. Deighton modernizes as: 'Don't you wish you may get it?'

40, 41. **they will along . . . charge**, 'they will like to have company, for they carry merchandise of worth'.

43. **At hand, quoth pick-purse.** A proverbial expression. Cf. *Appius and Virginia* (1575):

"At hand, quoth pick-purse, here ready am I.
    See well to the cut-purse, be ruled by me".

49. **franklin**, a small freeholder. See the description of the Franklin in the *Prologue to the Canterbury Tales*.

49, 50. **the wild of Kent**, the open country, the Kentish weald.

56, 57. Saint Nicholas' clerks, thieves, highwaymen. This is not the St. Nicholas who was the patron-saint of scholars, nor the Santa Claus of Christmastide, but the "Old Nick" whom Sir John Harrington calls "Saunte Satan". See Nares' *Glossary*.

62, 63. old Sir John, sc. Falstaff.

63. starveling. Cf. Starveling the tailor in *Midsummer-Night's Dream*.

64. Trojans. A cant term for *thieves*.

68. foot-land rakers, vagabonds who travel over the country on foot and commit paltry thefts.

long-staff sixpenny strikers, men who, armed with the long-staff, rob travellers of paltry sixpences.

69. mad mustachio purple-hued malt-worms, purple-faced drunkards who wear fierce-looking moustaches.

70. nobility and tranquillity, high-born nobles who live in ease and luxury.

70, 71. great oneyers. Various emendations have been suggested for this, the best of them being *moneyers*. Malone contends that *oneyers* are public accountants, and that to *ony* meant to settle accounts, *ony* being a corruption of *o. ni*, which in its turn is an abbreviation of the Latin phrase, *oneratur, nisi habeat sufficientem exonerationem*.

71. hold in, hold together, keep their ground.

76. boots. Deighton sees a pun here, interpreting *make her their boots*, as (1) use the commonwealth as something to tread on, (2) turn it to their advantage.

78. in foul way, on a muddy road.

79. liquored, greased with tallow. Cf. *Merry Wives of Windsor*, iv. 5. 100: "They would melt me out of my fat drop by drop, and liquor fishermen's boots with me".

80, 81. fern-seed. Fern-seed, perhaps because scarcely visible itself, was popularly believed to render invisible those who possessed it. Cf. Jonson's *New Inn*, i. 6:

> "I had
> No med'cine, sir, to go invisible,
> No fern-seed in my pocket".

82. beholding, used quite generally by Shakespeare for the modern *beholden*.

85. purchase, capture, booty.

88. "homo" is a common . . . men. It has been suggested that this statement of Gadshill's is a quotation from some Latin Grammar. The relevance of the remark is not very clear, but Prof. Hereford comments as follows: "In other words, 'thief' is not an antithesis to 'man', as 'false' is to 'true'".

Scene 2

The plot of the comic scenes advances more rapidly than the historic plot. In the scene before us we see the Gadshill robbery committed, and the robbers robbed in their turn; everything falls out as Poins has foretold. Falstaff is again the central figure, and once more dazzles us with his vivacious humour. His cries to the waylaid traveller—"bacon-fed knaves! they hate us youth: . . . What, ye knaves! young men must live"—are amongst his best-inspired sallies. The question of Falstaff's cowardice, concerning which Maurice Morgann had so much to say in his *Essay on the Character of Sir John Falstaff*, calls for consideration at this point. Poins' words in i. 2—"and for the third, if he fight longer than he sees reason, I'll forswear arms"—are borne out in the present scene, where we learn that whereas Falstaff's comrades decamp on the first appearance of the prince and Poins, Falstaff himself does not flee until he has struck "a blow or two" and has recognized that the better part of valour is discretion. Compared with Gadshill, Bardolph, and Peto, Falstaff is an almost heroic figure; compared with the warlike son of Edward III, Prince Henry's own grandfather, he is less imposing: "Indeed, I am not John of Gaunt, your grandfather; but yet no coward, Hal".

2. gummed velvet. An allusion to the practice of mixing gum with velvet and taffeta to stiffen them.

12. by the squier, measured by the foot-rule.

14. for all this, in spite of all this.

17, 18. medicines, love-philtres.

20. starve. The word is used in its original sense, 'to die'.

36. to colt me thus, to befool me thus. The prince puns on the word, alluding to the fact that Falstaff is horseless.

42. Go, hang . . . garters! "He may hang himself in his own garters" was a proverbial expression of the time.

43, 44. ballads made on you. Cf. *Antony and Cleopatra*, v. 2:

> "Saucy lictors
> Will catch at us like strumpets, and scald rhymers
> Ballad us out of tune".

49. setter; cf. Falstaff's words in i. 2. 97: "Now shall we know if Gadshill have set a match".

50. **what news?** All the early editions of the play make the speech of Poins end with the words *Bardolph, what news?* But Johnson's suggestion to make Bardolph the speaker of the words 'what news' and to ascribe the following speech to Gadshill is a good one. Gadshill, whom Poins speaks of as the 'setter', is the one who would naturally furnish the information as to the travellers.

51. **Case ye,** put on your masks.

55. **make.** Gadshill uses this verb in the sense of 'make our fortunes for life'; Falstaff, who follows, treats it as a causative auxiliary.

70. **Now cannot I strike him.** I have not the heart to strike him (Poins). Falstaff is throughout jealous of Poins, who, he realizes, comes between him and the prince.

73. **happy man be his dole,** may happiness be ours. The phrase, which was a proverbial one, occurs again in *Winter's Tale*, i. 2. 163:

> *Mamillius.* No, my lord, I'll fight.
> *Leontes.* You will! Why, happy man be his dole.

81. **caterpillars,** devourers of substance. Cf. *Richard II*, ii. 3. 166, where Richard's favourites are called by Boling-broke, "the caterpillars of the commonwealth".

84. **gorbellied,** fat-paunched. The terms of abuse which Falstaff showers down upon the travellers have, without exception, a singular application to himself.

85. **chuffs,** clowns, boors; a word of uncertain origin not connected with *chough*.

88. **true men.** In Elizabethan English the *true man* is the opposite of the thief. Cf. *The Four Prentices of London*:

> "Sweet wench, embrace a true man, scorn a thief".

90. **argument,** subject-matter.

Scene 3

This scene, of which there is no suggestion in Holinshed, was inserted by Shakespeare probably in order to diversify his characterization by the introduction of Hotspur's wife. Female characters are for obvious reasons somewhat rare in Shakespeare's historical plays, yet we find that he seized every opportunity for introducing them which his material offered, and on certain occasions—the present is one of these—made openings himself for such introductions when history failed to furnish them. The insight into Hotspur's domestic life here revealed is full of charm: we feel that beneath the feigned nonchalance of his bearing towards his wife there is deep sympathy and love. Hotspur will not tell her his secret, yet he declares: "Whither I go, thither shall you go too". Husband and wife are well matched, and the sprightliness which comes from high spirits is almost as much the portion of Lady Percy as of her husband. It is interesting to compare with this scene that more sedate one in *Julius Cæsar* where Portia entreats her husband Brutus to make her a sharer in his secret and, unlike Lady Percy, does not entreat in vain.

Stage Direction. **Warkworth.** Warkworth is in Northumberland, 30 miles north of Newcastle. Warkworth Castle, the seat of the Percies, was founded in the reign of Stephen.

a letter. The writer of the letter is not indicated. Two suggestions have been made as to his identity: (1) George Dunbar, Earl of March; (2) Sheriff Rokeby. The latter suggestion is based on information given to Sir Walter Scott by Mr. Morfitt of Rokeby. See Clarendon Press Edition of *1 Henry IV.*

1. But, for mine own part . . . &c. The impetuousness of Hotspur, which opposition changes to peevish impatience, is well brought out in his comments on the letter he is reading. We must imagine him striding up and down the room as he reads, with that peculiar gait of which Lady Percy tells in *2 Henry IV.* His contempt for the writer of the letter is expressed in every word and gesture. The man is a "fool", "a shallow cowardly hind", "a lack-brain", "a dish of skim milk", "a frosty-spirited rogue", "a pagan rascal", whom Hotspur threatens to "brain with his lady's fan". Incidentally, we learn of the progress made by the conspirators, who now number, in addition to the Percies, Edmund Mortimer, the Archbishop of York, Owen Glendower, and Hotspur's old enemy, Douglas. The king is as yet in the dark, and Hotspur is prepared to march the same evening.

11. unsorted, ill adapted.

17. expectation, promise.

18, 19. my lord of York. This was the Archbishop of York, Richard Scroop, who appears in iv. 4, and is one of the leaders of the later conspiracy. (See *2 Henry IV.*)

20, 21. I could brain . . . fan. A similar fancy, perhaps suggested by these words of Hotspur, occurs in Beaumont and Fletcher's *Wit at Several Weapons*:

> "Wer 't not better
> Your head were broke with the handle of a fan".

And again in Webster's *White Devil*:

> *Marcello.* If I take her near you, I 'll cut her throat.
> *Flamineo.* With a fan of feathers?

In all three instances the extreme weakness of the person against whom the threat is breathed is forcibly suggested.

23, 24. the Douglas, Archibald, Earl of Douglas, the late enemy of Hotspur, but now reconciled to him through common hostility to Henry IV.

29–31. I could divide . . . an action. I could cut myself in half, and make one half fisticuff the other for bringing so splendid an undertaking before the notice of such a coward.

33. Kate. Lady Percy's real name was Elizabeth.

34. O, my good lord . . . &c. We scarcely need Lady Percy's description of Hotspur's troubled dreams to realize the excitability of his temper. But how vivid a picture she gives us of her husband's frame of mind! The loss of appetite and colour, the sudden starts, the sleep so troubled—

> "That beads of sweat have stood upon thy brow
> Like bubbles in a late-disturbed stream",—

all serve to indicate how foreign to Hotspur was the position in which he now found himself, how unfitted his open, generous nature was to take part in a conspiracy which was as yet kept secret. We may compare with Lady Percy's words those uttered by Portia to Brutus (*Julius Cæsar*, ii. 1. 252):

> "It will not let you eat, nor talk, nor sleep,
> And, could it work so much upon your shape
> As it hath much prevail'd on your condition,
> I should not know you, Brutus. Dear my lord,
> Make me acquainted with your cause of grief".

38. stomach, appetite.

42. my treasures, that which you treasure in me.

43. thick-eyed, dull of vision, gloomy.

44. thy faint. The later Quartos changed *thy* to *my*, quite needlessly.

46. Speak terms of manage, give directions.

48. retires, retreats.

49. palisadoes, entrenchments made of stakes; **frontiers,** outworks.

50. basilisks, pieces of ordnance. See Glossary.

   culverin. This was also a form of cannon. See Glossary.

52. currents, courses. Some editors read *'currents, i.e.* occurrents, occurrences.

   heady, impetuous.

59. On some . . . hest, on suddenly receiving some important command.

66. crop-ear, a horse whose ears have been docked.

68. back, mount.

straight, straightway.

Esperance! This was the motto of the Percy family, and Hotspur makes it his war-cry. Holinshed, describing the battle of Shrewsbury, says: " The adversaries cried *Esperance Persie*, and so the two armies furiouslie joined".

72. carries you away. Lady Percy seems to use the words in reference to Hotspur's absent-mindedness. ' What is it that makes you pay no attention to my question?' Hotspur, however, interprets the words literally.

74. Out, you mad-headed ape! . . . As yet Lady Percy has spoken seriously and feelingly; now, finding that Hotspur will not treat her seriously, she quickly changes her mood, and assumes a light bantering tone, which enables her to meet her husband on his own self-chosen ground.

75. A weasel . . . spleen. The spleenishness of the weasel seems to have been proverbial. Cf. *Cymbeline*, iii. 4. 162:

> " Ready in jibes, quick-answer'd, saucy, and
> As quarrelous as a weasel ".

79. his title, his claim to the throne. See i. 3. 155.

80. To line, to support. Cf. *Macbeth*, i. 3. 112:

> " Whether he was combined
> With those of Norway, or did line the rebel
> With hidden help or vantage. . . ."

82. paraquito, little parrot. The allusion is to the ceaseless and inconsequent chatter of the parrot kind.

84. break, pinch. " To ' break ' or ' pinch ' the little finger was ' a token of amorous dalliance '."

85. An if. See Glossary, *sub. an.*

89. mammets. The usual meaning of this word is ' puppets ', ' dolls ', and Shakespeare uses it in this sense in *Romeo and Juliet*, iii. 5, applying the term to a woman, as he does here:

> " And then to have a wretched puling fool,
> A whining mammet, in her fortunes tender,
> To answer I 'll not wed—I cannot love".

Gifford, however, suggested that Hotspur's *mammet* was a different word, based upon the Latin *mamma*, and signifying ' breasts '. This would of course make the connection between this and the following phrase: " tilt with lips "= kiss, somewhat closer.

91. And pass them current too. The phrase is intelligible only when it is borne in mind that the word *crowns* is used in a double sense: (1) the crown of the head; (2) a five-shilling

piece. It is the latter meaning which is used in the above phrase—"and circulate them too".

91. **God 's me.** God is for me, God is on my side.

101. **whereabout,** on what errand.

108. **Thou wilt not . . . know.** This is a proverbial saying, and finds a place in Ray's *Proverbs* under the form: "A woman conceals what she knows not". Chaucer has something very like it in his *Tale of Meliboeus*: "Ye sayn that the janglerie of wommen can Hyde things that they wot not of".

114. **of force,** necessarily, perforce.

Scene 4

This famous scene will be estimated by many as the most mirthful scene in the whole range of dramatic literature. Falstaff engages here in his hardest fight, in which the weapons are not swords but words; and though at last he is forced to cry, "Ah, no more of that, Hal, an thou lovest me", we feel that he comes out of a conflict, in which the odds have been so heavy against him, crowned with glory. The opening of the scene is, at least to the reader, dull enough, and it is hard to force a laugh at Francis' "Anon, anon, sir"; but the appearance of Falstaff, who is throughout the play a whetstone to the prince's wit, lifts us at once into the region of high comedy. In the narrative of the men in buckram, told with Falstaff's splendid command of exaggeration, the knight plays the braggart; but in a moment the whole situation is changed by the prince's "plain tale", and Falstaff finds himself at bay and hard bestead. Then it is that his resourcefulness and powers of evasion are brought into full play. Nor does the banquet of wit end here; Falstaff's impersonation of the king and then of the Prince of Wales is conceived in the most humorous fashion; the parody of the "Cambyses vein", and that of the euphuistic jargon in fashion at the Elizabethan court, is delightful, while the ease with which the knight plays either part and turns it to his own advantage reveals yet further the versatility and brilliance of his wit. That wit seems inexhaustible; he resents the interruption of Bardolph telling of the approach of the sheriff, and exclaims: "Play out the play: I have much to say in the behalf of that Falstaff".

The play-acting of Falstaff and the prince in the second part of the scene may have been suggested to Shakespeare by a scene in *The Famous Victories*, in which Dericke and John Cobler act over again the scene in which the Prince of Wales gave the Lord Chief Justice a box on the ear, and was forthwith committed to prison. A quotation of a part of the scene will bring out the points of resemblance:

Dericke. Faith John, Ile tell thee what, thou shalt be my
Lord Chiefe Justice, and thou shalt sit in the chaire,
And ile be the yong Prince, and hit thee a box on the eare,
And then thou shalt say, to teach you what prerogatives
    meane, I commit you to the Fleete.
John. Come on, Ile be your Judge,
But thou shalt not hit me hard.
    Der. No, no.
    John. What hath he done?
    Der. Marry he hath robd Dericke.
    John. Why then I cannot let him goe.
    Der. I must needs have my man.
    John. You shall not have him.
    Der. Shall I not have my man, say no and you dare.
How say you, shall I not have my man?
    John. No marry shall you not.
    Der. Shall I not John?
    John. No Dericke.
    Der. Why then take you that till more come,
Sownes, shall I not have him?
    John. Well I am content to take this at your hand,
But I pray you who am I?
    Der. Who art thou, Sownds, doost not know thy selfe?
    John. No.
    Der. Now away simple fellow,
Why, man, thou art John the Cobler.
    John. No, I am my Lord Chiefe Justice of England.
    Der. Oh John, Masse thou saist true, thou art indeed.
    John. Why then, to teach you what prerogatives mean, I
    commit you to the Fleete.

Stage Direction. **The Boar's-Head Tavern.** This is the
tavern to which the prince and his comrades resort after their
robbery of the king's receivers in *The Famous Victories of
Henry V.*

1. fat. The exact force of the adjective is not easy to determine. The reference is possibly to a room in which lard was
kept. Prof. Herford suggests that *fat* is another form of *vat*.

1, 2. lend me thy hand, help me.

5, 6. base-string. The figure is drawn from stringed instruments, the base-string being the string which produces the
lowest bass-note. "*The base-string of humility*" means therefore *the depths of degradation*.

8. take it upon, swear by.

11. a Corinthian, a prince of topers; the word must not be
interpreted exactly in the sense of "debauchee", as many of
Shakespeare's commentators have interpreted it. The words

which follow—"a lad of mettle, a good boy"—indicate that the term is one of compliment.

15. watering, drinking.

16. play it off, drink it down.

16–18. **To conclude, I am . . during my life.** In whatever light we may regard the prince's tap-room indulgences, we must recognize the ease with which he can place himself on a level with those beneath him, and by mastering their "language", see life from their standpoint. In the play of *Henry V* we recognize the value of this. The king associates with the humblest of his soldiers, learns to appreciate their manner of life, and wins their sympathy and confidence. His conduct is a deliberate reaction from that of his father, whose aim was to assume "the grand air" on all occasions, and to suffer nothing to lower the formal dignity of his kingly state.

16. a proficient, an expert.

20. action, combat.

21. pennyworth of sugar. It was the custom for drawers to keep pennyworths of sugar wrapped up in paper, ready for placing in a glass of sack.

22. under-skinker, tapster's boy.

25. bastard, a sweet wine from Spain.

25, 26. **Half-moon.** This, like the Pomgarnet a little farther on, is the name of a special room in the tavern.

33. **Thou art perfect,** you act the part perfectly.

35, 36. **Pomgarnet,** Pomegranate.

47. books, Bibles.

62. **Anon, Francis?** The prince humorously applies Francis word to his offer of a thousand pounds.

66–68. **Wilt thou rob . . . Spanish-pouch.** The prince is here describing the vintner or landlord of the house, who appears immediately afterwards. The epithets used are descriptive of the vintner's dress and person: thus the leathern jerkin with buttons of crystal glass was frequently worn by men of this calling: not-pated is usually explained as 'with close-cropped hair'. In Chaucer's description of the yeoman (*Prologue to Canterbury Tales*, v. 109), we read: "A not-heed hadde he with a broun visage", where Skeat interprets *not-heed* as 'crop-head', and gives several instances of the verb *to nott* in the sense of 'to cut', 'to poll'.

67. agate-ring. This was a ring of small value worn by the vintner on his finger.

puke - stocking, wearing stockings of a dull gray colour.

caddis-garter, a garter of worsted lace.

68. Spanish-pouch. This has been regarded as equivalent to 'fat-bellied' by some: others explain it as 'wine-bag', *i.e.* drunkard. Like the other terms, however, it may be taken to indicate simply a characteristic feature of the vintner's dress, the pouch being the purse or bag in which he placed his money.

70. brown bastard. Bastard wine was of two colours, brown and white.

72. in Barbary . . . so much. The statement is quite irrelevant, and is uttered only to detain Francis.

86. match, device. The Francis episode is a little tiresome, but it would seem from this question of Poins's that it was intended to lead up to something. Such, however, is not the case.

89. goodman Adam. Cf. 'goodman Verges' (*Much Ado*). The word is used, like 'gaffer', as a mark of easy familiarity.

90, 91. the pupil age . . . midnight, the modernity of this present midnight hour.

95-97. His industry . . . reckoning. 'He employs his time in running upstairs and downstairs, and his powers of speech do not extend beyond enumerating the particular items in the bill'.

97-103. I am not . . . a trifle. Hotspur has already (i. 3. 230) given us his opinion of Prince Henry, and we, who know the truth concerning the Prince of Wales, recognize how false that opinion is. The prince's reference to Hotspur, on the other hand, is as shrewdly penetrating as it is full of delightful humour.

98. me. See Glossary.

105. brawn. The reference is to Falstaff, and the meaning is 'that mass of flesh'.

Rivo! A common cry of tipsy revellers, the origin of which is obscure. Its association with the word *Castiliano* suggests that it hails from Spain. Cf. *The Jew of Malta*·

"Hey, *rivo, Castiliano*, a man's a man".

110. nether stocks, stockings. The threat is similar to the wish expressed a little later: "I would I were a weaver". See note to l. 124.

112. virtue, valour, manliness.

114, 115. pitiful-hearted Titan . . . sun. Warburton suggested that the words "pitiful-hearted Titan" should be placed in parenthesis. This would make the relative *that* refer back to the *butter* which melted when the sun-god, the Titan Hyperion, approached it to tell his story and imprint his kiss upon it. It seems to be a ludicrous application of the Greek myth of

Icarus. Steevens proposed to read *his son*, and saw in the passage a reference to Apollo and his son Phaëthon.

116. here's lime in this sack. The practice of putting lime or gypsum into wines was not to adulterate, but to preserve them. Thus, in Sir R. Hawkins *Voyages* we read: "Since the Spanish sacks have been common in our taverns, which for conservation are mingled with lime in the making, our nation complains of calentures, of the stone, of dropsy, and infinite other distempers not heard of before this wine came into frequent use ".

121. a shotten herring, a herring that has spawned, and is in consequence of little value.

123. the while, the age we live in.

124, 145. I would I were . . . or any thing. When the Calvinists in Flanders were subjected to persecution by the Spanish under the Duke of Alva, in the latter half of the sixteenth century, many of them fled to England and set up their weaving looms in Norfolk and in the district of London called Petty Flanders. Like the Lollards, these refugees were famous for their singing of psalms. Cf. Jonson's *Silent Woman*, iii. 4: "He got this cold with sitting up late, and singing catches with cloth-workers ". In the Folio editions the words "psalms or anything" are changed to "all manner of songs", and the change indicates the way in which the Act forbidding the use of scriptural language was carried into effect.

128. a dagger of lath. Such a dagger was carried by Vice in the Morality plays, and with it he belaboured the characters on the stage, and provided the spectators with a source of merriment. Cf. *Twelfth Night*, iv. 2. 116:

> " *Clown [singing]* I am gone, sir,
>   And anon, sir,
>   I'll be with you again,
>   In a trice,
>   Like to the old Vice,
>   Your need to sustain;
>
>   Who, with dagger of lath,
>   In his rage and his wrath,
>   Cries, ah ha! to the devil:
>   Like a mad lad,
>   Pare thy nails, dad;
>   Adieu, goodman Drivel ".

The harlequin of the modern pantomime is similarly equipped.

146. All's one for that. It's all the same to me.

150. this day morning. Only the first two Qq. have this reading. The later Qq. omit *day*.

155. at half-sword, at close quarters.

159. ecce signum! These were the words used by the priests in the Catholic churches in the moment of raising the cross.

170. an Ebrew Jew. "The natives of Palestine were called *Hebrews* by way of distinction from the *stranger Jews*, denominated Greeks" (Steevens).

173. come. Q8, F3 and F4 read *came*.
     other, others.

176. a bunch of radish. In *2 Henry IV*, iii. 2. 234, Falstaff compares Shallow to "a forked radish".

181. paid, killed.

183. ward, guard at fence.

189. mainly, mightily.

195. hilts. Properly the hilt or hand-guard of a sword, but often used for the sword itself, as in Jonson's *The Case is Altered*, ii. 7: "Fetch the hilts; fellow Juniper, wilt thou play?"

199. mark. The word is probably used in the double sense of (1) pay heed to, (2) keep count: 'I keep count of the number of your men in buckram'.

203. points. The word has the double meaning of (1) sword-points, (2) tagged laces, used for suspending the breeches.

205. me. See Glossary.

208, 209. eleven buckram men grown out of two! Professor Bradley, in an article on "The Rejection of Falstaff", contributed to the *Fortnightly Review* for May, 1902, makes the following suggestive comment on Falstaff's story of the men in buckram:—"Again, the attack of the prince and Poins on Falstaff and the other thieves at Gadshill is contrived, we know, with a view to the incomprehensible lies it will induce him to tell. But when, more than rising to the occasion, he turns two men in buckram into four, then into seven, and then nine, and then eleven, almost in a breath, I believe they partly misunderstand his intention, and the great majority of his critics misunderstand it altogether. Shakespeare was not writing a mere farce. It is preposterous to suppose that a man of Falstaff's intelligence would utter these gross, palpable, open lies with the serious intention to deceive, or to forget that, if it was too dark for him to see his own hand, he could hardly see that the three misbegotten knaves were wearing Kendal green. No doubt, if he *had* been believed, he would have been hugely tickled at it, but he no more expected to be believed than when he claimed to have killed Hotspur."

211. Kendal green. Suits of green cloth made at Kendal, in Westmoreland, were worn by foresters. There is a reference to these suits of Kendal green in the Robin Hood Ballads.

6*   (B 101)

216. knotty-pated. This is probably another form of the *not-pated* in l. 67.

217. tallow-ketch, barrel of fat. This is Hanmer's emendation for the *tallow-catch* of the early editions.

226. strappado. A Spanish method of torture which Randle Holmes, in his *Academy of Arms and Blazons*, describes as follows:—" The strappado is when the person is drawn up to his height, and then suddenly to let him fall half-way with a jerk, which not only breaketh his arms to pieces, but also shaketh all his joints out of joint; which punishment is better to be hanged, than for a man to undergo".

230. sanguine. The word is probably used in its literal sense of red, red-faced.

233. elf-skin. This is the reading of the early editions, for which Hanmer proposed to substitute *eel-skin*, which is actually used by Falstaff in describing Shallow in Part II. ii. 4: "You might have thrust him and all his apparel into an eel-skin". But *elf-skin* is not impossible, for in *Midsummer-Night's Dream* Shakespeare, as Clarke points out, represents his elves as dressed in the cast-off skins of snakes:

> " And there the snake throws her enamelled skin
> Weed wide enough to wrap a fairy in" (ii. 1. 255).

234. neat's tongue, ox-tongue.

235. tailor's-yard. The word 'yard' means literally 'stick'. A stick of a certain length came to be known as a 'yard-measure'. The *tailor's yard* is the tailor's stick for measuring.

236. standing-tuck, rapier standing on end.

244. out-faced, frightened.

250, 251. starting-hole, way of escape. The literal reference is to the holes into which a rabbit runs to escape its pursuer.

257. beware, pay heed to, respect.

258. the lion . . . prince. "This belief, current in the Middle Ages, was the basis of a recurring *motif* in the early English Romances" (Herford).

262. clap to, shut.

273-277. a nobleman . . . a royal man. A pun is intended by reference to the two coins: a noble = 6*s.* 8*d.*, a royal = 10*s.*

283. packing, hurrying off.

295, 296. tickle our noses . . . bleed. In the *Famous Victories of Henry V* we read: "Every day when I went into the field, I would take a straw and thrust it into my nose, and make my nose bleed".

297. true men, the honest men with whom they—the thieves —had been fighting.

301. taken with the manner, caught in the act.

302. fire. The reference is to Bardolph's red nose.

305, 306. meteors and exhalations. By these are meant the carbuncles and eruptions on Bardolph's face.

309. Hot livers and cold purses, drunkenness and poverty.

310, 311. Choler . . . halter. There is a double pun here— a play on the words *choler* and *collar*, and on the double meaning of *rightly taken* = (1) rightly understood, (2) well captured.

313. bombast, unprepared cotton used for stuffing quilts, &c.

317. alderman's thumb-ring. It was the custom for aldermen and persons of dignity generally to wear a plain gold ring on the thumb. Cf. Glapthorne's *Wit in a Constable*, 1639: "An alderman—I may say to you, he has no more wit than the rest of the bench, and that lies in his thumb-ring".

318, 319. There's villanous news abroad. Amid the East-cheap revelry Shakespeare does not let us forget the progress of the serious plot. What in act ii, scene 2 was a secret conspiracy is now open rebellion. Tidings of the Percy rising have reached the court, and the king, if Falstaff is to be believed, is in terror. The prince receives the news with his usual calm. The thought of coming battle is not allowed to restrain even for a moment the mirthfulness of the hour. From the story of the robbery we glide easily into that delightful scene of personation in which Falstaff stands for the king and then for the prince.

319. Sir John Bracy, apparently a fictitious person.

321, 322. that gave Amamon the bastinado. That cudgelled Amamon. Amamon, or Amaimon, is the name of a fiend to whom reference is also made in *Merry Wives*, ii. 2. 311; "Amaimon sounds well, Lucifer well; yet are they devils' additions, the names of fiends".

Falstaff's references to Glendower's sorcery and mystery-mongering are delightful.

323, 324. a Welsh hook. Whalley says in his *Remains*: "The Welsh hook, I believe, was pointed like a spear, to push or thrust with, and below had a hook to seize the enemy if he should attempt to escape by flight."

330. pistol. Dr. Johnson points out an anachronism here. The use of the pistol was not known in England in the time of Henry IV.

342. blue-caps. The reference is to the blue bonnets of the Scotsmen.

356. state, chair of state.

364, 365. King Cambyses' vein. The reference is in all probability to an early Elizabethan tragedy, entitled "A Lamentable Tragedy mixed full of Pleasant Mirth containing the Life of Cambises, King of Persia". The author of the play was Thomas Preston, and it is thought to have been first acted *circ.* 1561. A reprint of the play is found in the fourth volume of Dodsley's *Old Plays*.

366. here is my leg. I make my bow. References to the *leg*, i.e. to a bow made by throwing out the leg, are very frequent in the plays of Shakespeare and his contemporaries.

369. Weep not, sweet queen; . . . vain. This is Falstaff's representation of the "Cambyses' vein". In a marginal note to that play we read: "At this tale tolde, let the queen weep".

370. how he holds his countenance! how he maintains his gravity.

371. tristful, sad.

372. For tears . . . eyes. Cf. *Cambyses*: "These words to hear make stilling teares issue from chrystall eyes".

375. tickle-brain. This was the name of a kind of spirituous liquor. Falstaff is, of course, addressing the hostess.

377-379. for though the camomile . . . wears. This is the first of several parodies of the style of Lyly's *Euphues* which occur in this scene, and are placed on the lips of Falstaff and the prince. The most characteristic feature of Euphuism is its use of similes drawn from a more or less fanciful natural history. Of the camomile Lyly tells us: "Though the camomile, the more it is trodden and pressed down, the more it spreadeth; yet the violet, the oftener it is touched and handled, the sooner it withereth and decayeth". But it is not only in the allusions to natural history that Euphuism is ridiculed in this speech of Falstaff. A little later in the same speech we meet with a number of rhetorical questions, and we come upon them again at the close of the prince's speech (ll. 429-433). Rhetorical questions of this sort are as frequent in *Euphues* as fanciful allusions to natural history. Thus we read in the first part of that work: "If thou diddest determine with thy selfe to be false, why diddest thou sweare to be true? If to be true, why art thou false? If thou wast minded both falsely and forgedly to deceive me why didst thou flatter and dissemble with me at the first? If to love me, why dost thou flinch at the last?" It will be observed that in addition to the rhetoric questioning there is an antithetical structure in these sentences, and this again is imitated by the prince in the passage referred to above. But a more striking instance of euphuistic antithesis, the antithetical words being also alliterative, is furnished in Falstaff's speech: "I do not speak to thee in drink, but in tears", &c., with which may be compared the following passage from *Euphues*: "As Lucilla was caughte by fraude, so shall she be kept by force, and as thou wast too simple to espye my crafte, so I thinke thou wilt be too weak to with-stande my courage ".

385. micher, truant.

389, 390. this pitch . . . doth defile. In *Euphues* we read: " Hee that toucheth pitch shall bee defiled ". The saying was a proverbial one, and occurs in Spenser's *Shepherd's Calendar* (*May*), under the form: " Who toucheth pitch mought needes be defilde". Its original is to be found in *Ecclesiasticus*, xiii. 1, " He that toucheth pitch shall be defiled therewith ".

412. rabbit-sucker, a suckling rabbit. In Lyly's *Endymion* we read : " I prefer an old cony before a rabbet-sucker, and an ancient henne before a young chicken peeper ".

poulter, poulterer.

418, 419. I 'll tickle . . . prince, I 'll play the part of the young prince to your cost.

424. bolting-hutch, trough; literally, according to Steevens, the wooden receptacle into which the miller ' bolted' his meal.

426. bombard, properly a machine for hurling blocks of stone in the bombardment of a castle, &c. A secondary meaning, which is the one required here, was that of a large leather drinking-vessel.

427. Manningtree ox. The oxen fed on the rich pasture-land at Manningtree, in Essex, were famous for their size. Manningtree was also famous for its fairs, at which, in addition to the roasting of oxen, stage-plays were performed which are said to have retained many of the allegorical characters of the Morality plays, including Vice, Iniquity, Ruffian, and Vanity mentioned in the next sentence.

431. cunning, skilful.

434. take me with you, explain your meaning to me.

450. therefore, for that very reason.

460, 461. Heigh, heigh! . . . matter? The first three Quartos give this speech to Prince Henry; the later Quartos and the Folios ascribe it to Falstaff. The words, "The devil rides upon a fiddle-stick ", were proverbial, and occur again in Beaumont and Fletcher's *The Lieutenant* under the form, " The fiend rides on a fiddle-stick ".

464, 465. never call . . . a counterfeit. Falstaff's thoughts are still running in the direction of his self-defence, and he refuses to countenance the interruption caused by the approach of the sheriff and his watch. He says: " My character is of sterling worth; do not make me out to be spurious metal. If you do, you prove that you are mad, however sane you may appear."

465. mad. This is the reading of the third and fourth Folios only ; all other early editions read *made*.

468. major, major premiss, viz. that Falstaff is a coward. A pun on the two meanings of major is intended.

so, very good.

469. if I become not a cart, if I do not adorn a hangman's cart.

472. arras, tapestry, originally made at Arras, in Picardy. The Elizabethan stage was partly hung with arras, and the part it plays in Hamlet's slaughter of Polonius will be familiar to every reader.

475. their date is out, their period of existence is over.

479. hue and cry, "the pursuit of a felon by horn and voice, a process then recognized in common law" (Herford).

484, 485. The man . . . employ'd him. "Every reader must regret that Shakespeare would not give himself the trouble to furnish Prince Henry with some more pardonable excuse without obliging him to have recourse to an absolute falsehood, and that, too, uttered under the sanction of so strong an assurance" (Steevens).

492. three hundred marks, £200.

498. Paul's, St. Paul's Cathedral.

500. *Peto.* Falstaff! &c. Dr. Johnson proposed to transfer to Poins this and the following speeches ascribed to Peto in the old editions, on the ground that Poins, and not Peto, is the prince's comrade, and that there was no reason for Poins to run away. Malone agrees with Johnson. But it must be noted that the name Peto occurs not only to indicate the speaker of these words, but also in the text itself in line 520. It is hardly likely that a printer's error could have reached so far.

511. ob., obolus, a half-penny.

514. at more advantage, at a more suitable time.

518. twelve-score, twelve score yards.

519. advantage, interest. Cf. *Merchant of Venice*, i. 3:

"Methought you said you neither lend nor borrow
    Upon advantage".

In iii. 3. 169 the prince informs Falstaff: "the money is paid back again".

Act III—Scene 1

With the opening of the third act we pass from London to the provinces. The rebellion, the outbreak of which we have already witnessed, has now spread; an alliance has been formed between the Percies, Mortimer, and Glendower, and this meeting at Bangor has been summoned for the purpose of dividing the kingdom of England between them after they shall have met and overcome the king. Up to this point Shakespeare has probably enlisted our sympathies on the side of the rebels: we have felt that their grievances are real, and that the king's bearing towards them has been tyrannical. But their plans for the partition of England, whereby the integrity of the nation is to be wholly destroyed, bring us as patriots back to the side of the king. We feel, too, the madness of this plan of division, and are at the same time made aware of the ill-success which must result from the union of these three allies. All the patience of Mortimer is needed to prevent Hotspur—who has not that great gift of leadership which enables a man to endure fools gladly—from quarrelling with Glendower. Glendower's superstitious self-esteem and Hotspur's masterfulness act and react upon one another with ill-boding results. The politic Worcester endeavours to school Hotspur into good behaviour and a sense of respect for his associates, but the lesson is not taken deeply to heart. The amorous toying of Mortimer and his Welsh wife rouses him to amused contempt, and the scene ends with another delightful peep into the marital relations of Hotspur and Lady Percy which is in exact keeping with what has gone before. It is a Benedick and Beatrice scene after marriage.

Shakespeare's magic art in breathing life into the dry bones of Holinshed is nowhere better displayed than in this scene, which is evolved out of the following brief passage in the *Chronicle*: "Heerewith, they by their deputies in the house of the archdeacon of Bangor, divided the realme amongst them, causing a tripartite indenture to be made and sealed with their seales, by the covenants whereof, all England from Severne and Trent, south and eastward, was assigned to the earle of March: all Wales and the lands beyond Severne westward, were appointed to Owen Glendouer: and all the remnant from Trent northward to the lord Persie.

"This was done (as some have said) through a foolish credit given to a vaine prophesie, as though King Henrie was the moldwarpe, curssed of Gods owne mouth, and they three were the dragon, the lion, and the woolfe, which should divide this realme betweene them. Such is the deviation (saith Hall) and not the divination of those blind and fantasticall dreames of the Welsh prophesiers."

In respect of historic fact it may be mentioned that Shakespeare and Holinshed are wrong in representing this "tripartite convention" as having been held before the battle of Shrewsbury. In reality it took place nearly three years later, the division of the land being made between Glendower, Mortimer, and Northumberland. See Wylie's *History of England under Henry IV*, vol ii, chap. 60. It will be noticed also that

whereas Holinshed represents this tripartite division as carried
into effect by deputies, Shakespeare brings the leaders themselves to Bangor, and thus enriches the bald story with highly
dramatic incident.

2. **our induction**, the inauguration of our enterprise.

8. **For.** The force of the conjunction may be expanded
into something like this: "I call you Hotspur and not Percy,
because . . .".

13-17. **at my nativity . . . Shaked like a coward.** This is
Shakespeare's expansion of the following words of Holinshed:
"Strange wonders happened at the nativity of this man, for
the same night he was born, all his father's horses in the stable
were found to stand in blood up to their bellies".

15. **cressets**, open lamps placed upon poles; they were used
in the play-houses.

16. **huge.** The adjective is found only in Q 1.

18. Pope proposed to read this speech of Hotspur's as verse,
making the verses end at *done*, *cat*, and *born*. A verse-setting
is also possible in the case of other speeches of Hotspur, but I
have preferred to abide by the prose diction of the Qq. and Ff.
The sudden transitions of Hotspur in this scene from verse to
prose and prose to verse are not without dramatic value.

23. **as fearing you**, because it was afraid of you.

31. **enlargement**, liberty.

32. **beldam earth**, grandmother earth; cf. *grandam earth*
in l. 34.

34. **distemperature**, disorder.

41. **mark'd me extraordinary**, singled me out as an extraordinary being.

44. **clipp'd in with the sea**, living within this island.

45. **chides**, chafes against.

46. **read to me**, instructed me.

48, 49. **Can trace . . . experiments**, who can follow me in
the pursuit of the toilsome paths of magic art, or keep pace
with me in the researches of alchemy.

53. **vasty.** Cf. 'the vasty fields of France' (*Henry V*,
Prol. 12).

59. **tell truth . . . devil.** This is a proverbial saying
which finds a place in Ray's *Proverbs* under the form, "Speak
the truth and shame the devil".

64, 65. **Three times . . . my power.** Here at any rate
Glendower tells the truth. The first occasion was in 1400,
when the king waged war in person with Glendower, who,
withdrawing to the mountains of the Snowdon district, escaped

capture. In the following year war broke out again, and resulted in the victory of Glendower over the Lord Grey of Ruthen, who was captured. The third occasion was in 1402, when, after the Earl of March had been taken prisoner by Glendower, the king himself again entered Wales, but again, as Holinshed says, "lost his labour". The word *weather-beaten* probably refers to the storms which King Henry encountered on this last expedition, and of which Holinshed writes as follows: "Owen conveied himselfe out of the waie, and (as was thought) through art magike, he caused such foule weather of winds, tempest, raine, snow and haile to be raised, for the annoiance of the kings armie, that the like had not been heard of".

70. **right,** rightful possessions.

71. **threefold order.** The reference is to what Holinshed calls the 'tripartite indenture', Hall, the 'tripartie endenture', and Shakespeare, the 'indentures tripartite', in l. 80.

72. **The archdeacon hath . . .** Daniel tells the story of the tripartite division of England very succinctly in the *History of the Civil Wars*, iv. 23:

> "With these the Piercies them confederate,
> And as three heads conjoin in one intent;
> And instituting a triumvirate,
> Do part the land in triple government;
> Dividing thus among themselves the state:
> The Piercies should rule all the north from Trent;
> And Glendour, Wales: the Earl of March should be
> Lord of the South, from Trent—and so they 'gree ".

74. **hitherto,** up to this point. Mortimer's finger is on the map.

80. **drawn,** drawn up.

81. **sealed interchangeably.** The meaning is that there are three copies of the agreement, each of which will bear the signatures of the three men.

89. **you may have drawn together,** you have the opportunity of assembling.

96. **moiety,** share; literally a half-share (Latin *medius*, *medietas*).

98. **comes me cranking in,** bends in upon my share of the land. Cf. *Venus and Adonis*:

> " He cranks and crosses with a thousand doubles ".

The river is the Trent, which, after flowing as far as Burton in a south-east direction, then turns north-east towards the Humber. The "huge half-moon" would accordingly be formed of Lincolnshire and a part of Nottinghamshire.

100. cantle, slice, share. Cf. *Antony and Cleopatra*, iii. 8:
> " The greater cantle of the world is lost
> With very ignorance ".

102. smug, smooth.

104. indent, indentation.

105. bottom, valley-bottom.

108, 109. runs me up . . . side, flows in a southerly direction on the other side (*i.e.* before reaching Burton), to your advantage and my disadvantage.

110. Gelding the opposed continent, cutting off from the country south of the Trent.

112. charge, expense (in constructing dams).

114. And then . . . even. The verse is imperfect, and has been amended in various ways. The best emendation seems to me the following:
> " And then he runneth straight and evenly ".

The words " fair and evenly " occur in l. 103.

121. For I was train'd . . . court. Holinshed writes of Glendower's upbringing as follows: " He was first set to studie the lawes of the realme and became an utter [outer, external] barrister, or an apprentice of the law (as they terme him), and served King Richard at Flint castell, where he was taken by Henrie duke of Lancaster ". It would seem as though Shakespeare, in deference to the Welsh devotion to the harp, altered Glendower's legal studies to studies in music.

124. And gave the tongue . . . ornament. Some editors have paraphrased *tongue* as 'the English language', but I think the meaning is—'furnished the songs with a graceful musical accompaniment'. This is in close keeping with the words, " I framed to the harp many an English ditty ".

129. metre ballad-mongers, ballad-singing rhymesters. Had Shakespeare in mind the Act of 1597 which classed minstrels as vagabonds?

130. a brazen canstick turn'd, a brazen candlestick in the turning-lathe.

132. nothing, not at all.

133. mincing, walking with affected unnatural steps. Hotspur's contempt for the fine arts is Shakespeare's own idea. Brandes, speaking of Shakespeare's love of music, and of the characters which are represented as lovers of music, bids us also " note the characters whom Shakespeare makes specially unmusical: Shylock, who loathes 'the vile squeaking of the wry-necked fife'; then Hotspur, the hero-barbarian; Benedick, the would-be woman-hater; Cassius, the fanatic politician; Othello, the half-civilized African; and, finally, creatures like Caliban, who are nevertheless enthralled by music as though by a wizard's spell" (G. Brandes' *William Shakespeare*, chap. xxi).

135. **Come, you shall have Trent turn'd.** Glendower yields at last from pure exhaustion. The question of having Trent turned is no longer under discussion, and Hotspur, as we learn from his next words, cares no longer about it. But the masterful "crossings" of Hotspur have broken the Welshman's spirit, and so, to secure a moment's peace, he yields the point which he fancies Hotspur has deeply at heart.

142. **the writer,** the notary or clerk who was to draw up the indentures.

143. **Break with,** inform.

148. **the moldwarp,** the earth-thrower, the mole. See the quotation from Holinshed given above.

149. **Merlin.** Shakespeare seems to have regarded the Arthurian legends, and more especially the miraculous powers of Merlin, with scepticism.

151. **moulten,** past participle of 'moult'. Pope suggested *moulting*.

152. **couching,** couchant; **ramping,** rampant. Both are heraldic terms.

153. **skimble-skamble stuff,** wishy-washy nonsense. The exact meaning of *skimble-skamble* is 'disconnected'; *scamble* being a secondary form of the verb *scramble*.

154. **faith,** faith in him.

156, 157. **the several . . . lackeys.** Falstaff has already referred to Glendower's dealings with the spirit Amamon. See ii. 4.

162. **cates,** delicacies. See Glossary.

163. **summer-house.** The building of summer-houses or garden-houses a little way out of London was a common practice with persons of means in Elizabethan times. It is of these houses that Stubbes writes in his *Anatomy of Abuses*: "In the fields and suburbes of the cities they have gardens either paled or walled round about very high, with their harbers and bowers fit for the purpose. And least they may be espied in these open places, they have their banquetting houses with galleries, turrets, and what not, therein sumptuously erected."

165, 166. **profited In strange concealments,** proficient in secret arts.

176. **you are too wilful-blame,** you deliberately make yourself deserving of blame. Cf. *King John*, v. 2: "The Dauphin is too wilful-opposite".

180. blood, spirit.

181. the dearest grace, the utmost credit.

182. present, reveal.

184. opinion, obstinacy. This meaning is preserved in the modern *opinionative*.

188. Beguiling . . . commendation, cheating them of the approval which they would otherwise command.

195. my aunt Percy. She was really his sister.

197. harlotry, hussy.

200. swelling heavens, swollen eyes. The reference is to "their beautiful blue, and to rain falling from heaven" (Deighton).

202. In such a parley, in such language, *i.e.* of the eyes.

204. a feeling disputation, a conversation of the senses.

207. highly, in high-flown diction.

209. division, melody; literally "a variation of melody upon some given fundamental harmony" (Dyce). Cf. *Romeo and Juliet*, iii. 5:

> "Some say the lark makes sweet division".

211. in this, in not knowing Welsh.

212. She bids you on the wanton rushes lay you. Lady Mortimer's sleep-song, as rendered by Glendower, is as truly lyrical in feeling and expression as the famous epithalamium of Juliet:

> "Gallop apace, you fiery-footed steeds . . . ".
> —*Romeo and Juliet*, iii. 2. 1.

The beautiful imagery of the passage was recognized, as Steevens has shown, by Beaumont and Fletcher. In their *Philaster* (iii. 2) Arethusa asks:

> "Who shall take up his lute,
> And touch it till he crown a silent sleep
> Upon my eyelids, making me dream, and cry,
> 'Oh, my dear, dear Philaster!'"

wanton, luxuriant.

rushes. Rushes served as a covering for the floor before carpets came into general use. It should be borne in mind that the Elizabethan stage was strewn with rushes.

215. crown, place as king.

217-220. Making such . . . east. Dr. Johnson paraphrases these verses as follows: "She will lull you by her song into soft tranquillity, in which you shall be so near to sleep as to be free from perturbation, and so much awake as to be sensible of pleasure; a state partaking of sleep and wakefulness, as the twilight of night and day ".

222. book, schedule of indentures.

224-226. And those musicians . . . be here. The meaning is, I think, as follows: 'And the musicians which are to delight you with their music, even though at present they be suspended in the air a thousand leagues from here, shall straightway by my magic arts be summoned to attend upon you'. Such a reading will require a comma after *you*.

227. Come, Kate, thou art perfect . . . Hotspur's parody makes us turn abruptly from the delicate sentiment and lyricism of the Celtic nature to the studied coldness of the Saxon temper, which conceals strong feeling beneath outward indifference to emotion. The antagonism of the Celtic and Saxon natures, as embodied in Glendower and Hotspur respectively, is strikingly illustrated throughout the scene.

231. humorous, whimsical, capricious. See Glossary.

236. Lady, my brach, my bitch, Lady.

240. Neither, 'I will not do that either'. Hotspur is probably satirical in describing *stillness* as a woman's fault.

246. comfit-maker's, confectioner's.

249. sarcenet surety, feeble surety. *Sarcenet* is the name of a thin silk, originally manufactured by the Saracens, whose name it bears.

250. Finsbury. Finsbury, in Elizabethan times, was a favourite pleasure-resort of the London citizens. There was a famous archery-ground there, and it was also a place of exercise for the London train-bands.

253. pepper-gingerbread. Hotspur is still thinking of the "comfit-maker's wife".

254. To velvet-guards . . . Sunday-citizens. To citizens in their Sunday clothes with velvet trimmings.

257, 258. 'T is the next way . . . teacher. Singing is the surest method of becoming a tailor or a teacher of music to robins. For the musical proclivities of the tailor, cf. Beaumont and Fletcher's *Knight of Burning Pestle*, ii. 8: "Never trust a tailor that does not sing at his work".

Scene 2

This scene between the prince and his father, the formality of which is in direct opposition to the free and easy converse of the prince with his Eastcheap associates, gives us further insight into the character of the two men, and also marks an advance in the historical plot. The king, in his anxiety to teach his son a lesson, so far puts aside the mask of kingship as to reveal the means by which he won the crown from the unfortunate Richard. We see throughout the skilled diplomatist, whose every step is deliberate and for whom spontaneous action is impossible. When he lays bare the steps by which he gained the throne, we are tempted to accept those terms of abuse—"this king of smiles . . . this fawning greyhound"—which Hotspur heaped upon him in act i, scene 3. Studied diplomacy has become so firmly engrafted into the king's nature that he is unable to understand the open honesty of his son. He sees in the prince another Richard, and fears that after his own death the House of Lancaster will fall a victim to the House of Percy. The dignity and manly openness of the prince's bearing in his father's presence win our hearts, and at last the heart of his father: "A hundred thousand rebels die in this". So far we have seen the prince almost exclusively in the company of his taverners, but the scene before us reveals that other side of his nature into which we gained a momentary insight during his soliloquy in act i, scene 2. The king here, as on previous occasions, draws a comparison between his own son and Hotspur, greatly to the disadvantage of the former. The prince's reply is altogether noble. His father has suggested that he is guilty of the basest treachery of which a Prince of Wales could be capable, but he takes no offence. Drawn by the king into comparison with Percy, he declares that Percy is only his factor, his agent, "to engross up glorious deeds on my behalf". He utters in this speech no idle boast, but speaks with the full conviction of the man who knows himself far better than others know him. From certain words of the king, and more fully from the speech of Blunt, we learn of the progress of the rebellion. Hotspur and his father, Archbishop Scroop, Earl Douglas, and Mortimer, are all in the field, and the proposed meeting-place of the different contingents is Shrewsbury.

Stage Direction. The palace. Westminster Palace.

1. give us leave, leave us alone.

6. my blood, my offspring.

8. passages of life, course of life.

11. my mistreadings. The king is conscious of the wrong he has committed in compassing the crown, and sees in his son a divine instrument of vengeance. With this reference to his "mistreadings" may be compared those words spoken to the prince in Part II, iv. 5. 184:

> "God knows, my son,
> By what by-paths and indirect crook'd ways
> I met this crown".

A righteous Nemesis pursues Henry IV throughout his reign, but that he should see that Nemesis working in the person of

his son is strange irony. The shrewd and diplomatic Bolingbroke, who won his way to the throne by keen insight into the
minds and characters of men, persists in misunderstanding the
true nature of his own son.

13. **lewd.** The word here means simply 'vulgar', 'low'.

15. **As thou . . . withal,** "as thou takest part in as an
equal" (Herford).

16. **blood,** descent.

19. **Quit,** exculpate.

20. **doubtless,** certain.

23. **in reproof of,** in refuting.

25. **pick-thanks,** flatterers; literally those who are always
on the look-out for opportunities of winning the gratitude of
others by their servility. Cf. Fairfax's *Tasso*:

> "With pleasing tales his lord's vain ears he fed,
>   A flatterer, a pick-thank and a lyer".

Holinshed uses the word himself. See Introduction.

  newsmongers, tale-bearers.

26-28. **I may . . . submission.** Taken with what goes
before, the meaning is: 'Refuting much of that which has
been laid to my charge, let me beg such mitigation of my
faults as may enable me, acknowledging my sins, to obtain
pardon at your hands for those real faults which in the wantonness of youth I have committed'.

30. **affections,** propensities.

  hold a wing, pursue a course.

31. **Quite from,** quite apart from.

32. **Thy place . . . lost.** This dismissal of Prince Henry
from the Privy Council, if indeed it happened at all, is of much
later date. It is, in fact, connected with the famous story of
the box on the ears given by the prince to Lord Chief-Justice
Gascoigne, which is set forth in great detail in *The Famous
Victories of Henry V*. Shakespeare introduces the matter at
this point in the story deliberately; Holinshed places the event
in its right order.

33. **thy younger brother.** Cf. Holinshed: "The king after
expelled him out of his privie councell, banisht him the court,
and made the duke of Clarence (his yoonger brother) president
of councell in his steed".

36. **thy time,** the time when thou shouldst come to the
throne.

38. **do;** *does* and *doth* have been suggested as emendations.

43. **possession,** the actual possessor, *i.e.* Richard II.

45. likelihood, prospects.

50. I stole ... heaven. The idea of acquiring surreptitiously must not be pressed here; the king means that his courtesy was so great that it seemed to men as though it had come direct from heaven. With the whole of this speech compare Richard's words in *Richard II*, i. 4. 23–36, and see Introduction.

59. wan, won. This form of the past tense, though common in Elizabethan English, is not found elsewhere in Shakespeare.

61. bavin. This is a word used for faggots of brushwood of a highly combustible nature. The following verse explains the metaphor.

62. carded; *to card* meant to debase by mixing, and is used literally in Greene's *Quip for an Upstart Courtier*: " You card your beer, if you see your guests begin to be drunk, half small, half strong ". See Glossary.

63. capering. This is the reading of Q 1; read in the light of the adjective *skipping*, which precedes, it is much better than the *carping* of the other editions.

65–67. And gave ... comparative; 'to the detriment of his kingly name and dignity, he joined in the merriment of jesting youths, and exchanged wit-combats with every beardless boy who was vain enough to match himself against the king '.

69. Enfeoff'd ... popularity, gave himself up wholly to the pursuit of popularity. The word *enfeoff'd*, which dates from feudal times, means literally ' to invest with possession '.

77. community, commonness, familiarity.

83. cloudy, gloomy.

87. With vile participation, by mixing with vulgar people.

91. Make blind itself. The king means that in his tender love for his son his eyes are blinded with tears.

98, 99. He hath ... succession. ' His worthiness furnishes him with a higher claim to the kingly power than is found in your shadowy right of succession '.

100. of no right, without any legal right.

colour like to right, semblance of right.

101. harness, armed men. See Glossary.

102. the lion, the king.

105. bruising arms, weapons of war.

109. majority, pre-eminence.

110. capital, supreme.

115. Enlarged, set him at liberty.

116. **To fill . . . defiance up,** in order to defy us in the completest manner possible.

120. **Capitulate,** draw up their grievances. Holinshed gives a list of these grievances as formally drawn up and presented to the king.

124. **vassal,** base-born, cowardly.

125. **start of spleen,** malicious impulses.

136. **favours,** features. The use of the word in the same sense occurs in *Richard II*:
> " Yet I well remember
> The favours of these men ".

142. **For,** as for, concerning.

147. **factor,** agent.

148. **engross up,** accumulate.

151. **worship,** honour.

157. **bands,** bonds.

159. **parcel,** portion.

160. **A hundred thousand rebels die in this.** The prince's noble defence forces his father to take him to his heart and give up his suspicions. Yet even after this, and after the prince's splendid achievements at Shrewsbury, the king fails back upon his old suspicions. In *Part II.* he becomes a slave to them.

161. **charge,** a responsible position.

164. **Lord Mortimer of Scotland.** Shakespeare makes the mistake of giving the name Mortimer, which belonged to the English Lords of March, to the Scottish family of Dunbar, who also held the title of Lords of March. The person in question is George Dunbar, who fought with Henry against the Percies at the battle of Shrewsbury.

168. **If promises . . . hand.** 'If all the rebels keep their promise'.

172. **advertisement,** intelligence.

177. **Our business valued,** if the work we have to do is rightly estimated.

180. **Advantage . . . delay.** " The favourable opportunity grows fat and lazy, loses its elasticity, when men are dilatory" (Delius).

Scene 3

The scene before us has something in common with act ii. scene 4. Falstaff puts forward the same extravagant claims in the matter of the pocket-picking as before anent the men in buckram, and here again it rests with the Prince of Wales

to unmask him and show the preposterous character of those
claims. If we were disposed to regard Falstaff seriously, and
to bring his conduct to a moral test, the charges brought
against him by the hostess of the Boar's Head would serve
to show the unscrupulousness of his character. When brought
to book by the prince in regard to this matter, the knight
shows a skill in evasion almost equal to that of the men-in-
buckram scene. To the prince's indignant question: "Sirrah,
do I owe you a thousand pound?" his ready answer is: "A
million: thy love is worth a million; thou owest me thy love".
A little later, when the prince puts his treatment of the hostess
in the true light, he shields himself from the charge of disgrace
by pleading: "Thou knowest in the state of innocency Adam
fell, and what should poor Jack Falstaff do in the days of
villany", and then with magnificent effrontery proceeds to
forgive the hostess whom he has maligned. The change from
prose to verse in the prince's concluding speech serves to remind us of the other side to his character. He can dally with
Falstaff in moments of leisure, but is not unmindful of the great
issue which is impending.

2. **bate**, lose flesh.

4. **apple-john.** The apple-john or John-apple was an apple
whose skin, owing to long keeping, became very wrinkled
John Philips describes this apple very exactly in his *Cider*:

> " Nor John-apple, whose wither'd rind, entrench'd
> By many a furrow, aptly represents
> Decrepid age ".

5. **in** some **liking**, in good condition.

8. **peppercorn.** Referred to by Falstaff because of its small
size.

a brewer's horse; a *malt-horse* was a common term of
reproach in Shakespeare's time; cf. Jonson's *Bartholomew
Fair*: "I am a dull malt-horse, I know nothing".

9. **spoil**, spoiling.

16. **in good compass**, moderately. Bardolph applies the
word in the phrase *out of all compass* in the sense of grasp,
embrace—'thou art unable to be embraced'.

22. **admiral**, admiral's ship. Cf. Milton's *Paradise Lost*,
i. 294:

> "His spear, to equal which the tallest pine
> Hewn on Norwegian hills, to be the mast
> Of some great ammiral, were but a wand".

See Glossary.

23, 24. **Knight of the Burning Lamp.** A humorous allusion to the quaint titles assumed by knights-errant. Cf. Beaumont and Fletcher's play, *The Knight of the Burning Pestle*.

31, 32. this fire, that's God's angel. Cf. Dekker, *Satiro-mastix*: "by this candle, which is none of God's angels".

36. purchase, purchasing power.

37. triumph, a triumphal procession accompanied by torches.

41. me, at my cost.

as good cheap, as cheap. See Glossary under *cheap*.

42. salamander, a kind of lizard, popularly supposed to live in fire.

48. Dame Partlet the hen. This is the name of the hen in *Reynard the Fox* and in Chaucer's *Nonnes Preestes Tale*. The word *partlet* means, literally, a ruff, and was applied to the hen because of the ruff of feathers on its neck.

65. Dowlas. A coarse linen made in Britanny.

66. bolters, canvas sieves.

69. by-drinkings, drinkings between meals.

75. denier, a French copper coin of the value of a tenth of a penny.

younker, greenhorn.

76. take mine ease . . . inn. The saying was a proverbial one. The word *inn* meant originally any place of abode, and this is its meaning in the old saying. Falstaff, however, uses the word in its modern sense as well.

78. mark. The value of the mark was 13s. 4d.

81. Jack, a common term of contempt.

sneak-cup, a coward in his potations; literally, one who sneaks from his cups.

84. is the wind . . . door, is this [marching to battle] the order of the day.

86. Newgate fashion, *i.e.* like criminals.

108. a drawn fox, a fox that has been drawn from his hole and is therefore cowed and spiritless.

109. Maid Marian. Maid Marian was a personage associated with the May-day games, and especially with the morris-dance, which was chiefly connected with May-day. The performers of this part in later times were often women of ill-fame, and this ill odour clings to the name in its use here, and again in Harrington's translation of Ariosto's *Orlando Furioso*, xlii. 37:

> "Not like a queene, but like a vile maide Marian,
> A wife, nay slave, unto a vile barbarian".

Maid Marian was also associated with Robin Hood, and here, curiously enough, she shines as a model of chastity.

109, 110. **the deputy's wife of the ward**, the wife of the police officer of the town-ward, *i.e.* a woman of respectability.

122. **where to have her**, in which class ("fish or flesh") to place her.

128. **ought**, owed. Cf. Heywood's *Edward IV*:
   " I had not ought thee so much as I do ".

See Glossary.

145. **I pray God . . . break.** Steevens sees in this an allusion to the old proverb, "Ungirt, unblessed", which is quoted by Dekker in his *Witch of Edmonton*.

150. **embossed**, swollen. See Glossary.

153. **injuries**, objects the loss of which might seem a grievance.

155. **pocket up wrong**, tamely submit to injustices.

165. **I am pacified still, I am always a peacemaker.** Hanmer placed the full-stop after pacified, and read ' Still?' *i.e.* "Are you still unsatisfied?"

175. **with unwashed hands**, *i.e.* immediately.

181. **rebels.** The reference is to Hotspur and his confederates.

182. **I laud . . . them.** He praises the rebels because they have procured him "a charge of foot".

185. **Go bear this letter . . .** In the Qq. and Ff. the whole of the prince's speech is given as verse, the first six lines ending with the words Lancaster . . . Westmoreland . . . and I . . . time . . . hall . . . afternoon. It was Pope who first suggested that as far as the word *afternoon* the diction was prose, and most modern editors have accepted this change. It must, however, be pointed out that there is little or nothing in the substance of the speech, or in the manner of its delivery, which would suggest a change from prose to verse after the word *afternoon*, and it is therefore possible that a verse-rendering of the whole passage is what Shakespeare intended. The change of diction indicates a change in the direction of the prince's thoughts.

189. **temple hall;** probabl a hall in the Temple, one of the Inns of Court.

192. **furniture**, equipment.

193. **burning.** The word is not to be taken literally, but in the metaphorical sense of ' consumed with warlike ardour '.

196. **my drum**, my rallying-place, my recruiting-station. "I could wish that it was here I had to enlist my soldiers (as was done by beat of drum) instead of having to march about in quest of them " (Deighton).

Act IV—Scene 1

Each scene brings us nearer to that engagement at Shrewsbury which gives to the play its dramatic unity. The epic
character of this, as of most of the history-plays, does not permit of a regular rise and fall—strophe and catastrophe—of the
action such as we find in many of Shakespeare's tragedies, but
the Percy rebellion, or at least that section of it in which Hotspur is the chief actor, gives to *1 Henry IV* a singleness of
theme, and furnishes it with a crisis. In the scene before us
the sense of impending failure, which we foresaw already in
act iii, scene 1, is deepened; we learn of Northumberland's
excuses and of Glendower's inability to unite his forces with
those of the other rebels. The high spirits of Hotspur rise
above these disappointing tidings, but to the more prudent
Worcester they bear "a frosty sound". Even Hotspur's
optimism is tinged with misgivings, and the last words which
he utters in this scene—"Doomsday is near; die all, die
merrily"—suggest that he also foresees defeat. Holinshed's
account of the meeting of Worcester and Hotspur, and of the
illness of Northumberland, is as follows:—" Howbeit when the
matter came to triall, the most part of the confederates aban-
doned them, and at the daie of the conflict left them alone.
Thus after that the conspirators had discovered themselves,
the lord Henrie Persie desirous to proceed in the enterprise,
upon trust to be assisted by Owen Glendouer, the earle of
March, and other, assembled an armie of men of armes and
archers foorth of Cheshire and Wales. Incontinentlie his
uncle Thomas Persie earle of Worcester, that had the government of the prince of Wales, who as then laie at London in
secret manner, conveied himselfe out of the princes house, and
comming to Stafford (where he met his nephue) they increased
their power by all waies and meanes they could devise. The
earle of Northumberland himselfe was not with them, but being
sicke, had promised upon his amendement to repaire unto them
(as some write) with all convenient speed."

3-5. **Such attribution . . . world,** ' such a tribute of praise
should you win, Douglas, that no soldier of this present age
should be so well received by men throughout the world '. **so
general current,** in such universal currency. The metaphor is
of a coin which passes current among every nation.

6. **defy,** refuse, renounce. The word is used with a similar
meaning by Hotspur in i. 3. 228, 229:

"All studies here I solemnly defy,
    Save how to gall and pinch this Bolingbroke".

7. **soothers,** sycophants.

9. task me to my word, put my words to the test.

approve, prove.

11. No man so potent . . . Shakespeare's Douglas, though brave, is a boaster and a shallow egoist. In this scene he shows little intellectual power, boasts of his valour, and harps on the word 'fear' to the last degree of childishness.

12. beard, encounter.

18. justling, jostling, bustling.

24. He was . . . physicians, his physicians were alarmed about him.

28. this sickness doth infect, &c. Hotspur, though he chafes at his father's absence, is too generous to attribute that absence to its real cause—cowardice. Here we are informed that Northumberland was 'sick'. In *Part II*, when the battle is over, and Hotspur dead, we learn that he was "crafty-sick".

30. 'T is catching hither. The infection reaches as far as this camp.

31. inward sickness, internal disease. Hotspur is too impetuous to finish the sentence.

32. by deputation, by sending a representative instead of going himself.

35. On any soul removed, on any stranger.

36. advertisement, advice.

37. conjunction, allied force.

39. there is no . . . now, there must be no hesitation now.

40, 41. possess'd Of, acquainted with.

44. And yet, in faith, it is not . . . Optimism and eagerness for the fray make a sophist of Hotspur. He proceeds to find reasons why Northumberland's absence is an advantage to them, but succeeds in convincing only Douglas, whose intellect is weak, while his devotion to Hotspur is very strong.

his present want, his failure to join us now.

46, 47. To set . . . cast, to stake at one throw all that we have: **states,** worldly positions, fortunes. Cf. *As You Like It*, v. 4:

> "Shall share the good of our returned fortune
> According to the measure of their states".

47. main, a hand of cards (Fr. *main*).

48. nice hazard, precarious chance.

49, 50. **for therein . . . hope,** 'in doing this we should realize that all our hopes were fixed on a single encounter'.

51. **list,** limit, boundary. Cf. *Hamlet*, iv. 5:

> "The ocean overpeering of his list".

53. **Where,** whereas.

reversion, a hope in store for us. Compare the phrase "A comfort of retirement" (l. 56).

54, 55. **We may boldly . . . to come in,** we may boldly use up our present forces, having the prospect of reinforcement afterwards.

56. **A comfort of retirement,** the consolation that we have something to fall back upon.

58. **look big,** loom ominously.

61. **hair,** complexion, character. For this metaphorical use of the word, cf. Beaumont and Fletcher's *Nice Valour*:

> "A lady of my hair cannot want pitying".

69. **offering,** challenging, attacking.

71. **loop,** loophole.

73. **draws,** draws back.

78. **A larger dare,** a greater boldness.

83. **Yet,** so far.

90. **No harm;** that will do us no injury.

92. **Or hitherwards . . . speedily,** or is planning a march hither very soon.

95. **madcap Prince of Wales.** Hotspur's opinion of Prince Henry is still the same as it was in act i, scene 3.

96. **daff'd the world aside,** thrust on one side all the serious concerns of life.

98, 99. **All plumed . . . lately bathed.** The reading of the Qq. and Ff. is as follows:

> "All plumed like estridges that with the wind
> Baited like eagles having lately bathed".

This conveys no meaning, and Malone accordingly suggested that some such verse as—

> "Run on, in gallant trim they now advance"

had fallen out after *wind*. Douce's suggestion, however, of reading *bated* (=fluttered their wings) for *baited*, and of placing a comma after it, makes sense of the passage without any such addition. 'All are equipped and under arms, all are in full feather like ostriches which have been fluttering their wings in the wind, or like eagles which are shaking the moisture from their wings after their bath.' This use of the word *bated* occurs elsewhere in Shakespeare, and also in the following letter of Bacon: "Now I am like a hawk that bates when I see occasion of service, but cannot fly because I am ty'd to another's fist". Douce declares further that by *estridges* are meant not *ostriches* but *goshawks*, and quotes the following verse from *Antony and Cleopatra* in support of this:

"And in that mood the dove will peck the estridge".

100. images. These would be images of the Virgin Mary and of saints which in Catholic churches are decked in splendid apparel on festive occasions.

104. I saw young Harry . . . Of all the historic characters of the play Vernon alone discerns the true nature of the Prince of Wales. He paints for us an heroic prince, and his genuine admiration for his noble foe gives an heroic quality to the words he utters. His whole speech is deeply poetic and kindled with the fire of exalted imagination. Hotspur chafes at these words of praise, and betrays a strain of ungenerousness in an otherwise generous nature. Yet the thought of the coming battle fires his imagination, and his speech takes on some of the ardour of his temper.

beaver, helmet. See Glossary.

105. cuisses, thigh-guards.

106. feather'd Mercury. Statues of the Greek god Hermes, the Roman Mercurius, represent him as having little wings springing from his sandals, suggestive of rapid flight.

107. vaulted. Malone suggests that we should read *vault it*.

110. witch, bewitch, charm.

113. They come . . . trim, they come like victims decked for sacrifice.

114. the fire-eyed maid of smoky war, Bellona.

118. reprisal, capture, prize.

119. taste, test. The Ff. read *take*.

126. cannot. This is the reading of the Ff.; the Qq., curiously enough, read *can*.

129. battle, battalion, army.

132. The powers of us, our powers, forces.

may serve, shall be sufficient for.

Scene 2

The king's forces are now on the march towards Shrewsbury, and amongst them is Falstaff with the charge of foot
with which the prince has supplied him.   The gross unscrupulousness of the knight's character is here completely
laid bare. He is devoid of all sense of honour, and stands out
by his own confession a bare-faced rogue. The use which he
has made of his commission is unpardonable; at the king's
expense he has acquired " three hundred and odd pounds ",
and has provided himself with a company of soldiers of whom
the best that even he can say is that they are " food for
powder ". The prince does not reproach him, but the incident
is assuredly remembered by him, and bears fruit in those
words spoken by Henry as king at the close of *2 Henry IV*;
" I know thee not, old man; fall to thy prayers ".

3. **Co'fil'**, the local pronunciation of Coldfield; Sutton Coldfield is a village in Warwickshire.   This is the Cambridge
Editors' emendation for the *Sutton cophill* of the Qq. and Ff.

5. **Lay out**, spend freely.

6. **makes** an angel, brings our wine-bill to an angel. The
angel, which bore the figure of the archangel Michael slaying
a dragon with his spear, was equal to about ten shillings at
this time. Shakespeare elsewhere plays with the double meaning of the word, and it is very likely that such word-play is
intended here.

8. **I'll answer the coinage**, I'll find the money.

11. **If I be not ashamed of my soldiers . . .**   Falstaff
professes shame for his conduct, and then gives an exhibition
of his shamelessness by describing in detail the condition of
his tatterdemalion company. The description is given with a
realism which conceals nothing, but lingers fondly over every
disgraceful detail.

      soused, pickled in vinegar. " Soused gurnet " was con-
sidered a vulgar dish, and the phrase is used rather frequently
as a term of reproach in Elizabethan literature.

12. **the king's press**, the king's orders to impress or enlist
soldiers.

15. **contracted**, affianced.

17. **commodity**, collection.
      warm, amorous.

18. **caliver**, a small musket.

19. **a struck fowl**, a wounded wild-fowl.

20. **toasts - and - butter**, literally eaters of buttered toast, *i.e.*
pampered persons.   In Moryson's *Itinerary* (1617) we read:

"Londiners and all within the sound of Bow-bell are in re-proach called cocknies and eaters of buttered toastes".

22. **ancients**, ensigns. Pistol is called "ancient Pistol" in *Henry V*. See Glossary.

23. **gentlemen of companies**, subordinate officers.

24. **the painted cloth.** Cloth or canvas, with pictures or mottoes painted upon it, served as a hanging for council-rooms and the rooms of dwelling-houses. In Shakespeare's *Lucrece* there occurs the couplet:

> "Who fears a sentence, or an old man's saw,
> Shall by a painted cloth be kept in awe".

26. **unjust**, dishonest.

27. **revolted**, out of employment.

27, 28. **trade-fallen**, out of service.

28. **the cankers . . . peace.** The force of these words is made clear by the following quotation from Nash's *Pierce Penniless*, 1592: "All the canker-worms that breed on the rust of peace".

29. **faced**, patched. The Ff. and some modern editors read *old-fac'd*.

ancient. Here ancient is not the standard-bearer, but the standard itself.

33. **draff**, refuse.

mad, whimsical.

37. **flat**, certain.

37, 38. **the villains . . . gyves on.** 'The wretched creatures walk with their legs far apart, as though they had fetters on their ankles.'

39. **There's but.** This is Rowe's emendation of the *There's not* of the Qq. and Ff.

44. **Daventry**, a municipal borough in Northamptonshire, on the road from London to Shrewsbury.

45. **linen . . . on every hedge.** The stealing of linen hung out to bleach on the hedges was one of the accomplishments of Autolycus:

> "The white sheet bleaching on the hedge,—
> With, heigh! the sweet birds, O, how they sing!—
> Doth set my pugging tooth on edge;
> For a quart of ale is a dish for a king".
>
> —*Winter's Tale*, iv. 2.

46. **blown**, inflated, fat.

quilt, flock-bed.

49. **I cry you mercy.** I crave pardon for not addressing you before.

52. **powers,** soldiers, forces.

53. **looks for,** expects.

53, 54. **away all night;** the Ff. read *away all to-night.*

62. **good enough to toss,** good enough to be impaled on the enemy's pikes. Cf. *3 Henry VI,* i. 1:

" The soldiers should have toss'd me on their pikes,
    Before I would have granted to that act ".

63. **pit,** grave.

70, 71. **three fingers on the ribs,** with ribs covered with fat to the thickness of three fingers.

76, 77. **To the latter . . . guest.** 'One who is a poor fighter but a good eater had better arrive when the fighting is over and the feast about to begin.'

Scene 3

We have now reached the eve of the battle of Shrewsbury. Hotspur, seconded by Douglas, who is in many ways an understudy to the famous Percy, urges that the battle shall be fought the same evening. Worcester and Vernon counsel delay, and, thanks to the arrival of Sir Walter Blunt, bearing messages from the king, they carry their point, though Hotspur and Douglas remain unconvinced of the wisdom of such delay. The charges brought by Hotspur against the king, like the similar charges of Worcester in act v, scene 1, are unanswerable: the whole conduct of the play of *Richard II* bears witness to their truth. Their formal statement here serves to connect the two plays more closely.

7. **You speak it out of fear and cold heart.** Douglas, who is a mere war-dog, can see in strategic policy only an exhibition of fear.

10. **well-respected honour,** dictates of honour duly considered.

17. **leading,** generalship.

19. **expedition,** ability to make a rapid advance.

21. **horse,** cavalry.

22. **their pride and mettle is asleep,** their high spirits and keenness are dulled.

26. **In general,** for the most part.

journey-bated, tired with the journey.

36. **quality,** fellowship, party.

38. **defend,** forbid.

7*   (B 101)

39. out of limit and true rule, acting in defiance of law and good government.

40. You stand against anointed majesty. Sir Walter Blunt's allegiance to Henry IV is something more than a personal matter. He sees in Henry "anointed majesty", the divinely-chosen representative of the common-weal.

41. charge, commission, duty.

The king hath sent to know . . . We discover from Blunt's words that Henry has the interests of England much more at heart than the rebels, who have proposed to divide the country between them. He shrinks from the thought of bloodshed and civil war, desires to know the grievances of his enemies, and is ready to treat them with the utmost generosity, if war may thereby be prevented.

42. griefs, grievances.

whereupon, upon what charges.

51. suggestion, instigation.

56. was not six and twenty strong, had less than twenty six followers. Holinshed mentions "three score" as the number of Bolingbroke's followers on his arrival at Ravenspur.

57. Sick in the world's regard, despised by the world.

62. To sue his livery, to seek the handing over of his inheritance. During Bolingbroke's exile, his father John of Gaunt, Duke of Lancaster, had died (see *Richard II*), and by the laws of feudal tenure the property of the dead man was in the hands of the court of wards until such time as the heir should come to claim it. The heir who thus put in his claim was said to "sue out his livery". Cf. *Richard II*, ii. 3:

> "I am denied to sue my livery here,
> And yet my letters patent give me leave".

68. The more and less, the nobles and the common people.

with cap and knee, submissively, kneeling before him cap in hand.

70. Attended him, waited upon him.

72. Gave him . . . follow'd him. This is Malone's punctuation of the verse; the Qq. and Ff. read, "Gave him their heirs as pages follow'd him".

74. as greatness knows itself, when his importance came to be recognized; knows itself, makes itself known.

79. certain, particular; **strait,** exacting.

82. by this face, by this appearance of clemency.

85. me. This is one of the many instances in the play of Shakespeare's use of the Ethical Dative. See Glossary.

87. **In deputation**, as his deputies.

88. **was personal in**, was personally engaged in.

92. **in the neck of**, following immediately upon. This phrase, like the phrase *at heel of*, which occurs in *Antony and Cleopatra*, is a metaphor from the race-course. Cf. Sonnet, cxxxi:

> "A thousand groans . . .
> On one another's neck do witness bear
> Thy black is fairest in my judgment's place".

task'd, taxed.

95. **engaged**, kept as a hostage. The word is used with the same meaning in v. 2. 44: "And Westmoreland, that was engag'd, did bear it". Pope proposed to read *encag'd*.

98. **intelligence**, spies.

103. **This head of safety**, this band of conspirators raised as a means of safety.

108. **impawn'd**, given as a pledge.

Scene 4

This scene, except in as far as it shows the weakness of the confederates, has no very direct bearing upon the play. It serves, however, as a useful connecting-link between *1 Henry IV* and *2 Henry IV*, the Archbishop of York being one of the chief leaders of the second part of the rebellion with the story of which the latter play is concerned.

1. **Sir Michael.** This was probably the Archbishop's chaplain, to whom 'sir' is used as a title of courtesy. Cf. *Sir* Oliver Martext, the hedge-parson in *As You Like It*.

brief, letter, document.

2. **the lord marshal.** This was Thomas Mowbray, Duke of Norfolk, whose quarrel with Bolingbroke is set forth at the beginning of *Richard II*. *Marshal* is a trisyllable here; see Metrical Notes.

10. **Must bide the touch**, must be put to the test.

13. **Lord Harry**, Harry Percy.

15. **in the first proportion**, of the first magnitude.

17. **a rated sinew**, a highly estimated source of strength.

31. **moe**, more. See Glossary.

corrivals, knights that emulate each other in deeds of prowess.

dear, prized.

Act V—Scene 1

As we enter upon the last act, we find the two armies in the neighbourhood of Shrewsbury in the early morning of the day of battle. Shakespeare is fond of referring to the climatic conditions of the day on which some great battle is to be fought. We find the same reference before the battle of Bosworth Field at the end of *Richard III*. There is, too, a suggestion here of a certain accord between the forces of Nature and the armed forces of the two combating parties. The scenic background to the battle-field is one of wind and tempest, and Nature is represented as sympathizing with the turmoils of men.

The charges brought by Worcester against the king are substantially the same as those with which we are already acquainted, and in adducing them at this point Shakespeare is only amplifying Holinshed's story. The offer of the Prince of Wales to engage in single combat with the peerless Hotspur bears witness to his gallantry, as his high praise of Hotspur does to his generosity of mind. Chivalrous as Hotspur is, the chivalry of the prince is of a finer temper. While the latter pays a high tribute to his rival's valour, Hotspur refuses to see in the prince anything but a madcap and a libertine.

The rapid progress and the martial excitement of the latter half of the play does not allow whole scenes to be allotted to the Falstaff prose comedy. The most that Shakespeare can grant us is a prose episode at the close of the scenes. But though confined to a narrow compass, the wit and humour of Falstaff are as dazzling as in the longer scenes laid in the Boar's Head Tavern. His catechism on the tyranny of honour is a noble *apologia* for his conduct when brought face to face with the " hot termagant Scot, Douglas ".

The historical incidents of this scene are recorded by Holinshed as follows:—" Now when the two armies were incamped, the one against the other, the earle of Worcester and the lord Persie with their complices sent the articles (whereof I spake before) by Thomas Caiton, and Thomas Salvain esquiers to King Henrie, under their hands and seals, which articles in effect charged him with manifest perjurie, in that (contrarie to his oth received upon the evangelists at Doncaster, when he first entred the realme after his exile) he had taken upon him the crowne and roiall dignitie, imprisoned King Richard, caused him to resigne his title, and finallie to be murthered. Diverse other matters they laid to his charge, as leviing of taxes and tallages, contrarie to his promise, infringing of lawes and customes of the realme, and suffering the earle of March to remaine in prison, without travelling to have him delivered. All which things they as procurors and protectors of the

commonwealth, tooke upon them to proove against him, as
they protested unto the whole world.

"King Henrie after he had read their articles with the defiance
which they annexed to the same, answered the esquiers that he
was readie with dint of sword and fierce battell to proove their
quarrell false, and nothing else than a forged matter, not doubt-
ing but that God would aid and assist him in his righteous
cause, against the disloiall and false forsworne traitors. The
next daie in the morning earlie, being the even of Marie
Magdalene, they set their battels in order on both sides, and
now whilest the warriors looked when the token of battell
should be given, the abbat of Shrewesburie, and one of the
clearks of the privie seale, were sent from the king unto the
Persies, to offer them pardon if they would come to any reasonable agreement. By their persuasions, the lord Henrie Persie
began to give eare unto the kings offers, and so sent with them
his uncle the earle of Worcester, to declare unto the king the
causes of those troubles, and to require some effectuall reformation in the same."

2. busky, bushy, woody. " I do not know whether Shakespeare ever surveyed the ground of the battle-field, but he has
described the sun's rising over Haughmond Hill from that spot
as accurately as if he had. It still merits the name of a *busky*
hill " (Blakeway).

3. his, *i.e.* the sun's.

　　distemperature, disordered colour.

4. Doth play . . . purposes, announces the sun's inten-
tions.

13. our old limbs. King Henry was in reality only thirty-
seven years of age at the time of the battle of Shrewsbury,
Prince Henry being a boy of fifteen: but Shakespeare makes
father and son a good deal older than this.

17. orb, orbit; ' will you return to that path of obedience?'

19. an exhaled meteor. The king contrasts the erratic
course of the meteor with the regular course of the planets
moving in their " obedient orb ". The belief was that meteors
were exhalations or evaporations from the earth caused by the
sun's heat. Cf. *Romeo and Juliet*, iii. 5:

　　" It is some meteor that the sun exhales ".

21. broached . . . times, mischief which will run its course
in the future. The figure is that of *broaching* or tapping a cask
of ale.

24. entertain, occupy.

26. the day of this dislike, this unpleasant day.

28. Rebellion lay . . . found it. It is instructive to notice

that Falstaff is present on this formal occasion and associating
with the highest in the land.   We are prone to connect Falstaff
with Bardolph and Dame Quickly, and to forget that a wide
social gulf separated him from these.   In reality Falstaff was
a knight of high standing.   In his youth he had been page
to Mowbray, Duke of Norfolk, and had lived on terms of
familiarity with the great John of Gaunt himself (see *2 Henry
IV*, iii. 2).

29. chewet, chough, jackdaw; Fr. *chouette*.   The word is
thought to be used in the sense of 'chatterer'.

32. remember, remind.

34. my staff of office. Cf. *Richard II*, ii. 2:

Bushy. Why have you not proclaimed Northumberland
And all the rest revolted faction traitors?
Green. We have: whereupon the Earl of Worcester
Hath broke his staff, resign'd his stewardship,
And all the household servants fled with him
To Bolingbroke.

The staff of office which Worcester broke at this time was that
of steward of the king's house.

44. new-fall'n right, the claim to the Duchy of Lancaster,
which was Bolingbroke's on the death of his father.

49. the absent king.   Richard was then in Ireland.

51. sufferances, sufferings.

58. Forgot . . . at Doncaster.   Holinshed's account of this
is as follows:—"At his comming unto Doncaster, the earle of
Northumberland, and his sonne sir Henry Persie, wardens
of the marches against Scotland, with the earle of Westmer-
land, came unto him, where he sware unto those lords, that
he would demand no more but the lands that were to him descended by inheritance from his father, and in right of his
wife".

60. that ungentle gull.   A gull in Elizabethan English
usually means a fool, a dupe, as in the title of Dekker's well-
known work, *The Gull's Hornbook*.   Here, however, it is used
in the sense of 'nestling'.   References to the nesting habits
of the cuckoo are common in Shakespeare, the following verses
uttered by the Fool in *King Lear* coming very near to the
passage here:

    "The hedge-sparrow fed the cuckoo so long,
        That it had it head bit off by it young" (i. 4).

64. of swallowing, of being swallowed.

69. dangerous countenance, threatening demeanour.

71. younger enterprise, your undertaking since you became
king.

72. **articulate,** articulated, set forth in articles. Holinshed and Hall give a long list of grievances, formally drawn up by the rebellious party, and submitted to the king.

74. **To face,** to overlay. The reference is to the ornamental facings of coats, &c.

76. **discontents,** discontented persons.

77. **rub the elbow:** This was a way of expressing satisfaction. Cf. *Love's Labour's Lost*, v. 2:

    " One rubb'd his elbow thus, and fleer'd and swore
      A better speech was never spoke before ".

78. **hurlyburly,** tumultuous.

79. **want,** lack.

80. **water-colours.** The reference is to the faintness and transitoriness of water-colour paintings as compared with those in oil.

81. **starving for,** dying for, longing for.

82. **pellmell.** See Glossary.

87. **by my hopes,** I swear by all that I hope for.

88. **This present . . . head,** taking no account of his share in this insurrection.

96. **Yet this,** *sc.* I assert.

100. **Try fortune with him in a single fight.** The prince's offer to engage in single combat with Hotspur is Shakespeare's own addition to the story. The offer shows alike the prince's bravery and his desire to spare the lives of the people. For the delivering of the challenge see v. 2. 47.

101. **so dare we venture thee,** we dare to stake your life in this encounter.

103. **No, good Worcester.** The king harks back to the thought with which his last speech ended.

104. **We love our people well . . .** These words furnish yet another indication of the king's love for his subjects, loyal or rebellious, and of his desire to spare their lives. His bearing in the scenes of negotiation before the battle is wholly kingly.

105. **upon your cousin's part** through the influence of your cousin Hotspur.

111. **Rebuke,** punishment.

    wait on us, are our attendants.

116. **both together,** united as they are.

119. **on their answer,** after receiving their refusal to submit.

121, 122. **bestride me,** stand above me and defend me.

122. so, good.

friendship, act of friendship.

130. prick me off, slay.

131. set to a leg, mend a broken leg.

137. insensible, unable to be grasped by the senses.

138. suffer it, suffer it to live.

139. scutcheon, a coat of arms borne in funeral processions and hung upon the walls of churches.

Scene 2

The story of Worcester's treachery in not imparting the king's terms to Hotspur is based on the words of Holinshed, but the motives which are ascribed to Worcester for keeping the matter secret are of Shakespeare's own devising. Holinshed writes: "It was reported for a truth, that now when the king had condescended unto all that was resonable at his hands to be required, and seemed to humble himselfe more than was meet for his estate, the earle of Worcester (upon his returne to his nephue) made relation clean contrarie to that the king had said, in such sort that he set his nephues hart more in displeasure towards the king, than ever it was before, driving him by that meanes to fight whether he would or not".

8. Suspicion. The Qq. Ff. read *supposition*. The emendation is Rowe's.

stuck full of eyes. "An allusion to Argus, son of Agenor, who had a hundred eyes, which, after his death, Hera transplanted to the tail of the peacock, her favourite bird" (Deighton).

12. sad, seriously.

13. misquote, misread.

18. an adopted . . . privilege, a privileged nickname, viz. Hotspur.

19. govern'd by a spleen, mastered by an impetuous disposition.

21. train, lure.

29. Deliver up . . . Westmoreland. Westmoreland had been in Percy's hands as hostage during the negotiations. See iv. 3. 108.

31. bid, offer.

32. Defy . . . Westmoreland, let the returning hostage carry to him our defiance.

35. no seeming mercy, no sign of mercy.

44. **engaged,** delivered up as hostage.

45. **Which cannot choose but,** which cannot do other than.

49. **draw short breath,** gasp in the fight.

51. **tasking.** This is the reading of the first Q. only; the later Qq. read *talking*. If we accept the reading 'tasking', the sentence means, 'How does his summons (his call to the task of fighting) sound?'

52. **I never in my life . . .** Vernon's praise of the prince, and Hotspur's contemptuous and ungenerous reply, is in almost exact imitation of the passage in iv. 1. 105–124.

57. **Trimm'd up,** decked out, recounted.

60. **By still . . . with you,** 'by always declaring that words of praise were not sufficient to represent your merits'.

62. **cital,** recital, statement.

64, 65. **As if . . . instantly,** 'as though he had suddenly acquired the power both of learning himself and of teaching others'.

66. **but let me tell the world . . .** It is interesting to compare this prophecy of Shakespeare's Vernon with that delivered by the prince's contemporary, Thomas Occleve, in his poem *De Regimine Principum*, written about 1411:

> "O worthy prynce, I trust in your manhode,
> Medled with prudence and discrecioun,
> That ye shulde make many a knightly rode,
> And the pride of our foes threste adowne".

67. **envy,** ill-will, malice.

68. **owe,** own, possess.

69. **So much . . . wantonness,** whose riotous behaviour has been so wrongly interpreted.

72. **libertine.** This is Capell's judicious emendation of the *libertie* of the Qq.

75. **That he . . . courtesy,** 'so that he shall tremble at the reception I shall give him'.

77–79. **Better consider . . . persuasion.** 'You can yourselves prepare your minds for the fight much better than I, who am no orator, can kindle your ardour by the force of my eloquence.'

83–85. **To spend . . . hour.** 'If the life of man did not extend beyond a single hour, it would still be of too long duration to permit meanness to enter into it.'

87. **brave death,** it will be a brave death.

88. for our consciences, as far as our consciences are concerned.

89. the intent of bearing them, the purpose for which we bear them.

92. For I . . . talking, talking is not my profession.

97. Esperance, a word of four syllables, as in French verse. See note to ii. 3. 67. Holinshed, in describing the battle of Shrewsbury, writes: "Then suddenlie [they] blew the trumpets, the kings part crieng S. George upon them, the adversaries cried *Esperance Persie*, and so the two armies furiouslie joined".

100. heaven to earth. I wager heaven against earth.

Scene 3

In his representation of the battle of Shrewsbury, Shakespeare claims the dramatist's license of altering in some measure the historical narrative to suit his dramatic purpose. It is Prince Henry's hour of triumph, and Shakespeare, in his great love for the prince, makes every incident in the fight contribute to that triumph. Of the prince's rescue of his father, and his subsequent victory over Hotspur, Holinshed says nothing, though he speaks eloquently of his valour. The portion of Holinshed's narrative which Shakespeare has used reads as follows:—"The prince that daie holpe his father like a lustie yoong gentleman: for although he was hurt in the face with an arrow, so that diverse noble men that were about him, would have conveied him foorth of the field, yet he would not suffer them so to doo, least his departure from amongst his men might happilie have striken some feare into their harts: and so without regard of his hurt, he continued with his men, and never ceassed, either to fight where the battell was most hot or to incourage his men where it seemed most need. This battell lasted three long houres with indifferent fortune on both parts, till at length, the king crieng Saint George victorie, brake the arraie of his enimies, and adventured so farre, that (as some write) the earle Dowglas strake him downe, and at that instant slue Sir Walter Blunt, and three other, apparreled in the king's sute and clothing, saieng: I marvell to see so many kings thus suddenlie arise one in the necke of an other. The king in deed was raised, and did that daie manie a noble feat of armes, for as it is written, he slue that daie with his owne hands six and thirtie persons of his enimies. The other on his part,[1] incouraged by his doings, fought valiantlie, and slue the lord Persie, called sir Henrie Hotspurre. To conclude, the king's enimies were vanquished, and put to flight, in which

[1] The rest of the king's men.

flight, the earle of Dowglas, for hast, falling from the crag of an hie mounteine, brake one of his cullions, and was taken, and for his valiantnesse, of the king freelie and franklie delivered." In treating his material Shakespeare's plan was to withdraw from the king his share in the victory and give it to the prince. Shakespeare tells us nothing of the king's gallant bearing in the fight, of which Holinshed gives so full an account: we hear only of the prince's heroism: further, the act of pardon granted by the king to Douglas is in the play (v. 5) the gift not of the king but of the Prince of Wales. Holinshed, again, makes no mention of Prince John's share in the battle, but Shakespeare introduces him in order that his bravery may serve as a foil to the greater bravery of his elder brother.

2. **crossest me**, crossest my path.

3. **Upon my head**, at my cost.

7, 8. **The Lord . . . likeness.** 'Lord Stafford has purchased his resemblance to thee at the cost of his life.'

21. **Semblably furnish'd like**, resembling in his equipment.

22. **A fool . . . goes.** 'Thou bearest the name of fool with thee (for pretending to be the king) whether thou art destined for heaven or hell.'

25. **The king hath many . . .** Daniel, in his *Civil Wars*, iv. 51, is still more precise:

> "For Henry had divided (as it were)
> The person of himself into four parts;
> To be less known, and yet known everywhere,
> The more to animate his people's hearts".

marching. Dyce proposed to read *masking*.

in his coats, in armour like his own.

30. **shot-free.** This is another form of *scot-free*.

31. **scoring.** Falstaff uses the word in the two senses of: (1) keeping an account of money owed; (2) hacking.

32. **there's honour for you.** Falstaff is thinking of his catechism on honour.

33. **here's no vanity.** Said ironically for 'here is vanity indeed'.

35. **I have led my ragamuffins . . .** It has been pointed out by those who are eager to defend Falstaff from the charge of cowardice that he has not shrunk from the perils of the fight, but has led his men where the battle was hottest. But is Falstaff to be believed?

37, 38. and they are . . . life, 'and they will have to live at the gates of London and maintain themselves by beggary'.

42. Whose deaths, the antecedent is 'many a nobleman'.

44. Turk Gregory. Falstaff has in mind the famous Hildebrand, who took the papal name of Gregory VII, and who, while friar, astonished Europe with his military exploits.

53. What, is it . . . now? For once Falstaff's pleasantry does not prove welcome to the prince.

54. pierce, pronounce 'perce'.

56. carbonado, a rasher of meat. Cf. *Coriolanus*, iv. 5: "Before Corioli he scotched him and notched him like a carbonado".

57. grinning honour, the honour of grinning death. Falstaff harps on the word honour, mindful of his catechism on honour in v. 1.

Scene 4

The passage from Holinshed's *Chronicle* on which this scene is based has already been quoted, and the reader's attention drawn to the modifications made by Shakespeare. The dramatic action here arrives at its climax; the rival Harries meet in single combat, and victory rests with the "sword-and-buckler Prince of Wales", for whom Hotspur has shown such undisguised contempt. Hotspur's death, like his life, is honourable; the thought that death is imminent does not disturb him; his only regret is for the loss of honour which he has sustained through his defeat. The prince, generous as ever in his feelings for Hotspur, pays a chivalrous tribute to his dead foe:

"this earth that bears thee dead
    Bears not alive so stout a gentleman".

We reach here the region of the heroic; but Shakespeare, in the rare versatility of his mind, does not allow us to remain there long. There is, in fact, a rapid descent to comedy as the eye of the prince turns from the dead Percy to the seemingly dead Falstaff. The words, "I could have better spared a better man", exactly express the prince's attitude towards the knight, while the two verses which follow suggest that a reformation is beginning in the life of the prince; the old-time vanities of life are losing their charm for him. Falstaff's defence of his counterfeiting is conceived with the same superb humour as his catechism on honour; his taking upon himself the credit of Hotspur's slaughter is a delightful piece of make-believe. Incidentally, it throws some light upon Falstaff's character. It shows that the main purpose of all his lying is the playing of a huge joke; to maintain, as some have main-

tained, that he wishes his lies to be believed is in the present
instance preposterous, and the same is true in the case of the
lies which he tells after the Gadshill robbery. He lies from a
keen sense of humour, and not with an intent to deceive.

2, 3. Harry . . . thou . . . Lord John of Lancaster . . . you.
The king addresses his eldest son simply as Harry, and then
uses the familiar *thou*; the younger son is given his full title
and addressed as *you*. It would seem as though Shakespeare
wished to indicate a real sense of comradeship between father
and eldest son at this critical hour.

2. thou bleed'st too much. Holinshed relates that the
prince was wounded in the face by an arrow.

5. make up, advance to your post as commander-in-chief.

6. amaze, alarm.

13. stain'd, blood-stained.

15. We breathe too long, we take too long a respite.

21. at the point, at spear's distance.

22. lustier maintenance, sturdier endurance.

23. such an ungrown warrior. Prince John was in reality
only fourteen years old at this time, and Holinshed makes no
reference to him in his account of the fight.

25. like Hydra's heads. The reference is to the well-known
fable of the Lernean hydra, the cutting-off of whose nine heads
was one of the labours of Hercules.

41. Shirley. Holinshed mentions Sir Hugh Shorlie as one
of those slain on the king's side at the battle of Shrewsbury.

45, 46. Sir Nicholas Gawsey . . . Clifton. These are
Holinshed's Sir Nicholas Gausell and Sir John Clifton, both
slain at Shrewsbury while fighting for the king.

48. thy lost opinion, the reputation which you lost through
your riotous conduct.

49. makest some tender of, hast some regard for.

52. hearken'd for, waited eagerly for news of.

54. The insulting . . . over you, the hand of Douglas,
which was audaciously raised above your head to slay you.

55. in your end, in accomplishing your death.

65. Two stars . . . sphere, "an allusion to the Ptolemaic
system of astronomy in which several spheres, each having a
planet set in it, were supposed to be swung bodily round the
earth in twenty-four hours by the top sphere, the *primum
mobile*" (Deighton).

77. my youth, my renown for youthful prowess.

81. But thought's . . . fool. 'Thought is in subjection to mortal life, and mortal life is the sport of time'. Q1 reads *thoughts, the slaves of life*, the words "the slaves of life" being in apposition to thoughts, while the predicate of this, as well as of what follows, is "must have a stop".

83. I could prophesy. The idea of the power of prophecy possessed by dying men is best illustrated by the speech of the dying Gaunt in *Richard II*, ii. 1.

92. thee dead. This is the reading of Q7 and Q8; the earlier Qq. read *the dead*.

95. dear, hearty.

96. favours. The prince covers Hotspur's face with the scarf which he was wearing as knightly adornment.

105. should have a heavy miss of thee, should deeply miss thee.

108. dearer, of greater worth, with of course a pun on *deer*.

109. Embowell'd. Embowelling was resorted to in order to preserve the body until it could be embalmed.

112. powder, salt, pickle.

114. termagant. Termagant or Tervagant is the Italian Trivigante, a name supposed to be based on that of Diana Trivia. In the crusading times Termagant was supposed by crusaders to be the name of a false god of the Saracens.

scot and lot. Still a current phrase with the force of 'utterly', 'out and out'.

121. gunpowder Percy. An admirable epithet to express the explosive outbursts which were so characteristic of Percy.

125, 126. Nothing confutes me but eyes. 'Only those who could see us could prove that I did not slay him.'

137. I am not a double man. Falstaff is carrying Percy on his back, and he applies the prince's words, "Thou art not what thou seem'st", to his seemingly double body.

148. I'll take it upon my death, I'll stake my life upon it.

155. do thee grace, help thee to win the king's favour.

158. the highest, the highest part.

Scene 5

The victory of the king is now complete, and all that remains is to pass judgment upon the prisoners. Worcester and Vernon are sentenced to death, but the Prince of Wales, generous in all things, procures the freedom of Douglas, and then, with graceful courtesy, hands over to his brother John the privilege of delivering the earl from prison. The closing speech, uttered by the king, reminds us that the rebellion is as yet only partly quelled, and we realize that the two parts of *Henry IV* form in reality only one play which the limitations of time divided into two halves.

2. Ill-spirited, malicious.

4. turn . . . contrary, misconstrue.

5. tenour, nature, the nature of the trust placed in you as kinsman of Percy.

15. Other offenders . . . upon. "We will pause before passing sentence upon the other offenders."

20. Upon the foot of fear, fleeing in fear.

29. His valour shown . . . Compare Daniel's *History of the Civil Wars*, iv. 56:

> "And Douglas, faint with wounds, and overthrown,
> Was taken; who yet won the enemy
> Which took him, (by his noble valour shown
> In that day's mighty work) and was preserved
> With all the grace and honour he deserved".

33. give away, announce.

44. leave, cease from action.

APPENDIX

METRICAL NOTES[1]

In the strictly dramatic portions of Shakespeare's plays we find blank verse, rhyming decasyllabic verse, rhyming octosyllabic verse, and prose. The use of octosyllabic verse is almost exclusively confined to supernatural beings, such as the Fairies in *A Midsummer-Night's Dream*, or the Witches in *Macbeth*. The rhyming couplets of decasyllabic verse, which in the early plays are very frequent—in *Love's Labour's Lost* there are almost twice as many rhyming as rhymeless verses,—become more and more rare as Shakespeare advanced in his career, until in what is his last, or almost his last, play, *A Winter's Tale*, they disappear entirely. In *1 Henry IV* rhyme is rare, and is chiefly reserved for the endings of some of the scenes, or of speeches which are followed by the departure of the speaker from the stage. (See i. 3. 301-302; iii. 2. 179-180; iv. 1. 131-136; v. 3. 28-29; v. 4. 105-110; v. 5. 41-44.) There remain for consideration only blank verse and prose. As a general rule, it will be found that the historical scenes are in blank verse, the comic scenes in prose. The king, who is throughout a formalist, always speaks in verse; Falstaff, except when he parodies the "Cambyses vein", or rounds off a scene with a single rhyming couplet, keeps to a prose diction; Prince Henry and Hotspur use both verse and prose, and turn from the one to the other with surprising ease and readiness. The blank verse of Prince Henry in his soliloquy in i. 2, coming as it does after a long scene of prose, furnishes an excellent illustration of the differences of character of these two forms of diction. Poetry is the diction of tension, prose of relaxation.

Blank Verse.—Blank verse appeared for the first time

[1] These notes are chiefly based on the "Outlines of Shakespeare's Prosody", appended to Professor Herford's *Richard II* (Warwick Shakespeare). The student is referred to these "Outlines" for a fuller treatment of the subject.

in English poetry in Lord Surrey's translation of the Second
and Fourth Books of the *Æneid* (*circ.* 1543). Employed
for dramatic purposes by the authors of *Gorboduc* (acted
1561), it was Peele and Marlowe who first established it
as the recognized metre of dramatic poetry.   At the hands
of Shakespeare, blank verse acquired a suppleness and ease
of movement unknown to his predecessors, and the means
by which these qualities were acquired calls for a moment's
notice.   The following verses, which form the prologue to
Marlowe's first play, *Tamburlaine* (1590), and also serve
as a defence of this new form of metre, represent the chief
characteristics of pre-Shakespearean blank verse:

> From jigging veins of rhyming mother-wits,
> And such conceits as clownage keeps in pay,
> We'll lead you to the stately tent of war,
> Where you shall hear the Scythian Tamburlaine
> Threatening the world with high astounding terms,
> And scourging kingdoms with his conquering sword.
> View but his picture in this tragic glass,
> And then applaud his fortunes as you please.

When we examine these verses, we find that their tendency
is to conform too closely to the normal type of blank verse,
in which unaccented and accented syllables follow each
other with exact regularity:

> From jig′ | ging veins′ | of rhym′ | ing moth′ | er-wits′.

Weak accents and stress-inversion, though not entirely
absent, are rare, and accordingly the tendency of a large
number of such verses is towards monotony.   It will
further be noticed that each verse ends with an emphatic
word, and that there is a pause at the end of every verse
except the fourth, and no pause whatever in the middle
of the verses.

Now let us compare with this the following verses of
1 Henry IV (iii. 1. 25-35):—

> O, then the earth shook to see the heavens on fire,
> And not in fear of your nativity.
> Diseased nature oftentimes breaks forth
> In strange eruptions; oft the teeming earth
> Is with a kind of colic pinch'd and vex'd
> By the imprisoning of unruly wind
> Within her womb; which, for enlargement striving,
> Shakes the old beldam earth, and topples down
> Steeples and moss-grown towers.   At your birth
> Our grandam earth, having this distemperature,
> In passion shook.

If these verses are read aloud immediately after those from *Tamburlaine*, the advance in flexibility must be at once apparent. Examining the passage more closely, we observe (i) that six of the eleven verses have no pause at the end of them; (ii) that on four occasions the pause falls in the middle of the verse; (iii) that there is an extra syllable at the end of the seventh verse, and that several of the verses end with unemphatic words like ' forth ' and ' down '; (iv) that a weak stress occurs in the first foot in verses 5 and 6; inversion of stress in the first foot of verses 8 and 9, and the third foot of verse 7; while the second foot of verse 8 has two equally accented syllables instead of one accented and one unaccented syllable. There are several other variations from the type in this passage, but the above will suffice to illustrate the varied rhythm of Shakespeare's blank verse at this period of his career.

We have next to consider the various devices practised by Shakespeare in order to give to his verse suppleness and ease. Some of these have already been hinted at, but it remains to consider them more exactly.

1. One of the simplest devices is the use of a *weak stress* instead of a strong stress at some point in the verse. Representing the weak stress by a grave accent, the following verses will be scanned thus:

As to` | o'er-walk' | a cur' | rent roar' | ing loud' (i. 3. 192).
Which' the | proud' soul' | ne'er pays' | but to` | the proud' (i. 3. 9).

2. As though to compensate for this weak stress, it will often be found that the same verse contains another foot in which both syllables are equally accented. The last quoted verse is a good illustration of this, as are also the following :—

And for' | whose death' | we in` | the world's' | wide' mouth' (i. 3. 153).
Of this` | proud' king', | who stud' | ies day' | and night' (i. 3. 184).
To pluck' | bright' hon' | our from` | the pale'- | faced' moon' (i. 3. 202).

3. Almost as frequent as the weak or light stress is *stress-inversion*, in which the foot is made up of an accented syllable followed by an unaccented, instead of *vice versa*. This inversion is chiefly found in the first, third, or fourth feet, and usually follows either a metrical pause or a pause in the sense. In the second foot it is unusual, and still more so in the fifth. The following are examples of its use :—

Find' we | a time' | for fright' | ed peace' | to pant' (i. 1. 2).
Our house', | my sov' | ereign liege', | lit'tle | deserves' (i. 3. 10).
Breath'less | and faint', | lean'ing | upon' | my sword' (i. 3. 32).

We rarely find two inversions in succession, and never three.

4. **Extra Syllables.** — An extra unaccented syllable is sometimes found in the middle of a verse before a pause, and quite commonly at the end of a verse. In the latter case the verse is said to have a *double* or *feminine* ending. Such double endings are comparatively rare in Shakespeare's early plays, but very common in his later ones, and still more so in the works of Beaumont and Fletcher. In *1 Henry IV*, as indicated in the Introduction (p. xxiii), the double ending is peculiarly rare, the percentage of such endings falling as low as 5.1, whereas in *2 Henry IV* it rises to 16.3, and to 20.5 in *Henry V*. The following are instances:—

On Wednes' | day next, | Har'ry, | you shall' | set for' | ward (iii. 2. 173).
Proclaim'd' | at mark' | et-cross' | es, read' | in church' | es (v. 1. 73).
But do' | not use' | it oft', | let' me | entreat' | you (iii. 1. 175).

Instances of its occurrence in the middle of a verse, before a pause, or at a break in the dialogue, are the following:—

Of my' | young Har' | ry.   O' that | it could' | be proved' (i. 1. 86).
Those pris' | (o)ners you' | shall keep'.
        Hotspur.   Nay, I will'; | that 's flat' (i. 3. 218).
Make' up | to Clif'ton: | I 'll' to | Sir Nich' | (o)las Gaws' | ey (v. 4. 58).

With regard to the last instance, it may be pointed out that Shakespeare allowed himself great license in his treatment of proper names. It is often impossible to subject verses in which proper names occur to the ordinary metrical rules: such verses must in fact often be treated as extra-metrical.

5. **Omission of Stresses.**—This is a far less usual variation from the normal blank verse than those noticed above, but instances are found here and there throughout Shakespeare's plays. The omission always follows a distinct pause, frequently that produced by a break in the dialogue:

Not' an | inch' furth' | er', | But hark' | you, Kate' (ii. 3. 110).
Before' | not dreamt' | of'. |
        Hotspur.   You strain' | too far' (iv. 1. 75).

6. **Pauses.**—In speaking of the pauses in blank verse, it is necessary to distinguish between (i) the metrical pause and (ii) the sense pause. In pre-Shakespearean blank verse the sense pause usually coincides with the metrical pause (see the quotation from *Tamburlaine*), but with Shakespeare this happens far less frequently. As we follow him through his career we find a growing tendency to make the sense pause fall in the middle of a verse instead of at the end. This non-coincidence of sense pause with metrical pause is called *enjambement* or overflow, and verses in which there is no sense pause at the end of the verse are called 'run-on' verses, in opposition to those which are 'end-stopt'. The percentage of run-on verses in *1 Henry IV* is 14.2, as compared with 2.9 in *Richard III*, and 18.3 in *Henry V*; in such late plays as *Cymbeline* and *The Winter's Tale* the percentage of run-on verses rises to between 40 and 50.

7. **Light and Weak Endings.**—Closely bound up with the use of run-on verses in Shakespeare is his use of light and weak endings.[1] Rare in the early plays, these become more and more frequent as Shakespeare's art developed, though they are always much rarer than the run-on verses. According to Prof. Dowden's table, they are most frequent in the Shakespearean portions of *Henry VIII*, where the percentage of weak and light endings together reaches 7.16. The following are instances of the light ending in *1 Henry IV*:—

> To Owen Glendower. and, dear coz, to you
> The remnant northward, . . .   (iii. 1. 78).
> And that his friends by deputation could not
> So soon be drawn.   (iv. 1. 32).
> So please your majesty, I would I could
> Quit all offences. . . .   (iii. 2. 18).

Weak endings are much rarer, and it is doubtful whether a single instance of such an ending occurs in our play.

8. So far it has been assumed that all of Shakespeare's verses contain five feet; this, however, is not the case. Short verses, containing four or less feet, occur quite occasionally, and here and there we find an *alexandrine* or verse of six feet. Short verses, consisting at times of a single foot, are found at the commencement of some of the

[1] For the explanation of these terms see Dowden's Primer, p. 41.

speeches, especially when the words are in the nature of
an address or an exclamation, *e.g.*:

> In faith, (i. 1. 76).
> Nay, (i. 3. 223).
> My good lord, (iv. 4. 6).
> Revolted Mortimer! (i. 3. 93).

Other instances of short verses are the following:—

> At Holmedon met (i. 1. 55).
> I tell thee (i. 3. 115).
> Had been alive this hour (v. 5. 8).

Note, too, the short, abrupt conversation of Hotspur and
Lady Percy in ii. 3. 70–76, where the shortness of the
verses adds to the studied abruptness of the conversation.

9. **Alexandrines.**—The use of true alexandrines is much
rarer; many verses which appear to contain six feet can
by means of an elision of unaccented syllables, be brought
within the compass of the normal blank verse of five feet.
But here and there occur verses which cannot be so com-
pressed, and which we must accordingly scan as alexandrines, *e.g.*:

On some | great sud | den hest. | O, what | portents | are these? (ii. 3. 59).
As you, | my lord, | or an | y Scot | that this | day lives (iv. 3. 12).
Suspic | ion all | our lives | shall be | stuck full | of eyes (v. 2. 8).

Syllabic Variation.—The Elizabethan dramatists, and
Shakespeare among them, were fond of employing such
syllabic variation as the language permitted, and the frequency with which such variations are introduced points
to the great flexibility of the English tongue in Shakespeare's time. The language was, in fact, much more
pliable than it is to-day, and the dramatists knew well
how to make the most of this pliability in order to secure
for their verse as complete a freedom of movement as
possible. The following points, some of which are commonly met with in modern poetry, indicate the chief directions in which syllabic variation was possible.

(i) Loss of vowel before a consonant at the beginning of
of a word (*aphæresis*), e.g. '*twixt* for *betwixt*, '*friend* for
befriend, '*scape* for *escape*, '*cross* for *across* (see Abbot's
Shakespearean Grammar, § 460). Abbot regards the use
of the form *cital* for *recital* as an instance of such aphæresis in *1 Henry IV*:

He made a blushing *cital* of himself (v. 2. 62).

A very common form of aphæresis is the dropping of the
initial vowel of unemphatic monosyllables like *is*, *it*. Thus
we find *of it* contracted into *of't* in i. 3. 124, *took it* into
took't (i. 3. 39), *that is* into *that's*, &c.

(ii) Loss of vowel before a consonant medially (*syncope*).
This frequently takes place in the case of inflections:
com'st for *comest*, *short'st* for *shortest*; also in the case of
the middle syllables of three-syllabled words, *e.g.*: a′ff(a)ble
(iii. 1. 167), a′bs(o)lute (iv. 3. 50).

An interesting feature of Elizabethan English is the use
made of what are called '*vowel-likes*', *i.e.* consonants
which partake of the nature of vowels, and acquire at
times a syllabic value. The letters *l*, *m*, *n*, and *r* could be
either syllabic or non-syllabic according to the requirements of the verse. The following are instances of the
syllabic use of such '*vowel-likes*':—

> Good uncle, tell your tale; I′ have done (i. 3. 256).
> So tell your cousin, and bring me word (v. 1. 109).
> You speak it out of fear and cold heart (iv. 3. 7).
> With winged haste to the lord marshal (iv. 4. 2).

Here *tale*, *bring*, and *fear* are rendered dissyllabic by means
of the vowel-likes, *l* and *r*, while *marshal* must be pronounced as though it were *marishal*.

Where the vowel-likes are non-syllabic, they show a
tendency to cause elision of unaccented medial vowels.
Thus we find *inn(o)cency* (iv. 3. 63), *ignom(i)ny* (v. 4. 100),
del(i)ver (i. 3. 260), *p(e)rempt(o)ry* (i. 3. 17), *Hol(y)-rood*
(i. 1. 52), *hostil(i)ty* (iv. 3. 44). Elision after a vowel-like
could take place between the unaccented syllables of different words. This is especially the case with the termina-
tion *-able*, *-ible*, *e.g.*:

> Let it be tenable in your silence still (*Hamlet*, i. 2. 248)

Another frequent form of contraction occurs in the case
of two adjacent vowels, which may, or may not, occur in
the same word. Here belongs the Shakespearean use of
the suffix *-ion*. Where a word with this suffix occurs at
the end of a line, the suffix is usually dissyllabic; in other
cases, monosyllabic, *e.g.*:

> To keep | his an | ger still | in mo | tion (i. 3. 226).
> Come cur | rent for | an ac | cusa | tion (i. 3. 68);

but

> Imag | ina | tion of | some great | exploit (i. 3. 199).

The same principle is often observed in the case of words ending in *-ience*:

> Drives him | beyond | the bounds | of pa | tience (i. 3. 200).

Note also (i. 3. 64):

> He would | himself | have been | a sol | dier.

Words such as *marriage, cordial*, are usually dissyllabic in Shakespeare, while in i. 2. 183 *being* is to be scanned as a monosyllable.

Where the adjacent vowels belong to different words, one of the vowels was often suppressed, *e.g.*: *th' earth* (iii. 1. 25), *th' irregular* (i. 1. 40), *th' one* (pronounced *thōn*).

Occasionally we find that an intervocalic consonant in a dissyllabic word undergoes a process of slurring when followed by an unaccented syllable. Instances of this are *spirit* (ii. 3. 52), *having* (iii. 1. 34), *either* (i. 3. 27), *devil* (i. 3. 116), *father* (iii. 1. 195).

Accent Variation.—In dealing with accent variation it is necessary to distinguish between the native words and those of foreign (Romance) origin. Pronominal and prepositional compounds of native origin have frequently a variable accent, e.g.: *there'by* and *thereby'*, *with'out* and *without'*, *some'what* and *somewhat'*. Instances of accent-variation in the case of other native compounds is less common: *man'kind* and *mankind'*, *straight'way* and *straight-way'*.

In the case of Romance words we find the accent in Shakespeare sometimes placed nearer the end of a word and sometimes nearer the beginning than is the case in modern English. Thus in *1 Henry IV* we find *portent'* (v. 1. 20), *aspects'* (i. 1. 97), but also *ex'treme* (i. 3. 31) and *miscon'strue* (v. 2. 69). In many of these words the accent, as is quite frequently the case with Chaucer, is variable in character, and follows the requirements of the metre. Thus Shakespeare uses *ex'treme* and *extreme'*, *se'cure* and *secure'*, *com'plete* and *complete'*. Cf. also:

> And be no more an *ex'haled* meteor (*1 Henry IV*, v. 1. 19)

with

> Let their *exhaled'* unwholesome breaths make sick (*Lucrece*, 779).

Such variations are chiefly found in the case of adjectives, but in *Richard II* we find the noun *record* accented as *re'cord* in i. 1. 30, and as *record'* in iv. 1. 230.

GLOSSARY

admiral (iii. 3. 22). An admiral's ship, a flag-ship. The word is from the Arabic, *amir*, commander, which appears in English under the forms *ameer* and *emir*; the final -*al* is the Arabic definite article, which is prefixed to the root in *alchemy*, *alkali*, &c. Like most other early borrowings from Arabic the word has come to us indirectly through some Romance language. The change from *amiral* to *admiral* is due to confusion with the Latin prefix *ad-*. In the M.E. oriental romances the connection of an admiral with the sea is not yet established. Its use in the sense of an admiral's ship dates from Elizabethan times, and is perhaps due to Italian influence. Florio renders the Italian *ammiraglia* as "an admirall or chief ship".

an (*passim*), if. This is simply another form of *and* and is spelt *and* in the Folios. Its connection with the Scand. *enda* (=if) is doubtful; it is most probably a development of the meaning of the simple copulative conjunction. A similar change of meaning occurs in the case of the German *und* in its older form *unde*. The conditional force of *and*, *an* is often strengthened by *if* (iv. 2. 7).

ancient (iv. 2. 22), standard-bearer, ensign. The word *ancient* meant originally the standard itself, the person who bore it being the "ancient-bearer"; etymologically the word is a doublet of *ensign*; in M.E. its form is *enseigne*, O.F. *enseigne*, Low Lat. *insigna*. Confusion has apparently arisen between the M.E. *enseigne* and *ancien* (old), O.F. *ancien*, L.L. *antianum*; the resultant form being *ancient* with excrescent -*t*.

antic (i. 2. 56), grotesque figure. Apparently from Ital. *antico*, old, but used as equivalent to Ital. *grottesco*, grotesque, an adjective formed from *grotta* (a cavern), and originally applied to the fantastic representations of human and other forms found in exhuming the Baths of Titus and other Roman remains. In England the word was at first closely associated with the grotesque forms of the gargoyles found on churches; cf. Hall's *Chronicle*: "Above the arches were made mani sondri antikes and divises". *Antic* is thus not developed from *antique*.

apprehends (i. 3. 209), lays hold of with the intellect. From Fr. *appréhender*, Lat. *apprehendere*, 'to seize'. The idea of seizing is still retained in Shakespeare's use of the word here, and he distinguishes between *apprehend* and *comprehend*. Deighton adduces the following passage from *Midsummer-Night's Dream* (v. 1.), in illustration of the difference:

"Lovers and madmen have such
        seething brains,
Such shaping fantasies that apprehend
More than cool reason ever comprehends",

and adds that "the mere appre-
hending, the seizing upon an idea,
is contrasted with the comprehend-
ing, the completing by logical con-
notation, of that idea".

arrant (ii. 2. 94), notorious.
This word, which Skeat derived
from *arghand*, a Northern English
present participle of the M. E.
argien, O.E. *eargian*, to fear, is
really merely a variant of errant.
Its original sense was 'wandering'
(cf. 'knight errant'), whence the
depreciatory meaning of 'vagrant'
arose. It was frequently associated
with the word *thief*—"An out-
lawe or a thef erraunt" (Chaucer),
—and thus acquired finally the
meaning of notorious, thorough-
paced.

assay (v. 4. 34), make trial of.
From O.F. *assayer*, < L.L.
exagiare, < L. *exagium*. The
form *assay* is older than *essay*,
which first appears in Caxton;
assay is now confined in its usage
to the testing of metals. The
original force of the L. *exagium*
is 'a weighing', whence came the
derivative meaning 'a testing';
examine and *examination* (L.
exāmen = exagmen) are from the
same root.

basilisk (ii. 3. 50), a large cannon made of brass, and discharging
a shot of about 200 pounds weight.
Literally a fabulous reptile. The
word is derived, through the Latin
basiliscus, from the Greek
Βασιλίσκος, a diminutive of Βασιλεύς,
a king. The reptile was so called,
according to Pliny, because of a
spot resembling a crown on its
head.

beaver (iv. 1. 104), the lower
part of the face-guard of a helmet.
The word is from the old French
bavière, orig. a child's bib, from
bave, spittle.

bombast (ii. 4. 313), cotton-wool
used for padding. The form *bombast* is a variant of the obsolete

bombace, from Fr. *bombace*, L.
bombax, *bombacem*, cotton, a corruption of L. *bombyx*, Gk. Βομβυξ,
silk-worm, silk. The use of the
word *bombast* in the sense of 'inflated language' is a figurative use
of this word and has not, as is
generally supposed, sprung from
the name of Bombast von Hohen-
heim, usually known as Paracelsus.

buckram (ii. 4. 184), coarse linen
stiffened with gum or paste. The
origin of the word is uncertain,
but it is found under varying forms
in most of the languages of Europe
between the twelfth and fifteenth
centuries, *e.g.* O.F. *bouquerant*,
Ital. *bucherame*, M.H.G. *buggeram*.
Some refer the word to the Ital.
bucherare, 'to pierce with holes',
and maintain that the word was
first applied to muslin. Another
suggested derivation is *Bokhara*.

capering (iii. 2. 63), skipping.
The verb 'to caper' is from the
noun *caper*, which is an abbre-
viated form of *capriole*, O.F.
capriole (cf. Ital. *capriola*), diminutive of Lat. *capra*, 'a she-goat'.

carbonado (v. 3. 56), a piece
of meat scored across and broiled
upon the coals (Murray). From
Sp. *carbonado*, Lat. *carbo*, *car-
bōnem*, coal.

carded (iii. 2. 62), mixed, de-
based by mixing, adulterated.
According to Murray, this is a
figurative use of *card*, 'to stir or
mix with cards', and the following
quotation from Topsell's *Four-
footed Beasts* (1607) supports this
view: "As for his diet, let it be
warm mashes, sodden wheat and
hay, thoroughly carded with a pair
of wool-cards". *Carded* is therefore not to be regarded as a contracted form of *discarded*.

cates (iii. 1. 162), dainty fare.
The singular *cate* which has under-
gone aphæresis from *acate* is rarely
found. The original meaning of
the word is 'purchase', being de-

rived from the O. Fr. *acat* (cf. Mod. Fr. *achat*) and Low Lat. *accaptum*, *accaptare*, to purchase. It is thus connected etymologically with *catch* and *chase* as well as with *cater*.

cess (ii. 1. 7). The word is probably connected with *assess*; its meaning being assessment, estimate. As a verb, meaning to assess, estimate, it occurs in Stow's *Survey*: "To the fifteene it is *cessed* at foure pound ten shillings"; *assess* is from the Lat. *assessus*, *assidēre*, to sit beside, to be assessor to a judge.

cheap (iii. 3. 41, "bought me lights as good cheap at the dearest chandler's in Europe"). Here *cheap* is used in its original sense as a noun. The word occurs under the form *ceáp* (barter, a bargain) in O.E., and has cognate forms in most Teutonic languages. The contraction of *good cheap* (cf. Fr. *bon marché*) into *cheap*, whereby the word acquired an adjectival force, took place in the sixteenth century.

cozening (i. 2. 115), cheating; a word of uncertain origin, the earliest trace of which occurs in 1561 under the term *cousoner*, 'a vagabond'. Cotgrave connects it with *cousin* and Fr. *cousiner*, which he renders "to clayme kindred for advantage or particular ends, and hence to cheat".

culverin (ii. 3. 50). This was originally a hand-gun, but in Shakespeare's time the word had come to be used in the sense of a long cannon. Like *basilisk* (see above) it means literally a reptile, being derived from Lat. *colubrinus*, through the Fr. *coulevrine*, Ital. *colubrina*.

daffed (iv. 1. 96), put aside. Daff is a secondary form of doff = do off. In Elizabethan English there were several such verbs formed by the union of *do* with a preposition; *dout*, = do out, occurs in *Henry V*, and *dup*, = do up, in *Hamlet*. Cf. the Mod. E. *don* = do on.

distemperature (iii. 1. 34), disorder. From Med. Lat. *distemperatura*, Lat. *dis* + *temperare* to mix in wrong proportions. The word is used first of all in a physical sense, and refers to unhealthy conditions of the atmosphere; thence it was applied to the disordered condition of the 'humours' of the body (Murray).

dowlas (iii. 3. 65), coarse linen. From Daoulas or Doulas, a town near Brest in Brittany.

embossed (iii. 3. 150), swollen. For the use of the word applied to persons cf. *King Lear*, ii. 4, 227:

> "thou art a boil,
> A plague-sore, an embossed carbuncle".

To emboss means literally to cut in wood (O. Fr. *bos*, *bois*) and the sense of 'swollen' is derived from that of 'protuberant', from the protuberances or bosses of wood-carving.

engross up (iii. 2. 148), amass. From the Fr. *en gros* 'in the mass'. Lat. *in* + *grossus*, stout, thick. There is also a French verb *engrosser*, Lat. *ingrossare*.

estridges (iv. 1. 98), ostriches. A variant of ostrich, M. E. oystryche, O. Fr. ostruche, Lat. *avis struthio*, *struthio* being from the Gk. στρουθός, a bird.

expedience (i. 1. 33), haste, a hasty undertaking. The word first came into use at the time of the Revival of Letters, coming through the French from the Lat. *expedire*, which means literally 'to disengage the feet', and hence 'to remove obstacles', 'enable to act freely and promptly'. The modern adjectives *expeditious* and *expedient* bring out the two ideas of haste, promptitude, and freedom from obstacles.

foil (i. 2. 202), setting. The

word is from the O.Fr. *foil*, Lat. *folium*, a leaf, and the original use of the word was for the metal surface in which jewels were set, and which was so arranged as to set the jewels off to the best advantage.

frets (ii. 2. 2), wears away; it is the O.E. *fretan* from an orig. Germanic *fra-etan*, 'to eat away' (cf. Goth. *fra-itan* and M.H.G. *fressen*). O.E. *fretan*, like its simple form *etan*, was originally strong, but became weak in M.E. From the physical sense of eating away has been derived the metaphysical force of the modern verb 'to fret'.

gage (i. 3. 173), engage, pledge. O.Fr. *gager* and *gage*, 'a pledge'. The word is of Teutonic origin, found in Gothic under the form *wadi* from an earlier *wadjo*, O.E. *wedd* (cf. *wedding*). The Mod. E. *wage* and *wager* are from the Anglo-Norman forms of the Continental French *gager*: cf. *warrant* and *guarantee*, *warden* and *guardian*.

gammon (ii. 1. 19), the ham or haunch of a pig. From N.Fr. *gambon* (cf. Mod. Fr. *jambon*), O.Fr. *gambe*, a leg.

grief (i. 3. 51), physical pain. M.E. *grief*, *gref*; O.F. *grief*, *gref*, Lat. *gravis*, heavy, sad.

harness (iii. 2. 101), armour, men in armour. The old sense of the word is armour generally, and with this the etymology of the word agrees. O.Fr. *harnas*, Breton, *houarn*, O. Welsh, *haiarn*= iron. The word was formerly used much more for the armour of men than of horses.

humorous (iii. 1. 231), whimsical. The word *humour* means literally moisture, and in ancient and mediæval physiology the *humours* were the four fluids (blood, phlegm, choler, melancholy) the relative proportions of which in any person determined his state of health. Hence the mental application of the word 'humour' (cf. "Every Man in his Humour") arose out of the physical. Thus *humorous* meant first 'moist', then 'subject to moods', 'whimsical', 'odd'; while from the idea of oddness arose the modern sense of 'jocular'.

hurlyburly (v. 1. 78), tumultuous. Shakespeare uses the word both as adjective and noun. Cf. *Macbeth*: "When the hurly-burly's done". The word is not found before the sixteenth century. *Hurly* is connected with *hurling*, violent, and the verb *to hurl*, and *burly* seems to be merely an initially varied repetition of the word (Murray). Cf. *Skimble-scamble* (*1 Henry IV*, iii. 1. 153).

impeach (i. 3. 75), bring a charge against. This word, which appears in the form *appeach* in *Richard II*, means literally 'to catch by the feet, entangle' (Murray), from an O.F. form of Mod. F. *empêcher*, Lat. *impedicare*, *pedicam*, 'a snare', *pes*, *pedem*, 'a foot'.

impressed (i. 1. 21). According to Wedgwood and Skeat this word is a derivative from *press*, and has no connection with the Lat. *impressare*. To press soldiers (cf. *press-gang*) did not mean to compel them to serve, but to give them earnest-money as a pledge of service. "It is quite certain", says Skeat, "that *press* is a corruption of the old word *prest*=ready, because it was customary to give earnest-money to a soldier on entering service, just as to this day a recruit receives a shilling. This earnest-money was called *prest-money*, *i.e.* ready-money advanced, and to give a man such money was to *imprest* him, now corruptly written *impress*."

lewd (iii. 2. 13), vulgar, base. M.E. *lewed*, O.E. *lǽwede*, 'lay,

unlearned', also used as a sub-
stantive, 'layman'. The word
looks like a formation from the
O.E. weak verb *lǣwan* (to betray),
but the difference of meaning is
against this. Possibly it is a derivative from the Lat. *laicus*, or
laicatus, though the appearance
of a *w* in O.E. for the Lat. *c* makes
this questionable.

lieve (iv. 2. 17), glad. Another
form of *lief*, M.E. *lief*, *leef*,
O.E. *leóf*. The phrase, "I had
as lief" arose in M.E. times, and
gradually replaced the older use
with the verb 'to be' and the
dative of the person. Thus the
Cotton MS. of the *Cursor Mundi*
reads *us lever ware*, the Fairfax
MS. *we had leyver*.

manage (ii. 3. 46), control,
direction. It is used here in its
original sense as a technical term
for horse-management. The word
is from the O. Fr. *manege*, and
ultimately from the Lat. *manun*.

me. Shakespeare preserves the
use of the old dative *me*, which
corresponds fairly closely to the
so-called ethical dative of Latin
syntax. Sometimes 'me' has the
force of 'to my cost', *e.g.*:

"See how this river comes *me* crank-
    ing in,
And cuts *me* from the best of all my
    land
A huge half-moon"
        (*1 Henry IV*, iii. 1. 98-100).

In other cases its meaning is far
less definite, and serves simply
to draw the attention to the personality of the speaker, *e.g.*:

"He presently, as greatness knows
    itself,
Steps *me* a little higher than his
    vow" (*1 Henry IV*, iv. 3. 74, 75).

Less frequently the other personal
pronouns are used in this way,
e.g.:

"And a' would manage *you* his piece
    thus, and
Come *you* in and come *you* out"
        (*2 Henry IV*, iii. 2. 304).

Here its use is probably intended

to give a familiar, colloquial air
to the speech. For other uses of
this dative see Abbot's *Shakespearean Grammar*, § 220.

moe (iv. 4. 31), more. M.E.
mā, *mo*, O.E. *mā*. The O.E.
mā is the neuter form of the
masc. and fem. *mara*, 'more', and
was also used adverbially. Shakespeare's use of it—"many moe
corrivals"—probably arose out of
its O.E. use with the partitive
genitive, *e.g. ma manna*, 'more
(of) men'.

muster (iv. 1. 133), a review.
M.E. *moustre*, O.F. *mostre*,
another form of *moustre*, a pattern.
From Lat. *monstrare*, to show.
The word is thus etymologically
allied to *monster*.

nonce, for the nonce (i. 2. 167),
for the once. Older forms of the
phrase are *for then ones*, *for then
anes*. The initial *n* of *nonce* thus
belongs properly to the definite
article, being the dative ending
(O.E. *tham*, *than*), while the *es* of
anes, *ones*, *once* is a genitive in-
flection.

ought (iii. 3. 128), owed. M.E.
owen, O.E. *ágan*. The original
meaning of the verb is 'to possess', cf. the Mod. E. adjective
'own' and the derivative verb 'to
own'. From the idea of possession
there developed in M.E. the idea
of obligation and also that of indebtedness. The verb appears
first of all as an auxiliary in Laya-
mon's *Brut* (*circ.* 1180), 'he *ah*
to don' = he must do, while the
use of *ought*, as Shakespeare uses
it here, is found as early as Wy-
cliffe—"that owgte to him ten
thousand talentis", which Tyndale
renders "whiche ought hym ten
thousande talenttes".

outlaw (iv. 3. 58). The word
occurs already in O.E. under the
form *útlaga*, but is a borrowing
from the Scand. *utlagi*. Cf. fellow > Scand. *félagi*.

passion (ii. 4. 364), strong emotion. M.E. *passiun*, O.Fr. *passion*, Lat. *passionem* > *pati*, to suffer. The original idea of 'suffering' has been partly merged in the idea of the strong feeling which accompanies the suffering.

pellmell (v. 1. 82), confused; usually an adv., confusedly. From O.Fr. *pelle-melle* (usually spelt *pesle-mesle*, cf. Mod. Fr. *pêle-mêle*), from *pelle*, a shovel, and *mesler* (Mod. Fr. *mêler*), to mix, Lat. *pala* + *misculare*, *miscere*.

popinjay (i. 3. 50), a parrot, thence a coxcomb. M.E. *popingay* > O.Fr. *papegai*; the *n* is excrescent as in *messenger*, > O.Fr. *messager*. The second part of the word is from O.Fr. *gai*, gay (cf. *jay* > Fr. *geai*), so called because of its *gay* plumage. The origin of the first part, *papa*, is uncertain; possibly it is a mimetic form. Cf. Bavarian *pappel*, a parrot, lit. a babbler. There is another form of the word in O. Fr. *papegau* (Ital. *papagallo*), where the second part of the word is clearly from Lat. *gallus*, a cock.

pouncet-box (i. 3. 38), a small box containing aromatic spices; *pounce* is another form of *pumice*, used in the sense of powdered pumice-stone, and then transferred to other kinds of powder, especially scented powders; Fr. *ponce*, *pierre ponce*, Lat. *pumex*, *pumicem*.

profited (iii. 1. 165), proficient; from M.E. *profit*, O.Fr. *profit*, Lat. *profectum*, *proficere*, to make progress. Shakespeare's use of the word here keeps close to the original (Latin) idea of making progress.

rascal (ii. 2. 5). The word means literally a hart under six years of age, and is used by Shakespeare in the sense of a lean deer in *As You Like It* (iii. 3. 58); the M.E. form is *raskaille*. The word, being a term of the chase, is probably of Norman French origin,

and Skeat connects it with O.Fr. *rascler*, to scrape, the rascal deer being the outcasts or 'scrapings' of the herd, unfit for shooting.

sad (*passim*), serious, grave. Under the form *sad* it occurs with many meanings in M.E., but the original sense is sated (O.E. *saed*), cf. Lat. *sat*, *satis*. From the idea of 'sated' seems to have sprung that of 'heavy' (still used in speaking of bread), thence 'serious', and finally 'sorrowful'.

scandalized (i. 3. 154), disgraced. The M.E. *scandal*, *scandle*, is from O.Fr. *escandle*, Lat. *scandalum*, Gk. σκάνδαλον, a snare. The metaphorical use of the word in the sense of a stumbling-block occurs in the Greek Testament (see Matthew xviii. 7).

Scot (i. 3. 214). There is probably a reference here to the phrase *scot and lot* which Falstaff uses in v. 4. 114. This phrase means literally 'contribution and share'. Skeat explains *scot* = contribution, as "that which is 'shot' into the general fund"; *scot* and *shot* are thus doublets.

strappado (ii. 4. 226), a form of torture; the word has assumed a Spanish form, but, according to Skeat, is from the Italian *strappata*, a pulling, wringing, Ital. *strappare*, to pull.

subornation (i. 3. 163), the crime of procuring another to do a bad action. From *suborn*, Fr. *suborner*, Lat. *sub* + *ornare*, to furnish in an underhand way.

tall (i. 3. 62), stout. M.E. *tal*, *tall*. Chaucer uses the word in the sense of docile ("So humble and tall", *Compleynt of Mars*), and this is not far from its original sense of fit, suitable. The O.E. form is found only in compounds, *e.g.* *ungetal*, inconvenient. Cf. Goth. *untals*, disobedient, and *gatils*, suitable. The change of meaning from docile to stout, and then to lofty, is not easily traced. Skeat adduces a Celtic word *tal* = lofty.

touch (iv. 4. 10), test; M.E. *touchen*, Fr. *toucher* (cf. Ital. *toccare*). The Romance forms of this word are usually traced to the Germanic *tiohan*, Goth. *tiuhan* (to draw). O.H.G. *ziohan*, also *zucchen* (cf. Mod. G. *zucken*, to twitch).

varlet (ii. 2. 23), scoundrel. From the O.F. varlet, vaslet, a diminutive of vassal, L.L. *vassallus*, a diminutive of *vassus*, 'a domestic'. The root is Celtic, the Breton form being *gwaz*, the Welsh *gwas*, 'a boy servant'. *Valet* as well as *vassal* are from the same Celtic root.

wanton (iv. 1. 103), unrestrained. From M.E. *wantogen* and *wantowen*, literally 'deficient in training,' M.E. *togen*, O.E. *togen* being the past participle of O.E. *téon*, (*tihan*) to draw, educate. For this use of the prefix *wan* cf. *wanhope* = despair.

INDEX OF WORDS

GENERAL INDEX TO NOTES

SHAKESPEARE'S STAGE IN ITS BEARING
UPON HIS DRAMA

§ 1. The structure and arrangements of the Elizabethan theatre are
still under discussion, and many points of detail remain unsettled. A
very extensive and highly technical literature on the subject is available, chiefly in England, America, and Germany. It is based especially
on the new evidence derived from (1) the original stage directions, (2)
contemporary illustrations and descriptions. The following summary
gives the conclusions which at present appear most reasonable, neglect-
ing much speculative matter of great interest.

§ 2. When Shakespeare arrived in London, soon after 1585, thea-
trical exhibitions were given there in (1) public theatres, (2) private
theatres, (3) the halls of the royal palaces, and of the Inns of Court.

Of the ' public ' theatres there were at least three: The Theater, the Curtain,
both in Shoreditch, and Newington Butts on the Bankside or Southwark shore.
About 1587, the Rose, also on the Bankside, was added. All these were occasionally used by Shakespeare's company before 1599, when their headquarters became
the newly built Globe, likewise on the Bankside. Of the ' private ' theatres the
principal, and the oldest, was the Blackfriar, on the site of the present *Times*
office. It was also the property of the company in which Shakespeare acquired a
share, but being let out during practically his whole career, does not count in
the present connexion. At court, on the other hand, his company played re-
peatedly. But his plays were written for the ' public ' theatre, and this alone
had any influence in his stage-craft.

§ 3. The ' public ' theatre differed from the other two types chiefly
in being (1) dependent on daylight, (2) open overhead, and (3) partially seatless; and from the court-stages also, in (4) not using painted
scenes. While they, again, had the rectangular form, the typical
' public ' theatre was a round or octagonal edifice, modelled partly on
the inn-yards where companies of players had been accustomed to
perform, prior to the inhibition of 1574, on movable stages; partly on
the arenas used for bear-baiting and cock-fighting;—sports still
carried on in the ' theatres ', and in part dictating their arrangements.

The circular inner area, known thence as the ' cock-pit ', or ' pit ', had accordingly no seats; admission to it cost one penny (6*d.* in modern money), and the
throng of standing spectators were known as the ' groundlings '. More expensive
places (up to 2*s.* 6*d.*) with seats, were provided in tiers of galleries which ran
round the area, one above the other, as in modern theatres; the uppermost being
covered with a thatched roof.

§ 4. **The Stage** (using the term to describe the entire scenic appa-
ratus of the theatre) included (1) the *outer stage*, a rectangular
platform (as much as 42 feet wide in the largest examples) projecting
into the circular area, from the back wall, and thus surrounded by
' groundlings ' on three sides. Above it were a thatched roof and hang-
ings but no side or front curtains. In the floor was a trap-door by
which ghosts and others ascended or descended. At the back were
(2) two projecting wings, each with a door opening obliquely on to
the stage, the *recess* between them, of uncertain shape and extent,
forming a kind of inner stage. Above this was (3) an upper room or
rooms, which included the actors' ' tiring house ', with a window or

SHAKESPEARE'S STAGE

windows opening on to (4) a *balcony* or gallery from which was hung (5) a *curtain*, by means of which the inner recess could be concealed or disclosed.

§ 5. The most important divergence of this type of structure from that of our theatres is in the relation between the outer stage and the auditorium. In the modern theatre the play is treated as a picture, framed in the proscenium arch, seen by the audience like any other picture from the front only, and shut off from their view at any desired moment by letting fall the curtain. An immediate consequence of this was that a scene (or act) could terminate only in one of two ways. Either the persons concerned in it walked, or were carried, off the stage; or a change of place and circumstances was *supposed* without their leaving it. Both these methods were used. The first was necessary only at the close of the play. For this reason an Elizabethan play rarely ends on a *climax* such as the close of Ibsen's *Ghosts*; the overpowering effect of which would be gravely diminished if, instead of the curtain falling upon Osvald's helpless cry for " the sun ", he and his mother had to walk off the stage. Marlowe's *Faustus* ends with a real climax, because the catastrophe *ipso facto* leaves the stage clear. But the close of even the most overwhelming final scenes of Shakespeare is relatively quiet, or even, as in *Macbeth*, a little tame. The concluding lines often provide a motive for the (compulsory) clearing of the stage.

In the *Tragedies*, the dead body of the hero has usually to be borne ceremoniously away, followed by the rest; so Aufidius in *Coriolanus*: "Help, three o' the chiefest soldiers: I'll be one ". Similarly in *Hamlet* and *King Lear*. In *Othello*, Desdemona's bed was apparently in the curtained recess, and at the close the curtains were drawn upon the two bodies, instead of their being as usual borne away.

The close of the *Histories* often resembles the dispersing of an informal council after a declaration of policy by the principal person; thus *Richard II*. closes with Bolingbroke's announcement of the penance he proposes to pay for Richard's death; *Henry IV*. with his orders for the campaign against Northumberland and Glendower; *King John* with Falconbridge's great assertion of English patriotism.

In the *Comedies*, the leading persons will often withdraw to explain to one another at leisure what the audience already knows (*Winter's Tale*, *Tempest*, *Merchant of Venice*), or to carry out the wedding rites (*As You Like It*, *Midsummer-Night's Dream*); or they strike up a measure and thus (as in *Much Ado*) naturally dance off the stage. Sometimes the chief persons have withdrawn before the close, leaving some minor character—Puck (*Midsummer-Night's Dream*) or the Clown (*Twelfth Night*)—to wind up the whole with a snatch of song, and then retire himself.

§ 6. But the most important result of the exposed stage was that it placed strict limit upon dramatic illusion, and thus compelled the resort, for most purposes, to conventions resting on symbolism, suggestion, or make-believe. It was only in dress that anything like simulation could be attempted; and here the Elizabethan companies, as is well known, were lavish in the extreme. Painted scenes, on the other hand, even had they been available, would have been idle or worse, when perhaps a third of the audience would see, behind the actors, not the scenes but the people in the opposite gallery, or the gallants seated on the stage. Especially where complex and crowded actions were introduced, the most beggarly symbolic suggestion was cheerfully accepted. Jonson, in the spirit of classical realism, would have tabooed all such intractable matter; and he scoffed, in his famous Prologue, at the " three rusty swords " whose clashing had to do duty for " York and Lancaster's long jars ". Shakespeare's realism was never of this literal kind, but in bringing Agincourt upon the stage of the newly built Globe in the following year (1559) he showed himself so far sensitive to criticisms of this type that he expressly appealed to the audience's imagination—" eke out our imperfections with your thoughts "—consenting, moreover, to assist them by the splendid descriptive passages interposed between the Acts.

It is probable that the Elizabethan popular audience did not need any such appeal. It had no experience of elaborate ' realism ' on the stage; the rude movable stages on which the earliest dramas had been played compelled an ideal treatment of *space* and a symbolic treatment of *properties*; and this tradition, though slowly giving way, was still paramount throughout Shakespeare's career. Thus every audience accepted as a matter of course (1) the representation of *distant* things or places simultaneously on the stage. Sidney, in 1580, had ridiculed the Romantic plays of his time with " Asia of one side and Africa of the other ", indicated by labels. But Shakespeare in 1593–4 could still represent the tents of Richard III. and Richmond within a few yards of one another, and the Ghosts speaking alternately to each. Every audience accepted (2) the presence on the stage, in full view of the audience, of accessories irrelevant to the scene in course of performance. A property requisite for one set of scenes, but out of place in another, could be simply ignored while the latter were in progress; just as the modern audience sees, but never reckons into the scenery, the footlights and the prompter's box. Large, movable objects, such as beds or chairs, were no doubt often brought in when needed; but no one was disturbed if they remained during an intervening scene in which they were out of place. And " properties either difficult to move, like a well, or so small as to be unobtrusive, were habitually left on the stage as long as they were wanted, whatever scenes intervened " (Reynolds).

Thus in Jonson's *The Case is Altered* (an early play, not yet reflecting his characteristic technique), Jaques, in III. 2, hides his gold in the earth and covers it with a heap of dung to avoid suspicion. In IV. 4, he removes the dung to assure himself that the gold is still there. The intervening scenes represent rooms in Ferneze's palace, and Juniper's shop; but the heap of dung doubtless remained on the stage all the time. Similarly in Peele's *David and Bethsabe*, the spring in which Bethsabe bathes; and in his *Old Wives' Tale*, ' a study ' and a ' cross ', which belong to unconnected parts of the action.

It follows from this that the *supposed locality of a scene could be changed* without any change in the properties on the stage, or even of the persons. What happened was merely that some properties which previously had no dramatic relevance, suddenly acquired it, and *vice versa*; that a tree, for instance, hitherto only a stage property out of use, became a *tree* and signified probably, a wood. The change of scene may take place without any break in the dialogue, and be only marked by the occurrence of allusions of a different tenor.

Thus in *Doctor Faustus*, at v. 1106 f., Faustus is in " a fair and pleasant green ", on his way from the Emperor's Court at Wittenberg; at v. 1143 f., he is back in his house there. In *Romeo and Juliet*, I. 4. 5, Romeo and his friends are at first in the street; at I. 4, 114, according to the Folio, " they march about the stage and serving-men come forth with their napkins "; in other words, we are now in Capulet's hall, and Capulet presently enters meeting his guests. This is conventionalized in modern editions.

§ 7. The Inner Stage.

—An audience for which the limitations of the actual stage meant so little, might be expected to dispense readily with the concessions to realism implied in providing an actual inner chamber for scenes performed ' within ', and an actual gallery for those performed ' aloft '. And the importance and number of the former class of scenes have, in fact, been greatly exaggerated.

Applying modern usages to the semi-mediæval Elizabethan stage, Brandl (*Einleitung* to his revised edition of Schlegel's translation) and Brodmeier (Dissertation on the stage conditions of the Elizabethan drama), put forward the theory of the ' alternative ' scene; according to which the inner and the outer stage were used ' alternately ', a recurring scene, with elaborate properties, being arranged in the former, and merely curtained off while intervening scenes were played on the outer, or main stage. But while this theory is plausible, as applied to some of Shakespeare's plays (e.g. the intricate transitions between rooms at Belmont and piazzas at Venice, in the *Merchant*), it breaks down in others (e.g. *Cymbeline*, II. 2, 3; *Richard II.*, I. 3, 4), and especially in many plays by other dramatists.

It is probable that the use of the ' inner stage ' was in general restricted to two classes of scene: (1) where persons ' within ' formed an integral though subordinate part of a scene of which the main issue was decided on the outer stage; as with the play-scene in *Hamlet*, or where Ferdinand and Miranda are discovered playing chess in *The Tempest*; (2) where a scene, though engaging the whole interest, is supposed to occur in an inner chamber. Thus Desdemona's chamber, Prospero's cell, Timon's cave, Lear's hovel, the Capulet's tomb.

§ 8. The Balcony.

—There is less doubt about the use of the balcony or gallery. This was in fact an extremely favourite resource, and its existence in part explains the abundance of serenade, rope-ladder, and other upper-story scenes in Elizabethan drama.

From the balcony, or the window above it, Juliet discoursed with Romeo, and Sylvia with Proteus (*Two Gentlemen of Verona*, IV. 2); Richard III. addressed the London citizens, and the citizen of Angers the rival Kings. From the window the Pedant in *Taming of the Shrew*, V. 1, hails Petruchio and Grumio below; and Squire Tub, in Jonson's *Tale of a Tub*, I. 1, puts out his head in answer to the summons of Parson Hugh. But whole scenes were also, it is probable, occasionally enacted in this upper room. This is the most natural interpretation of the scenes in Juliet's chamber (IV. 3, 5). On the other hand, though the Senators in *Titus Andronicus*, I. 1, " go up into the ' Senate House ' ", it is probable that the debate later in the scene, on the main stage, is intended to be in the Senate-house by the convention described in § 6.

For further reference the following among others may be mentioned:

G. F. Reynolds, *Some Principles of Elizabethan Staging* (*Modern Philology*, II. III.); A. Brandl, *Introduction* to his edition of Schlegel's translation of Shakespeare; V. E. Albright, *The Shakespearian Stage* (New York); W. Archer, *The Elizabethan Stage* (*Quarterly Review*, 1908); W. J. Lawrence, *The Elizabethan Playhouse and other Studies* (1st and 2nd series); D. Figgis, *Shakespeare, a study*.

From one or other of these, many of the above examples have been taken.

C. H. H.